A Time for Peace Between Muslims and the West

by Judith I. Shadzi

R&E Publishers, Inc.
Saratoga, California

R & E Publishers
P.O. Box 2008, Saratoga, CA 95070
Tel: (408) 866-6303   Fax: (408) 866-0825

Book Design by Diane Parker

Cover by A.S.C.I., Los Altos, California

Excerpts from Blood-Brothers printed with permission of Fleming H. Revell Company.

Library of Congress Card Catalog Number: 93-37239

ISBN 1-56875-068-4

To my husband, Bahram, for loving me, for taking me on a real life adventure, but most of all, for being my friend.

ACKNOWLEDGMENTS

I am deeply indebted to my family. My husband Bahram protected and worked with me in Iran while I learned a new language and culture, has endured being my life-long case study, and has wholeheartedly supported this project. My son Javad has been a valuable confidant. My daughter Taraneh has helped me overcome my fear of the computer. My son Peymon has had patience with my big project. My mother Laura has supported me with her faith and her valuable assistance.

Bob and Kari Malcolm have encouraged and tutored me from the beginning. Debra Stoesz has listened and helped bridge the two cultures for me. Joyce Slaughter has read and helped organize and critique my manuscript. Jean Schuler and Penny Nejad have given valuable assistance in editing. The prayer support and anticipation of all my Christian sisters in Bible Study Fellowship and other Christian friends has been greatly appreciated. The enthusiasm of all our Middle-Eastern family and friends has made this project a delightful experience. I would like to thank Robert Reed for the encouragement and support he provided throughout the publishing of this book.

CONTENTS

INTRODUCTION

Everyone thinks I'm crazy around here. Do you think they're right? Oh no madame, oh, no. Most of us go through life with blinders on, Madame, knowing only that one little station to which we were born. But not you Madame, on the other hand, have had the rare privilege of escaping your bonds for just a spell to see life with an entirely new perspective. How you choose to use that information Madame, is entirely up to you.

--Andrew the Butler's answer to Joanna in the film "Overboard."

My neighbors in Virginia have been wonderful to me, inviting me to share in their traditions like Thanksgiving and Christmas and coming to my home in the afternoons to take a cup of tea and chat. When Noha, her husband Hassan and their four children visited me in June of 86 along with Gamal, Dina and their daughter Tasmin, the neighbors lent me cribs, playpens and bicycles and invited the older children to go on trips to the beach.

--Jehan Sadat, former First Lady of Egypt

"Mommy, mommy, where is Grandma," cried our three year old daughter Taraneh as we exited our airplane and entered the Chicago airport.

"Darling, we have to go on the train to see Grandma. Grandma lives in another city."

"Mommy, Mommy, where is Disneyland?"

"*Azizam* (sweetheart), Disneyland is still far away from here; we cannot go there just yet." "That is what we get for making them all those wonderful promises about America," I thought. Poor little thing, she could hardly speak a word of English. All she could say was "I vant ice cr-ream." We said, "Taraneh, say I want water."

"No," she said, "I vant ice cr-ream."

We waited for our luggage and the custom official asked for my husband Bahram's passport. He showed them all our passports. "Iranians," said the official, "You'll have to wait over by the wall."

"What do they want?"

"I don't know, we'll just have to wait and see," Bahram said, looking a bit worried. When everyone on the plane had passed through customs the officials came to us and asked how many bags we had.

"We are four people, and we have six bags; we had to leave everything when we came out of Iran," I answered.

"It looks like quite a bit to me. You are going to have to open them and put everything out on the table," said the custom's clerk.

"What do you expect," I thought, "it has been only one week since the hostages were released." After they had gone through every item we had, I started stuffing things back in the suitcases. I felt as if the whole airport was watching us. We left the airport and flagged down a taxi.

"To the train station please," Bahram told the taxi driver. I looked up from the back seat of the taxi and couldn't believe my eyes. It had been over three years since I'd been in the states and everything looked so spread out. The cars looked so wide, and on such wide streets. It would take some getting used to.

We transferred our two sleepy little ones onto the train. The train stopped in Minneapolis and Bahram picked up a bag hoping it had some of his clothes left in it. As it turned out, not one pair of shoes ended up together. I sent him his *other* shoes later.

"I don't know how long it's going to be before we see each other again, honey; I'll try to get my old college job back for now. My brother, Hossein will let me stay with him. Say hello to Mom and Dad for me." He kissed each of us and turned and walked away. The children and I watched his back until he was out of sight. I had a very large lump in my throat. The reality was setting in that coming back to America would not solve all of our problems.

I called it, "Starting over with nothing but our talents." We went on to North Dakota; Grandpa and Grandma were waiting for us at the train depot. Taraneh had been so excited to see them but now acted quite shy. They had not seen her since she was two months old. But it wasn't long before she was chattering away at her Grandmother in Farsi, the Persian language. She would then get a confused look on her face, trying to figure out why Grandma didn't answer back. It took her a week or so to figure out Grandma couldn't understand her, and that she would have to learn another language.

I was thinking and dreaming in Farsi myself. Everyone was asking where I was from because I had an accent. It was a long story! Then they would ask me how I liked Iran. I would tell them I had a very nice time in Iran. Then they would ask, "Wasn't it dangerous?" I would answer, "not for me, I was taking the taxi all over Teheran with my children during the hostage crisis. People would apologize to me and they wouldn't even take my money." That was it! Whoever had asked me the question would turn away from me and never mention Iran again. I couldn't understand why they reacted like that. Now I know that my answer was so different than what they expected to hear they were afraid to hear anymore. But I wondered why they weren't curious about that. They just acted like they didn't want to know anymore.

Some people felt that the Middle Eastern political and social situation was just my problem. One lady told me, "You can't expect everyone to be interested in your problem all the time." I tried to tell them that this is going to be everyone's problem if attention is not given to it. Islam is the fastest growing religion in the United States and indeed in the world. The Iran Contra scandal, the 1991 Gulf War, and the bomb placed in the World Trade Center in 1993 has helped America come to that understanding. We cannot ignore Middle Easterners any longer.

It was three long months before Bahram and I got to see each other again, and it was six months before we were together again as a family. It was a very difficult time for me. My father was very old and not feeling well. I knew the children were too much excitement for him, but I had nowhere else to go.

I had not attended church for about 15 years; out of respect for my mother I went with her. One Sunday morning a guest speaker came and preached on Ezekial. While sitting there listening to Ezekial's story, I had a very soft touch from the Spirit of God. That touch was so sweet that my whole life after that became a quest to know God in a personal way.

I decided I needed to start studying the Bible. I was so confused and disappointed with the way men were handling this world.

After we were into our home in Minneapolis, I took the children to a church two blocks away. I was still quite reluctant about church people and thought I would keep a low profile. But something unexpected happened. Everyone stood up, held hands and sang, "We are one in the Spirit, we are one in the Lord, ...and they'll know we are Christians by our love, by our love. Yes, they'll know we are Christians by our love." For a minute I felt like I couldn't breathe. This was the kind of caring I needed to see between people. I decided to join my Bible Study with this group of people.

Hungrily I searched the scriptures to see what knowledge God had for me. I started to find answers for many of my questions. I had so often thought about how the Iranian people, in their oppressed and weakened state, pulled down a powerful world leader like the Shah. I had seen it happen; I was there, but I still didn't understand how it could happen. In I Corinthians 1:27 I read:

...but God chose what is foolish in the world to shame the wise, God chose what is weak in the world to shame the strong,

In Luke 4:18 Jesus said:

"The Spirit of the Lord is upon me, because he has anointed me to preach good news to the poor.

He has sent me to proclaim release to the captives and recovering of sight to the blind, to set at liberty those who are oppressed, to proclaim the acceptable year of the Lord."

The Shah once said it was not easy to be a king to such a poor people. That explained it; man's inventions of tyranny are powerless in the face of justice.

I discovered the Old Testament had a wonderful coverage on Persian history. In Isaiah 45, King Cyrus was actually called God's anointed and gave all his people religious freedom. He not only encouraged the Jews to go back to Jerusalem and rebuild their temple but returned all of the wealth that Babylon had taken from the temple. The prophet Daniel had been one of King Darius' favorite advisors. In Daniel 25-28 the story of Daniel's success is told:

Then king Darius wrote unto all people, nations, and languages, that dwell in all the earth; Peace be multiplied unto you. I make a decree, That in every dominion of my kingdom men tremble and fear before the God of Daniel:

for he is the living God, and steadfast forever, and his kingdom that which shall not be destroyed, and his dominion shall be even unto the end. He delivereth and rescueth, and he worketh signs and wonders in heaven and in earth, Who hath delivered Daniel from the power of the lions. So this Daniel prospered in the reign of Darius, and in the reign of Cyrus the Persian.

Daniel's monumental grave still stands in Susa, Iran.

In the Bible I met Queen Esther, who was also married to a Persian, and how she loved him. Her uncle Mordaci said to her, "...and who knows whether thou art come to the kingdom for such a time as this." I thought about that. God had a purpose for her. Could that mean that God had some purpose for me too? Would God allow me to have this intimate experience with Middle Easterners and not use it for good?

I began to regret the wasted years I had not walked with God, but I quickly came upon the verse in Joel 12:25 which says "I will restore to you the days the locusts hath eaten..." I decided if these were to be the days of my restoration I must work hard. I would study, pray, and fast from things that distracted me from seeing God's purpose for my life. I started by fasting from television commercials and billboards.

In the meantime, these were difficult, lean days for us. My Iranian sister-in-law helped us buy a house. We bought the largest house which we could possibly afford. Bahram's niece Mina, who had been studying in Germany was coming to live with us. The ban on Iranian travel was lifted in the spring of 1981 and she was there to help us move in by July 24, our son Javad's birthday.

The summers were busy with visitors from the Middle East. Then my father died in 1983, and my mother came to live with us. One summer we were 13 people. Some nights I would be cooking supper with my mother discussing American relatives in English and my mother-in-law discussing Iranian relatives in Farsi. As a lonely child, I had said, "When I grow up I am going to fill my home with people." Well, that prophecy had certainly come true.

Iran was under an economic blockade and the government was running short of foreign currency. This meant Iranians wanting to travel out of their country could no longer exchange Iranian money for foreign currency. The only place they could buy foreign money was on the black market and it had become ten times more expensive. The only way any Iranian could afford to travel to America was if they had someone to stay with. They could buy their airplane ticket in Iran with Iranian money, but Iran-Air did not fly to America after the revolution. That meant they would have to pay $10 for every $1 for airfare from Europe, not mentioning any other expenses. American garage sales became very popular.

God's very special purpose for me began to unfold the following summer. I helped translate for family and friends while they got visas, false teeth, social security cards, and had doctors' checkups. But most of all, I tried to be their friend. They seemed to value my friendship, and showered me with love and gifts. I represented America to them, and they needed to feel accepted by America. I soon realized there was an endless number of needs and I was only one person. An American friend, Linda, said to me one day, "Judith, you are the only person I have ever met who has penetrated another culture and have come back to tell us about it. It has opened up a whole new world for me. I'm starting to notice Middle Easterners everywhere I go." That really made me think. I could be a bridge between the East and the West, a means of helping people understand each other and become friends. But I needed to find a way to reach more people with my message.

We were thankful for our friends Kari and Bob Malcolm. They were former missionaries to the Philippines, and they loved Muslim people. Kari would give all my Muslim guests big smiles and hugs, even though she could not speak their language. Every year no matter how many of us there were, she and Bob would invite us all out to their Norwegian style home, *Solbakken. Solbakken* means sunny hill.

My Iranian family so enjoyed visiting their home every year. Middle Easterners love to visit over a hot cup of tea. They always comment, "Americans have such beautiful homes, why don't they ever invite anyone over?" Our church called that summer and said they had heard we had a houseful and would like to help. They wanted to know if they could send someone over to clean my house. "No thank you," I said. But I was too shy to say, "What we would really like is to have someone invite us over to tea."

This poem was written in California by an Iranian misplaced by the 1979 Revolution and here is my translation:

This is a pretty house,
  but it is not my home.
This is a beautiful land,
  but it's not my homeland.
How can I make my neighbor understand
  why my heart is aching.
  Who can be my friend?
I am a vagabond.

Middle Easterners need to be friends with Americans; they need to be integrated into the social system. There are so many areas that Middle Eastern Muslims need assistance when they first come to America. Christians and Muslims have similar moral convictions but Muslims are often unaware of the dangers in a free society such as ours. Americans are a very busy and productive people, and we don't always have time for reaching out to others. We don't know or understand these people. We may be frightened of rejection or just plain being put in an uncomfortable situation. Jesus spoke to us in Luke 14:12-14:

When you give a luncheon or dinner, do not invite your friends, your brothers or relatives, or your rich neighbors; if you do, they may invite you back and so you will be repaid. But when you give a banquet, invite the poor...and you will be blessed. Although they cannot repay you, you will be repaid at the resurrection of the righteous.

Middle Easterners needs are not usually financial, but rather social. Most of them are of higher income levels and are either already educated or in the process of getting their education. Forbes magazine describes the one percent of Iran's population now residing in California:

By and large, the homeland's loss has been our gain. To be sure, these Iranians are hardly your ordinary "tired and poor" refugees. They were the country's elite...Doctors, lawyers, architects, engineers, entrepreneurs, businessmen. [1]

Abraham believed God and acted upon it and God said that all the peoples of the earth would be blessed through him. (Gen 12:3) American Christians can share their blessings, and Middle Eastern Muslims make delightful friends. I knew then what I needed to do. I needed to find those Americans that were interested in making friends with Middle Easterners and share with them all the things I had learned. A successful Muslim-Christian relationship operates at a point of interaction which rises above politics, culture and theology; a point where the love of God penetrates the walls of misunderstanding and serves as a healing agent. Making friends with a Middle Easterner is an adventure in geography, history, ancient culture, and ethnic foods. This book is an attempt to give Americans some historical insights with social and political implications; to become informed and challenged to have relationships with the Middle Eastern Muslims around them. On the nightly news we generally receive negative information about the Middle Eastern people. This book is an attempt to balance our view of the Middle East. I found Middle Easterners warm, loving, and accepting of outsiders. But they have been deeply hurt by many of the actions of Western countries. Without knowledge of some of the unfair treatment Middle Easterners have received from the West, Americans go into a relationship with what seems to be a pious attitude. We appear naive and remain in a superficial relationship. If a Middle Eastern friend is brave enough to inform us, we may become hurt or angry and never recover from the shock of our country's role in that part of the world. It is necessary for us to hear their side of the story. We must go into these relationships equipped with all the information needed to prepare our hearts. Without this open heart and mind we are destined for failure.

My desire is to see Christ's love and justice reach to all people. I trust the information provided in this book will not be overwhelming, but will enrich and broaden each reader's spiritual perspective and effectiveness.

Notes: Welcome to Teheran, Calif: Forbes Magazine, December 12, 1988.

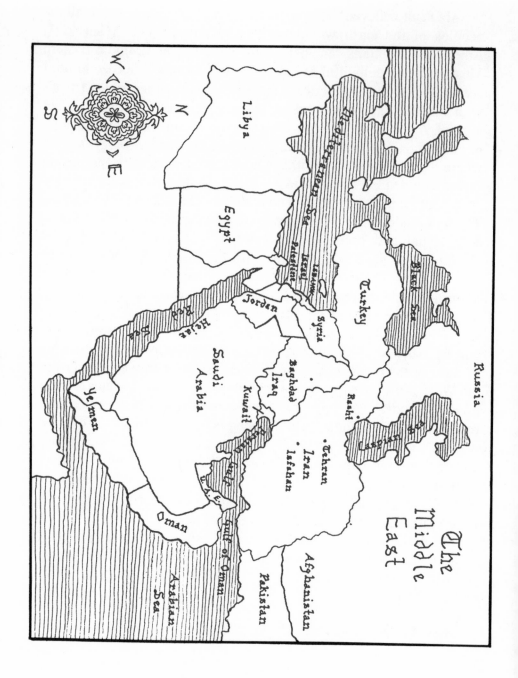

PART I

MIDDLE EASTERN
MUSLIMS IN AMERICA

SOCIALIZING WITH MIDDLE EASTERNERS

Few value friendship because few experience it....we can live and breed
without friendship. It has no survival value, rather it is one of those things
which gives value to survival.

--C. S. Lewis

If we truley desire truth, and a deeper understanding of one another, then
our mutual conversation must continue. This conversation should move on
many different levels... probably the most significant level of conversation
should be good neighborliness. We must learn to know one another as
friends. We must pray to God asking him to help us cultivate bridges of
love between ourselves. We must learn the conversation of love,
forgiveness, respect, good neighborliness, listening and witness.

--Badru D. Kateregga, David W. Shenk
Islam and Christianity

When my husband Bahram asked me to marry him in 1971, it was
with the understanding we would spend the rest of our lives in Iran. It
sounded like a great adventure to me.

By 1976, we had finished our college educations at the University
of Minnesota, and had one small child. Bahram had his master's
degree in chemical engineering and I had studied nutrition and Iranian
studies. The excitement was building.

Nixon had been President of the United States, and relations with
the Shah of Iran had never been better. The Iranian government was
calling their foreign graduates to come back home, and to bring all the
foreign goods they wanted with them, duty-free. Many of our friends
took new cars, but we decided to take household items. We took the
perfect souvenir from America, a bicentennial rocking chair. It had a
huge eagle across the back; it said 1776 to 1976.

We crated everything ourselves in our small apartment. On

Saturday nights, while everyone was out on the town, we pounded the nails in our crates. We were just waiting to start our new life.

As we stepped off Iran Air in Tehran, I breathed in the dry arid summer air. It felt different than anything I'd ever experienced.

After checking out our baggage in a modern flat-roofed building, we were greeted by ten eager faces. All the family had come to meet us, and there were lots of hugging, crying, and kissing. Our son seemed captivated by the constant attention he received from one member or another of the family. Javad was almost two and he instantly recognized a familiar sight, a garbage truck. He delighted everyone by loudly announcing "garbage truck" every time he saw one.

We were driven home on modern streets and autobahns to a lovely, modern two story brick home surrounded by a brick wall. Most homes in Iran have walls around them and even though the landscape is the color of khaki, there are colorful gardens and ponds inside the walls.

We were greeted by a servant girl who immediately brought us a cold Persian melon drink. The smell of steamed rice and lamb came from the kitchen. It was later served with tomato and cucumber lemon salad. Special occasions called for Pepsi with a meal.

Later over hot, sweet, spicy tea and bowls of fresh fruit, we were told the relatives would be coming the whole week to acknowledge our arrival.

I was amazed at the love and attention we received from a large extended family. Each visitor brought gifts of flowers, candy, lovely glass dishes, or Iranian artifacts. We would all wear our lovely flowing dresses and crisp shirts; we would sit together in the guest living room and sip hot, sweet tea, eat sweet cakes, fruit, and trail mix. Iranian trail mix is a combination of roasted seeds, roasted nuts, and dried fruit.

The children seemed to enjoy this special time more than anyone. They would dress in their best clothes and sit close together, giggling and smiling at their guests. The guest living room was usually off limits to children, because it was filled with expensive art pieces, finer Persian carpets, and decorative china. It was a novelty for them to be allowed in the room.

After one week we took the bus south to Isfahan, Bahram's hometown. It was an eight hour bus trip by TBT, which is similar to the American Greyhound bus service. Here though, it was quite different. The driver had an assistant, whose job was to socialize and meet the needs of the passengers. He was always ready with a pitcher of water for thirsty passengers, and served one round of Pepsi during the course of the trip. There were pretty curtains on the bus windows, and he would come and go pinning them up or letting them down as the sun shined in people's eyes.

There was a half-way stop at what they called a coffee house. This was an odd name because Iranians usually drink tea and coffee was not even on the menu. The coffee house served chelo-kabob, which was a plate full of rice with long strips of lamb filet pounded flat, and hot sweet tea.

Upon our arrival in Isfahan, more family members were there to greet us. It was what I called *dozens of cousins*. The following week was filled with more guests bringing gifts, drinking hot tea, eating cakes, fruit, and trail mix. This went on for a few weeks until all the cousins, to the fourth and fifth, along with groups of in-laws, visited us. When this process was completed, the invitations for dinner started. The custom was that we were to visit them all in return!

At times it was tiring, but I was touched by the love and affection of these people. They genuinely enjoyed just being together. Of course, this was the process of a journeying wayfarer returning home, and things would settle down to once a week or once a month.

Middle Eastern children from the time they are born, are with their mothers. If their mother is a professional person, they will be in the presence of another member of the extended family. Some working mothers may have a nanny in the home. Baby-sitters or day care centers are almost unheard of.

The child will learn his father may be big and huggable, but at the same time a strong authority figure. A father's word is final in the home. His image brings much security for the children and the loss of a father in death is devastating to a Middle Eastern family. Even though another male in the extended family will try to take the responsibility, it is just not the same. One Iranian psychologist pinpointed the main cause of mental instability among his people as the loss of a father in the family.

A child can look forward to many family socials. These socials are a great source of joy, because there are always plenty of cousins to play with, lots of good food, and much laughter and fun.

School may be a bit more traumatic because it is very difficult. The Iranian education system is based on the French model but with religious modifications made to accommodate spiritual reasoning. A good Muslim education combines the religious and secular experiences into one divine law of God. One's faith has a social, economic and political dimension. Learning is accomplished through memorizing historical lore and the traditional knowledge it carries. Sexes are segregated and educational success contributes to family honor.

While my husband and I were dating, one of our favorite pastimes was to sit on the college campus lawn while he recited long poems in Farsi, the Persian language. He would then translate them for me. Persian history and moral lessons are recorded in beautiful poetry.

Middle Eastern children are taught advanced concepts of mathematics and scientific theory at a much earlier age, but may be behind the western students in applying technology. Most Middle Eastern students that come to college in America are two years ahead in their mathematical skills, and that gives them time to get caught up in the English language. This knowledge of math and science is an excellent tool in getting them started in an engineering major.

It is very important that Christians understand the customs of the Middle East. Understanding of certain Bible passages depend on knowledge of Middle Eastern culture. Why did Joseph have the authority to put Mary away when he wasn't yet her husband? Why did Lot say he had two daughters who had never slept with a man and then five verses later say he had two son-in-laws who didn't come with him out of Sodom? How did Lot have the authority to take his daughters out of Sodom despite their husbands refusals? What does the parable of the ten young virgins mean? The answers to these questions become apparent when one understands the customs of the Middle Eastern marriage ceremony.

There is no dating in the Middle Eastern Muslim community. The large family gatherings are the extent of teenagers getting together. Even cousins must observe strict rules of social conduct since it is not forbidden for them to marry, although it is not as common as it once was.

One friend of ours felt he was becoming a little more modern. He had his eye on the daughter of a familiar family so he went to her father and asked if he could take his daughter to the movies. Her father said "Marry her and you can take her anywhere you like." He finally had to marry her to take her to the movies.

There is a certain betrothal procedure that is followed. Either a young man will see someone he is attracted to or his mother may pick out a suitable girl for him. The groom, with the women of his family, will visit the girl's home. The girl's family will accept them graciously into their guest living room, and the young girl must serve tea for them. Most loving fathers would not force their daughter to marry someone she doesn't like, but the daughter is obligated to be hospitable on the suitor's first visit.

If the groom and his family are pleased with the girl they will go ahead with the negotiations. Items to negotiate would be profession and income of the groom, dowry of the bride (household furnishings), place of residence, and the *mehrieh*. The *mehrieh* is like pledge money. It is the guarantee of the fulfillment of a commitment and obligation to the bride. It is usually a large sum of money, and if the groom would leave her for any reason she would receive this money. Two other obligations of the groom are that he must finance the wedding and give the bride's parents expensive gifts.

If the negotiations go well, the next step is to have a betrothal ceremony which is done by a religious leader and a notary public. What we would call the engagement ceremony is actually the legal contract in the Middle East. The bride does not move to her husband's home at this time; this is a time of getting to know each other. But if they were to decide they didn't like each other they would have to get a divorce. This is a custom in the Middle East that has held since before the time of Christ. Daniel-Rops describes the Jewish custom of betrothal in *Daily Life in the Time of Jesus:*

> *The fact is that the law recognized rights and obligations during the betrothal that were almost the same as those of marriage...a fiance*

who was found guilty of adultery was to be stoned, exactly as if she had been a wife. On the other hand, she did have the advantages of some legal rights: she might not be rejected except by a letter of divorcement; if her fiance should die, she was counted as a widow; and a child born during the betrothal was held to be legitimate. This preliminary state therefore had a very close resemblance to definitive marriage.[1]

Having made the commitment, the betrothal time is a time of romance and getting close. One year is a common betrothal period before a wedding celebration takes place, and then the groom gets to take his bride home for the consummation of the marriage. Weddings are the height of celebration with all the little girls dressed in long white dresses, dancing in native custom. The celebration may go on for more than one day and as it is traditionally held in the groom's home; many family members may spend a few days there. Men and women are usually seated in separate rooms but that would depend on the region and family preference.

The new bride and groom will most likely move into the groom's father's home. Years may pass until they have enough money to purchase their own house. In the Middle East, the only financial credit received would be through one's employment or from family members.

Those children born in the early part of the marriage will receive the love and attention of all the extended family because they are living in their grandparent's house.

Most people live in the same home or at least the same city all their lives. They have a very clear sense of who they are and enjoy existent and permanent relationships. Women develop close relationships with women, and men with men. Women either wear the veil, or dress in stylish but very modest clothing. The covering of women's hair is an ancient tradition that was once a sign of class distinction. In the ancient world, only upper class women were allowed to wear the veil. The Middle Assyrian law (circa 1100 B.C.) number 9 ordered the cutting off of the ears of a female slave who dared to veil herself. [2] Today, the Western world seems to feel the veil is a sign of oppression. Some people say, "It's not wearing a scarf that is so bad, but it is evidence of the restrictions put on women. To the Eastern men it is a sign of modesty and protection for their women. Some Middle Eastern women say there is a freedom in not having to wear makeup and fix your hair every time you go out, but other women feel covering oneself is an inconvenience. We have a friend that recently visited Iran, a country that has a law that women must cover their head. He saw many veiled American women in Teheran, and asked them why they were there. They answered, "This is my country now." He asked them if they were happy there. They all said, "Wearing the veil is inconvenient, but other than that, I am happy here."

It is not proper among Middle Eastern Muslims for men and women to have direct, personal conversations together like it is in the West. Exceptions would be professional women working side by side with men, such as in the medical field or educational and research situations.

In the Middle East, people visit each other more often, and spend more time just being together. There are a number of reasons that this is possible. One is that most women are in the home and can take the time for food preparation. Secondly, the work week is six days, instead of five days. Saturday through Wednesday the working hours are 7:30 a.m. to 2:30 p.m. Businesses all close at noon on Thursday, and Friday is the day of rest. The average family eats their large meal of the day at three o'clock in the afternoon; they have a nice nap and then five to eight is free time. They visit each other, take long walks in the park, or go to the movies. Life moves at a slower pace.

Isfahan was my favorite city in Iran. It was the ancient capitol of Persia and was once known as *half the world*. There are two ancient stone bridges crossing the famous Zayandeh Rud river. There are parks along the river, and people can rent row boats or paddle boats. It is a common sight to see people sitting on Persian carpets on the steps of the Khajou bridge in early evenings, drinking hot sweet tea and talking about this and that. There are professional photographers with Polaroid cameras to take one's picture for a small fee.

Many people in the Middle East still do not use furniture. They sit on their oriental carpets with a large pillow behind their back. They put a large tablecloth on the floor and everyone sits cross-legged around it to eat. They always take their shoes off at the door so the carpets stay very clean.

In Isfahan, my mother-in-law had a very nice neighbor, Mr. Kharazi, who used to invite us over. We learned early on to come on an empty stomach because we knew they would insist that we eat so much fruit and cakes. We would sit on the floor with a big pillow fluffed behind us and they would always say, "I'm sorry we don't have our furniture but it is out being cleaned."

We would say, "Oh that's alright, we are quite comfortable." The truth of the matter was that they didn't have any furniture because they didn't want any. The carpets we were sitting on were worth ten times the price of furniture. But because I was a Westerner, they were afraid I would think less of them if they didn't have any furniture.

There is quite a variety of Middle Eastern food. A variety of flat-breads is common throughout the Middle East and would be considered their staple food. Lamb or beef, lots of fresh vegetables, many dried beans and peas, and rice make up the diet. Foods are lightly spiced in the Arab and Persian areas and more heavily spiced in eastern Pakistan and India. Most third world countries have a natural prevention of bacteria and the Middle East puts dried limes or lemon juice in everything. Besides the fact that it makes everything taste delicious, the citric acid kills many germs.

They actually eat pretty much the same things we eat in the West but they are just put together differently. My children's favorite food is called *gourmet greens*. It is a stew with small pieces of meat, lots of chopped green leafy vegetables, red kidney beans, and lots of lemon juice. This is put over a plate of steamed long-grain white rice. Middle Eastern food is very healthy. When I was studying nutrition at the University of Minnesota we would put our weekly diet in the computer. The week I ate gourmet greens I consumed 400% of the daily recommended amount of vitamin A.

A typical breakfast is white goat's cheese (commonly known in America as Greek feta cheese), flat bread, and hot sweet tea. The large meal of the day is at three in the afternoon and usually rice with a stew over it, rice with beans and meat mixed in it, or Middle Eastern stews and soups. Meat is eaten in much lesser amounts than in the West, but when they do make it; they spice it exquisitely. A light, late evening meal is eaten around eight or nine o'clock. Soup, scrambled eggs, a type of souffle, or other easier to prepare foods are eaten in the evening. Milk is available, but most Middle Easterners prefer plain yoghurt.

In the Middle East, respect and authority come with age. The young bride keeps quite a low profile, especially if she lives in her father-in-law's home. But as the years pass, her words begin to carry more weight. Elders are never spoken to crossly, and the Middle Eastern languages have an honorific pronoun which is used to address parents.

I have been truly fascinated with the outlook of parents in the Middle East and especially the mothers. They seem to look at their children as an extension of their own lives, which truly they are. All their hopes are in their children and no sacrifice is too great. I believe many a child is kept on the straight and narrow by the knowledge of how easily his mother and father's hearts could be broken. My husband's father died when he was twelve but his influence was so strong that one night he dreamed his father came to him and asked him to be kinder to his younger brother and take responsibility as the oldest son. It left a lasting impression.

CULTURE SHOCK

The poorest of the poor are in America because there are many lonely people forgotten by society.

--Mother Teresa

With all this in mind, we see what a change it is for Middle Easterners moving to America. First of all, life moves much faster in America and things are much more complicated. The first thing that hits one is the large shopping areas, with hundreds of decisions to make every way one turns. There are so many kinds of bars of soap.

People are not interested in just being together anymore, they have to be doing, doing, doing. Everyone seems to be alone, the families are so small, and every member seems to be doing his own thing. No one talks about God but only the achievements and productivity of men. Crimes against the government are treated as though they are much more important than crimes against God. On the other hand, no one even speaks of them, crimes against God that is. Not paying taxes is a crime, but adultery isn't. Everyone is dressed so shamelessly and sexual activity is flaunted. People are talking about things, things, things, and money, money, money.

Oh well, let's slow down here. After all, America is the most comfortable country in the world. Americans welcome foreigners and treat them well. Personal achievement is respected and rewarded in the professional arena. One can borrow money from the bank to buy a car and a house. People in the stores are polite and helpful in making all those decisions. If one makes the wrong decision, the merchandise can be returned and one's money given back. There is lots of outside entertainment; people gather in the shopping centers and join clubs and organizations if they are lonely. There are nightclubs for dancing. Everything will be alright.

And everything is alright for awhile. The excitement of getting a job and moving into a home keeps the family occupied. They may become acquainted with a few people from their native country. They may even have some friendly neighbors. The children get settled into a new school that is very clean and has beautiful pictures on the wall. Cooking is easier for the lady of the house; the food is so clean and cooks so quickly.

But many of their native countrymen are becoming increasingly materialistic and are given to having large birthday parties, seeing who can bring the most elaborate gift. They don't do any reading, but spend all their time watching television and imitating Hollywood personalities. They talk long about money and think nothing of divorce anymore. These are not the same people they knew back home. They slowly try to drop out of the social activities and in doing so become more isolated than ever.

Joseph Campbell, who held the chair in comparative mythology at Sarah Lawrence College, describes the trauma of a person out of step with a society's dream:

> *They've moved out of the society that would have protected them, and into the dark forest, into the world of fire, of original experience. Original experience has not been interpreted for you, and so you've got to work out your life for yourself. Either you can take it or you can't. You don't have to go far off the interpreted path to find yourself in very difficult situations. The courage to face the*

trials and bring a whole new body of possibilities into the field of interpreted experience for other people to experience--that is the hero's deed. [3]

The problem is, in order to be a hero there must be some source of inner strength. These people have lost their spiritual support system. If there is a mosque in their area, it may have such a variety of nationalities involved in its activities that they cannot relate. Besides, the mosque was only a small part of their religious experience.

So the Middle Easterners begin to grieve for what they have lost. In a small book called *Good Grief*, Granger Westberg describes some of the stages people will go through after a great loss. The first process of grief is shock. [4]

Middle Easterners, upon arrival, will experience an extended period of shock. This is what we call *culture shock*. I myself experienced this upon our return from Iran. I was thinking and dreaming in the Farsi language, and had to translate everything to English in my mind. I had to deal daily with all new people that acted differently than what I was familiar with. All their values were different, and I had to be a different person in a different language. This may sound strange coming from a person who grew up in America but as a child one does not directly deal with main stream America. After I graduated from high school I went to the University and met and socialized with Middle Easterners. When I learned to cook; I learned Iranian and Lebanese foods from my roommate, who was a Middle Easterner. My return to America brought me to the suburbs for the first time and that can be a shock in itself.

Upon our immediate return, my two small children and I were staying with my mother and father. Bahram was living with his brother in another city. We had not been allowed to bring anything with us when we left Iran. The country was experiencing a war and an economic blockade, and did not allow any goods or money to leave the country. We were able to bring six suitcases and $2600. Teheran customs graciously gave us permission to air-freight one crate with a Persian carpet, some Iranian blankets, our pillows, and our silverware to Germany. I thought, "I'll imagine we are back on our honeymoon; we'll have silverware to eat with, some blankets to sleep with, and we'll get started all over again."

In Iran we were told if we air-freighted our crate to America the dock workers would not accept it, and we may never receive it. We freighted it to Germany, which meant we had to pay for further transportation with our limited foreign currency. We had to stay in Germany for one month in order for Bahram to get his American visa. We were thankful it wasn't any longer because $2600 doesn't go very far.

As much as we wanted to see the American hostages released; I was not very happy to hear they were coming to Frankfurt the very day of our appointment with the American consulate. We talked him into processing our paperwork the day before they arrived.

The hostages made it back to America one week before we did. At 33, Bahram went back to his college job until he could find another engineering job. He was very thankful for old friends. That was the end of January and by March, I had become quite emotional and isolated. It is acceptable for one to show emotion if they've lost a loved one, but not if they've lost a country, or in my case, a lifestyle. To make things more difficult, my seven year old son was going through a similar grieving process. Our three year old daughter seemed to breeze through that particular crisis, even though she couldn't speak a word of English with her grandparents.

In contrast to the loving welcome I had received in Iran, very few people came to see me or invited me over to their home in the whole six months I was at my father's home. I had only one aunt I felt comfortable to drop in on occasionally, and Javad's Sunday school teacher visited him a few times and had us over one day for tea. My mother was very patient with three live-ins who had no place to go.

Having had time to think about the difficult political climate in Iran, but also grieving for what we had lost, I continually slipped into a deeper depression.

It was about this time, an Evangelist named Ravi Zacharias came to my mother's church. He was originally from India, had married a Canadian girl, and was a professor at a Christian seminary. I looked up and saw black hair, olive skin, and dark almond shaped eyes. I felt the first spark of interest I had had for anything in a long time.

He preached on Ezekial. He told how God had shown Ezekial the sins of his own country; how God had taken something dear from him and he was not supposed to grieve. Ezekial was to tell his people that God was going to pronounce judgement on his country if they did not repent. So...no one was interested in hearing the information Ezekial had either. Something touched me that day, and I realized the only one who really understood how I felt was God. Ravi read the verses in Psalms that said, "The sacrifices of God are a broken and humble spirit that God will not despise." I knew then that God was the only one who would not turn away from me when I said that I loved the Middle Easterners and that they had loved me back, because He loved them too.

After the service Ravi was standing in the back with a big empty circle around him. The local people weren't sure they knew how to relate to him; he seemed so different. I walked up to him and said, "I think you were sent here just for me." Then I looked around, unable to believe I had really said that! I was thankful that Ravi took time to talk with me and help me understand what was happening. He helped me understand that as a family we needed spiritual guidance to get us through this difficult transition period.

By May, Bahram had an engineering job and by July we were in our own home. The very first thing he bought was a short-wave radio to listen to the overseas news reports. A couple of times I tried to explain to him what had happened to me, but the reality hit him when I wanted to go to church every Sunday. He was not quite sure what this change in the woman he married meant. I sat down one night and cried as I often did those days and said, "My fault is that I'm a woman that loves God." I was very involved in my own self-pity, but then I looked up and saw Bahram's face. He was dark red all around his eyes.

He said, "I wish I could cry like that." My heart really went out to him. He was a man, and in America men never cry. I realized he was in his own culture shock, and very much worse than what I was experiencing.

He was unable to show emotion so instead he moved into the next stage of grief, depression and loneliness. Many people at this stage will experience some sort of physical illness, but we are thankful that life was good to us. We met some new friends, refound some old friends, and found praying friends in the church. Most of all, we had new life. We had a baby boy that next year, and we named him Peymon, which means *oath* or *promise*. That was a new beginning for us and I knew things were going to be alright.

But for many Iranians things were not alright. There were suicides, and one fellow really panicked and went to Iran and married there. He must have been warned how difficult it was to get visas for Iranians that year, but went ahead with his plans anyway. He brought his bride to the American Embassy in Germany, and they told him it may take a year to get her visa. He did a very foolish thing and put his new bride in a suitcase with some bananas to eat. When he arrived at the Los Angles airport, he rushed to get his suitcase; he took it over in a corner to open it, but his new bride was dead. She had been crushed under the weight of all the suitcases. He left the suitcase there, went to Sacramento, and three days later committed suicide. It took the authorities a few days to relate these two deaths. Los Angeles Times reported the dead groom's roommate, Hadi, as lamenting, "The Romeo and Juliet story has come back in all this. She just wanted to be with her husband."

This fellow had been consumed by the next stage of grief which is a sense of guilt. This was an extreme case but most Middle Easterners will experience a deep sense of guilt for having left their friends and families. If the man was the oldest son, he will feel he shirked the responsibility of elderly parents, aunts and uncles, or nieces and nephews. If the foreigner is a war refugee, he will feel guilty about family or friends left behind in that dangerous situation.

When we left Iran, my two close friends clung to me and wept bitterly. I took Hesam, my Iranian friend Simin's little boy, in my arms. Hesam had become like one of my own children, and I couldn't help remembering the day I helped get a fish bone out of his throat. "Who would Simin call when she needed help after I was gone?" I wondered. They were looking to a future of insecurity and devastation, and the loss of a friend was taken very hard. That memory for me will always be mixed with a tinge of guilt.

After having been hard on themselves, the Middle Easterner may become angry and resentful of others. People have a tendency to try to figure out what went wrong and who is to blame for their situation. America, with its twentieth century colonialism activities is a prime target for being the cause. Granger Westberg describes it like this:

> Resentment is not a healthy emotion and, if allowed to take over, it can be very, very harmful. Yet it is a normal part of the grief process. It is to be expected, it is to be wrestled with, and it can, by the Grace of God, be overcome....When we have something precious

*taken from us we inevitably go through a stage when we are very
critical of everything and everyone who was related to the loss.*

With feelings of guilt and anger, it can be very difficult for the
Middle Easterner to have a good time. In fact, if they enjoyed
themselves they would feel more guilty. This feeling of not being able
to relax and become your *old self* may last for a very long time. They
may develop a feeling of mistrust for people around them.

The process of grieving is normal and healthy but people around
them have no idea what they are going through. Many Americans
make remarks like, "My, it must be quite a privilege for you to be in
this country." Another famous question is, "How do you like it here?"
At times it is difficult for them to respond to these questions. Some
Americans may wonder, "If it's so difficult why don't they go back to
their country?"

Usually there are real reasons why they cannot return, but Bahram
described the situation like this. "You become like a bird with two
homes who can't decide which one to go to. You just have to make a
decision and learn to live with it."

One day Bahram and I were having one of our philosophical and
sometimes heated discussions about the difference between
Christianity and Islam. Our son, Javad, who was by now fifteen years
old said, "What do you guys think you are accomplishing? Today I had
a kid ask me if I was a Buddhist!" This threw us all into a fit of
laughter. The situation can actually be comical at times.

We have much to be thankful for. Christian friends have
continually prayed for us and our Middle Eastern family. Not one of
our relatives was hurt in the ten year Iran-Iraq war, and they have had
many chances to visit us. But many other Middle Easterners are still
very isolated. Where do they find their hope and a new reality of life?

Christians can be that hope to help Middle Eastern Muslims find
their new reality. Muslims have more in common with Christians than
any other segment of our society. When they first come to the West
they are not so materialistic. They like nice things but still have the
basic understanding that things are to be used, and people are to be
loved.

Middle Eastern men will usually be educated, professional people.
Muslims are very moral people and enjoy what Americans call clean
entertainment: a picnic, a play, the zoo, museums, or just visiting in

each others homes. The men are usually very good at soccer and volleyball, and interested in learning about new sports. Most of all, they may just enjoy being with you over a cup of nice hot tea.

Much of Middle Eastern education is composed of memorizing historical lore, so they are steeped in literature and spiritual teaching. A Christian may discuss religion with a Muslim more comfortably than a next door neighbor.

Muslims need to see the model of a healthy God-worshipping family. Even the Muslim families that seem to have made a healthy adjustment will still be in a state of transition. They are in a position of re-evaluating beliefs, values, and practices. Many of their former ways of life are not workable in this new culture. They will be living in varying degrees of *sub-culture*. They are adopting many American practices but rejecting others. A Christian family's friendship, support, and guidance at a time like this would be very beneficial to them.

Middle Eastern women will be in their own state of transition. We must be careful not to judge Middle Eastern woman and their relationships with their families by current Western standards. They come from ancient societies with centuries of traditions. They grew up enjoying the company of the women in their extended family, and spending very little time alone. They have not been raised to think as individuals like we are in the West, but rather were a part of an interdependent society. Privacy is not even an issue in the Middle East. They identify very strongly with their families. Women are known by who their father is or who their husband is. If one's husband is an engineer like mine, for example: people called me Mrs. Engineer Shadzi. Women carry a sense of responsibility that their behavior is reflective on the family name. That is of paramount importance in the Middle East. Young men come looking for a bride based on the good family name. If an older sister shames the family name the younger sister may not have anyone ask for her hand in marriage.

Many of the Middle Eastern countries are making a special effort to provide education for the present generation of women. When we lived in Iran I wanted to continue learning Farsi. I had Farsi at the University of Minnesota, but in Iran I could not find a class at my level of language. I decided to go to illiteracy classes for women. I will never forget what a delightful experience that was. The teacher was a young lady and she maintained an excellent balance of kindness and discipline in her class. We had one young woman who would often come in late, and always had an excuse which obviously sounded very logical to her. To the teacher and the rest of the class, watching TV or taking a shower were not good excuses for interrupting the class. She was quite comical.

Everyone was fascinated by the illiterate foreigner in class, and they all spent a good deal of their time watching me. One nice girl named Esmat became my friend and seemed very intelligent. She noticed that I walked home seven blocks every night. It was late fall and it had started to get dark before class was over. Esmat said, "I notice you are attracting quite a bit of attention walking home every evening. Why don't you ride home with us. My brother picks me up and will be happy to drop you at Azar Street."

I thought to myself, "Yes, the group of curious young fellows following me was getting larger." I knew they meant no harm but it was getting embarrassing. I told her that I would appreciate that. The next day when I got to class everyone was very obviously watching me. "I wonder what's up today," I thought.

Finally someone came up to my desk and asked, "Did that strange car you got into last night take you outside of the city and bother you?"

So that was it! "No, that was Esmat's brother's car and they just gave me a ride home." They all shook their heads and I'm not quite sure if they believed me because they kept warning me not to ride with strangers. I would say, "I will never do that, thank you for your concern." I only stayed a few months in that class because they were studying much more slowly than I needed to, but I'm glad to have had the experience.

Educated women are going to work, in fact, everyone kept saying what a shame it was that I had a college education but was not pursuing a career. At the same time, women that made their home and family their career were still very much respected. One Pakistani friend made this comment about his mother. "My mother had seven children and they all became engineers, doctors, or lawyers. I consider my mother a very successful woman."

Even under Khomeini's Islamic Republic women have been included in educational advances. My sister-in-law, Shahla, is a biology Professor at the University of Isfahan. In 1988, she published a book on skin diseases. She was given an award for the best medical book of the year. She had to wear her veil, but she was honored on television by the President of Iran. Although there has been much publicity about the negative treatment of women by this new government, I was encouraged that they would honor a woman for this academic effort.

It may seem to a Westerner that women are over-protected in the Middle Eastern society. To myself, it felt very normal that the men should be attentive to where their women were and what they were doing. In fact, I was so impressed with what I saw, that I taught our little son that it was his job to care for his younger sister. He took his responsibility very seriously. One day I saw him herding her home and scolding her, "You are not allowed to go that far from the house, now you get home right this minute." He was only four and she was one year and a half, but she knew he was in charge. He saved her life twice when she was little. They have developed a loyalty to each other.

The transition of living in the West after such a sheltered lifestyle can be very confusing. Especially the younger women seem to be influenced by the materialism and romantic commercials on television. These young women could use an American woman friend to take them out to lunch, shopping, or introduce them to some of the cultural arts in America. Aminah al-Sa'id, a modern Egyptian feminist and journalist describes this transition:

> Thus, one of the most important challenges facing the Arab woman today is that of trying to equate her inner self, her thoughts and attitudes and feelings, with the contemporary social reality about her. It is not easy to resolve the contradictions, both personal and societal, which are bound to occur between the old inherited traditions and the new currents of thought.[5]

One very serious problem that eventually arises for Muslims in the West is the training of their children. Without spiritual education, their children are left to the mercy of television morals and advertising propaganda. They need to be advised that extended television viewing combined with this kind of societal freedom can be disastrous for their children. A Christian friend could encourage them to get their children in a Bible class so they can learn about God. They don't realize they will be more alienated from their children if they worship the god of materialism. The Muslim families we know that have sent their children to parochial schools have been very satisfied. The extra discipline is closer to the former system of education they were familiar with. This essay *Belonging to Two Worlds* by my son, Javad, reflects the struggle of Middle Eastern-American children:

> *Being a Middle Easterner and living in the United States is kind of like trying to melt water into lead, not much of a melting pot. It seems everywhere I go I have to wonder when someone is going to ask my nationality. If they do I tell them and wait for their reaction, or tell them that I don't know. But what's the use denying my own roots. It seems if you're not European in the United States, you are made to feel foreign. I'm as American as any German or Englishman and sometimes I'm glad of it; sometimes I regret it more than anything. When everyone is cheering on Desert Storm I think, "Why can't I just be happy and close my eyes and not care that it's fellow Middle Easterners they are killing?" Or when somebody starts bothering me because I'm part Iranian, I wish my Dad had never seen my Mom. Then there are times when I'm around other Iranian-Americans. We all share the same world and political beliefs and since there are so few of us, we are all greatly appreciated. It seems that we understand each other better and are more forgiving of each other's mistakes. All my best friends have been Iranian. By now you may be thinking, "If he likes Iran so much why doesn't he go live there." Well, for most of my life I've lived in America and I feel it may continue that way. No doubt, I'd love to visit Iran for a month or two, but living there would take some adjustment. I have no real problem with other Americans most of the time. The only times are when they let their ignorance of the world, and their ethnocentrism show through. The other half of me is Scottish but since the relatives on my Mom's side are third generation Americans, they've lost touch with their original heritage. I feel that my Iranian ancestry has made me a much better person, and I thank God for my Mom and Dad's meeting.*

What can you expect from a Muslim relationship? You can expect a polite, gracious, and loyal friend. C. S. Lewis says this about relationships from the old *country:*

> *To the ancients, friendship seemed the happiest and most fully human of all the loves; the crown of life and the school of virtue. The modern world ignores it....on a broad historical view, it is not*

the demonstrative gestures of friendship among our ancestors but the absence of such gestures in our society that calls for some special explanation. We, not they, are out of step.[6]

The Middle Easterners have a series of humble gestures that the Persians call *tarouf*. They involve placing the guest at the head of the table and saying all kinds of interesting phrases like "your face is like the moon," "I die for you," and many many more. During my Farsi classes at the University of Minnesota, I would ask our Farsi professor, Dr. Bashiri, to teach us *tarouf*. I learned that if someone gave you a compliment you would answer, "Thank you, but it is your eyes that behold beauty." When you left someone's home after dinner you would say, "You have made us ashamed with your wonderful hospitality." If someone thanked you for doing something nice for them, you would answer, "I am your servant." Learning the taroufs was like a game for me. When I stepped off the airplane in Iran and immediately started using them, my family squealed in delight that I had made such an effort.

These humble gestures of friendship are one of the things the Middle-Easterners miss when they move to the West. We Americans have a few of these gestures left, phrases like "How are you," "Did you have a good day?," "It was nice to have you or see you," etc. Feel very free to use these gestures with Middle Easterners; they will enjoy them very much. Middle Easterners look at these phrases as an effort to acknowledge another person and give him worth. Muslims are very hospitable people and readily open their homes. Remember, they enjoy *being* together rather than *doing* together, so things will move more slowly. They may enjoy some activities, but keep it simple.

You can expect your relationship to mean more to them than you realize, so don't get discouraged if things seem to be moving slowly. They did not grow up in the fast lane, instant everything, society of the West.

Eventually, as friends share everything, you will share your faiths also. As you share your faith, most Muslims will reject parts of it but will also add parts of it to their own religious knowledge. They will be deeply wounded if you reject their confession of faith. You do not have to agree with everything they believe but you do need to respect and encourage their faith in God. That is the thing you have the most in common. Remember the words of Paul in 1 Corinthians 13(TJB):

Love is always patient and kind; it is never jealous; love is never boastful or conceited, it is never rude or selfish; it does not take offense, it is not resentful. Love takes no pleasure in other people's sins but delights in the truth; it is always ready to excuse, to trust, to hope, and to endure whatever comes..... In short, there are thre e things that last: faith, hope, and love; and the greatest of these is love.

Notes:

1. Daniel-Rops, *Daily Life in the Time of Jesus.*

2. Edwin M. Yamauchi, *Persia and the Bible,* (Grand Rapids, MI: Baker Book House, 1990), p. 140.

3. Joseph Campbell, *The Power of Myth with Bill Moyers,* (New York, NY: Doubleday, 1988), p. 41.

4. Granger E. Westberg, *Good Grief,* (Philadelphia, Pa.: Fortress Press, 1971), p. 21.

5. Elizabeth Warnock Fernea and Basima Qattan Besirgan, *Middle Eastern Muslim Women Speak,* Austin: Univ of Texas Press, 1984. p. 380.

6. C. S. Lewis, *The Inspirational Writings of C. S. Lewis, The Four Loves,* (New York, NY: Inspirational Press, 1987), p. 244, 247.

THE PRACTICE
OF ISLAM

*Ye are the best community that hath been raised up for mankind. Ye enjoin
right conduct and forbid indecency; and ye believe in God.*

--Surah 3:110, Quran

Bahram and I had our first wedding in the Baptist church in a small
city in North Dakota. We assumed no pastor would marry us since
Bahram was Muslim and I was not affiliated with any church. So, after
four years of being best friends, we announced to my parents that we
were getting married at the justice of the peace. It was my
grandfather's idea that we get married back home in a church. As
destiny dawns, a Baptist pastor had a son who was studying in Iran at
the American University of Shiraz. This pastor was very kind and
offered to let us get married in his church. The pastor of my mother's
church agreed to marry us. He made the ceremony very religious; he
even had Bahram pass the ring to him and then to the best man and
take it back again in the name of the Father, the Son, and the Holy
Spirit. Bahram said that part very quickly. Our best Iranian friend,
Javad, drove up with us from Minneapolis to be our best man. He did a
very good job except he neglected telling us he didn't know how to
drive until we were in my father's car going up the wrong side of the
road.

We had our second marriage ceremony scheduled for the next
summer in Iran. Bahram didn't tell his family we were married. He
had received their approval but didn't want to spoil the Iranian
wedding for them.

That was our first trip to Iran and it was very traumatic for me. My
vocabulary of about twenty-five Farsi words was only enough to
communicate the mere essentials. The day we arrived in Isfahan I
couldn't get my feet on solid ground. The weather was so dry and arid,
and I felt like my balance was off. I went upstairs to lie down and

woke up a couple hours later not knowing where I was. There was someone standing over me but I did not recognize him. He had a worried look on his face. I finally realized it was my own beloved husband.

The house was busy with plans for the wedding. Everyone was rushing here and there but I couldn't understand a word.

"Bahram, what are we going to do at this wedding?"

"I don't know; I have never been married before!"

"Well, couldn't you translate a little bit for me?"

"Honey, I can't sit around and translate all day for you. But there is one thing we need to discuss. In Iran, in order to be a legitimate wife you must be a Muslim. If you decide not to become a Muslim we can have a contract marriage for as many number of years as we like."

"Well, if I weren't a wife, what would I be?"

"A concubine."

A concubine! I thought, Oh.., I've never been very good at being a concubine. I would much rather be his real wife. "What would I have to do to become a Muslim?" I asked.

"You would have to say, 'I believe in one God and that Muhammad is his prophet'."

Well, I thought, that sounded easy enough.

"In Arabic."

"In Arabic!" I exclaimed.

"Don't worry, I can write it down on a piece of paper and you can memorize it."

I was on the verge of tears that morning and every time Bahram's seven year old niece Mina saw me, she announced it to everyone.

By afternoon, all the guests started pouring into Bahram's mother's home, the women in one room and the men in another. Then Bahram's brother-in-law, Dr. Baluchi, came and said, "Judith, you must put on this chadour (veil) and come into the other room to talk to a Mullah."

"What does a Mullah want with me?"

"Oh, he just wants to ask you a few questions."

I went in and sat down with my long chadour and he asked me, "Why do you want to become a Muslim?"

Well, because I want to be a wife, I thought, but I probably shouldn't tell him that. So, I just gave him a blank look.

"Is it because you want to marry this boy?" I gave him my most polite smile.

Dr. Baluchi said, "She doesn't speak very good Farsi."

My, I thought as I got up to leave, these Mullahs are certainly perceptive people.

They set me in the middle of the women's room in front of a beautiful display of flowers, a large mirror, and dishes of candy, nuts, and pretty spices all laid on a tablecloth on the floor. The mirror, I was told, is reminiscent of a time when the groom was not allowed to see the bride's face until the wedding night (like Jacob and Rachael, or Leah I should say). Since all women were under the veil in public places, their faces were partially hidden to men outside the family. When a man was of marriageable age he would go to a respectable family and ask for one of his daughters, knowing full well it would be the oldest. The first tender look between the bride and groom would be through the reflection of a mirror in the marriage chamber.

My sisters-in-law brought a large sheet and two of them held it over my head. Two other ladies rubbed gigantic sugar lumps together over the sheet. This was supposed to make our life sweet together.

Bahram's sister had taken my wedding ring, and I looked down and saw it laying in the candy dish. "Oh," I said, "someone has dropped my ring in the candy."

Bahram said, "No silly, that's where it is supposed to be."

All in all, it turned out to be a lovely wedding. I was especially thankful to be a real wife. Nothing more was said to me about being a Muslim until I was over visiting with a neighbor. She said, "Now that you are a Muslim you must learn the five pillars of Islam."

"I think I better learn how to speak Farsi first. But what are the five pillars of Islam?" She said the pillars of Islam are profession of faith, prayer, fasting, alms, and the pilgrimage to Mecca.

Profession of Faith

Man is truly free only as he submits to God and works with his supreme will.   --Muhammad the Prophet

Let us consider the Muslims and their religious beliefs. Islam means *submission to God*, and Muslim means *one who submits to God*. The Muslims worship God, and Muhammad is the messenger of God's word.

We often hear that Muslims worship Allah. Muslim scholars feel the word God in English is not as all-encompassing in its meaning as Allah is in Arabic. For this reason they are reluctant to translate the word Allah to God. Some Muslims feel it may be a bit nationalistic on the part of the Arabs. Allah literally means *The Almighty and Merciful God, Creator of heaven and earth, to Whom all things return*, what the Christians would perceive more as *God the Father*. Arab Christians also worship Allah because it literally means *God* in the Arabic language.

Muslims prefer not to be called Muhammadans because it implies they worship Muhammad, which is not so. Muhammadans was a name put on the Muslims by European Christians, and Muslims have always been offended by it.

Islam is not only a religion but it is a way of life. We could compare this with the Christian phrase "walking daily with your Lord." Islam also has a complete system of government and social order.

The profession of faith is a simple creed of "I bear witness that there is no God but Allah and that Muhammad is the Prophet of Allah." Whoever makes this profession of faith becomes a Muslim.

Prayer

Islam could well be called the religion of prayer, for in no other faith is such strict emphasis placed on regular and frequent prayer.

--I.G. Edmonds
"Islam"

Muslim's must pray to God five times a day, but often combine the last two prayer times. The most common prayer times are before dawn, at noon (high noon), and after dusk. Before prayer each person must wash their face, their arms up to the elbows, and the front of their feet. In many parasitic disorders like microscopic mites (better known as scabies or the "seven year itch"), 60 percent of the mites stay on the hand to the elbow. This washing of hands to the elbow would prevent this kind of a disorder. This ritual washing is not only a practical reminder of cleanliness, but also symbolic of approaching God with a repentant and cleansed heart.

Each household keeps a prayer cloth, often adorned with hand embroidery. The cloth lies on the floor in front of the person praying. Each prayer cloth contains a small clay tablet from Mecca with Quranic scripture impressed on it, a string of beads and maybe a keepsake from a loved one. Standing toward Mecca, their holy city, the individual does a ritual kneeling down, prostration with forehead on the clay tablet, and standing with hands uplifted to heaven in prayer. It is fascinating to see a large group of Muslims with their faces on the ground in prostration to God.

The Muslims have a main prayer which they recite that could be compared to the Christian's "Lord's Prayer":

> In the name of God, Most Gracious, Most Merciful,
> Praise be to God,
> The Cherisher and Sustainer of the Worlds;
> Most Gracious, Most Merciful;
> Master of the Day of Judgement.
> Thee do we worship,
> and Thine aid we seek.
> Show us the straight way,
> The way of those on whom
> Thou hast bestowed Thy Grace,
> Those whose (portion)
> Is not wrath
> And who go not astray........ [1]

This is part of the prayer that is repeated by faithful Muslims at least seventeen times throughout their daily prayers.

Muslims often go to the Mosque for mass prayer. Friday is the one day off in the Middle East and large numbers come to the Mosques or Islamic Centers for corporate prayer. There is also a guest speaker and prayer leader at the Friday prayers.

One is never to break a prayer for any reason. I remember our two-year-old son going up to his grandmother during her prayer time and watching for a while; but then in his impishness, he grabbed her clay tablet and ran off with it. She would try to suppress her humor with just a smile but faithfully finish her prayers. She would then go find the little rascal and retrieve her sacred clay tablet.

Fasting

O ye who believe! Fasting is prescribed for you, even as it was prescribed
for those before you, that ye may ward off evil;　　--Quran, Surah 2:183

Muslim countries recognize the fasting month of Ramadan. It is the ninth month of the Muslim year shifting with the lunar calendar. It changes a few days every year, so Ramadan is sometimes in the winter; sometimes in the summer. From sunrise to sunset no one is to eat, drink, smoke, or indulge in life's pleasures.

When Ramadan falls in the long hot summer days it can be a very difficult task. Those physically unable are excused from fasting, but must abstain from eating openly in public as not to tempt others.

After the 1979 Revolution in Iran, the Khomeini government became especially strict about the practice of fasting. Shopkeepers dared not sell anyone open bottles of refreshment during the daylight hours. We were out shopping and our three year old daughter, Taraneh, was crying. She was thirsty but a number of shopkeepers refused to sell us any refreshments. Finally, one shopkeeper took pity on me and said, "I will give you a cold bottle of orange pop but you must hide it under your clothes until you get it in the car and out of sight." This was in due respect to hungry or thirsty fasters in the street.

Fasting is a spiritual discipline but also helps people identify with the poor and hungry. Muslims believe it is a training in self-discipline and atones for all the sins of the year. If one is unable to fast, feeding of one poor person for a month is prescribed for the financially able.

This may all sound very glum but Muslim families have special memories of the late evening dinners and prayers of that month. Sweet shops bake a special series of cakes similar to apple fritters in syrup to revive the hungry fasters. This time carries a special kind of excitement in a Muslim country.

Almsgiving

Prayer carries us half-way to God; fasting brings us to the door of His
palaces; almsgiving procures for us admission.　　--Early Muslim Scholar

The Arabic word for alms is zakat. It means purification. In Islam, the contribution to God's work makes the rest of ones wealth authentic.

Giving alms is an integral part of the Muslim obligation and could be compared to the Christian tithe. It is not a completely foreign term. We are all familiar with Walt Disney's Robin Hood dressed as a beggar calling, "Alms, alms, give alms to the poor."

No one knew better than the Prophet Muhammad what it was like to be in need; he was an orphan quite early in his life. In Islam, there is a big emphasis on helping the poor, the orphans, the slaves, and the travelers.

Different Muslim countries may handle alms in different ways. Alms is broken down into different categories; 10 percent of a farmer's unirrigated produce, 5 percent of irrigated produce, 2 1/2 percent of cash and precious metals, etc. Some Muslim governments have actually collected alms as taxes but other Muslim countries will leave tithing up to the individual's personal conviction. Iran uses the terms "khoms" and "zakat" together for the combination of giving money and material goods such as food or clothing. "Khoms" literally means 20 percent, as a guideline to the faithful.

Alms are to be primarily used for the poor, but the *Quran* gives a few other examples of administration such as facilities for health and education, facilities for travelers, redeeming debts, or ransoming Muslim war captives. Many of these services have been rendered through the mosque.

Another practice quite common is contributing to the poor in appreciation to God for a special grace bestowed. The first time I saw a women slip a bill under a pillow was when her daughter had fallen and hit her head on the cement. The child had acted unusually lethargic, and illness is very frightening to people in the Middle East because of the limited medical facilities. I asked Bahram, "Why did she put money under the child's pillow?" He said she would give it to the poor in appreciation to God for gracefully restoring her child's health. Islam teaches one should always be thankful to God for mercy.

The Pilgrimage to Mecca

Living on a day to day basis, the person lacks direction. His aim is only to live. What exists is a dead spirit in a living body. However, the Hajj experience alters this unhealthy condition!   --Dr. Ali Shariati

Our cousin Manuchehr had become quite wealthy through his clothing factory and had moved close to the University of Isfahan.

What a beautiful house he had bought; it was made from white stone that literally shown in the sunlight. It had two floors, with complete living quarters on each floor. The main floor was for serving guests and was elaborately furnished. Persian carpets throughout the whole house overlapped each other. Manuchehr and his wife, Batul Agha, slept on the first floor and the second floor was living quarters for the grandmother and five children. Outside was a lovely flower garden with a large water pool in front of the house and a tall brick wall around it.

One day Cousin Manuchehr announced he was going on his pilgrimage to Mecca. Everyone seemed very excited about this. He was gone for a few weeks, and upon his return a great celebration was planned. Cousin Manuchehr now received the title of Hajji. We were told to plan on staying at his home for four whole days.

It was a very interesting experience to say the least. All the aunts and uncles and their children stayed there for four days and other guests kept pouring in throughout the afternoon and the evening. One evening was particularly crowded. The main floor was full of men, and a Mullah had been invited to read from the *Quran*. The second floor was full of the women, and those of us that didn't wear the veil congregated into a room by ourselves. Of course, I, being a fair-eyed Westerner, was often the star attraction. I didn't always know how to handle so much attention.

Hajji Manuchehr and Bahram were very close and we were constantly being called down to the main floor living room to sit with a special guest. We decided we had never eaten so many cakes or drunk so many cups of tea as in those four days, and probably never would again.

I asked them what happened in Mecca to deserve such an elaborate celebration and this is what they told me:

It is prescribed for each Muslim once in his lifetime, provided he can afford it, to do a pilgrimage to Mecca. It occurs during the last month of the Islamic calendar. The Arabic word for the pilgrimage to Mecca is Hajj.

Before a person departs for Hajj, he must write a will, pay up debts to people, and go ask forgiveness for disagreements with others. This is symbolic of preparing oneself for death and God's judgment.

Muslims say "Go to Mecca and you will find yourself." It represents a return of man to God, to his origin, of visiting his creator and best friend.

Hajj is a journey through creation; it takes twelve days. The journey has two parts and six stops.

The show of creation begins at Miqat, a spot six miles south of Medina, Saudi Arabia. Several million people from all nations and tribes participate in Hajj. At this point each person must state his intention, as a form of verbal repentance, and then change his street clothes into the white burial shroud of the Muslim tradition. This act represents the shedding of self-centeredness and class distinction. Miqat emphasizes "we" rather than "I."

In Miqat, man visits his own grave, symbolic of burying the old self. Now, having buried the old self and wearing the white robes of righteousness, they move as a flood of white toward God's house in Mecca. The group walks the six miles through the desert and sleeps in tents at night. A medical staff accompanies them. This unity of believers is called the community, or Ummah.

The next stop is Mecca, which consists of the Kaaba, the skirt of Hagar, and the black rock.

The Kaaba is a cubical building and is believed to have been built by Abraham. It is constructed of stone and cement, is covered with a black cloth, and is empty inside. Dr. Ali Shariati, an Iranian theologian and philosopher explains the simplicity of the Kaaba in his book *Hajj:*

> *Why is the Kaaba so simple, lacking color and ornamentation? No pattern or visualization of God that man imagines can represent him being omnipotent and omnipresent, God is "absolute."*

To the west, facing the Kaaba, is a small semi-circular wall called the "skirt of Hagar." Hagar, the Egyptian slave girl who was the mother of Ishmael, is honored here. The fact that God chose such a humble being to be used for his purposes, and that she obeyed in returning to Sarah is the message of Hagar's skirt. The act of the participants is to circle the Kaaba and Hagar's skirt seven times. The circling of the Kaaba is symbolic of the continuing activity and turning of God's people toward him. God's presence in the Kaaba becomes the center of existence.

The pilgrims must enter and exit the area at the point of the black stone. The black stone signifies God's hand, and the person must put their right hand on the stone, making a promise to God. This symbolism comes from the traditional tribal practice of holding each other's right hand in commitment and nullifying all previous allegiances.

There is also a spot where one stops and prays in Abraham's footprints. At this point each person has completed the Hajj and moves on to the second part of the journey through creation. The group walks to neighboring mountains and must run seven times between two of them to signify the struggle of living out God's promises. This evolves from Genesis 21:14-19, where Hagar cries out to God to save Ishmael from thirst in the desert and from her struggle to find water for him.

Nine days have passed and the group travels to Arafat where Muhammad gave his last message. The pilgrims are to spend the day just leisurely discussing and interacting with each other, as this stop symbolizes "knowledge."

They leave at sunset for the next stop of Meshu which means "consciousness" and "understanding." The time spent here is in the quietness of night. The purpose is to reflect on what has been learned, and to prepare themselves in prayer for Holy War with Satan the following day. They are to collect seventy pebbles for the spiritual battle ahead of them. They pray and rejoice, preparing themselves for spiritual victory.

The next morning they enter the gate of their destination, Mina, meaning love and faith. Here the stations of Satan are located in the form of three statues or idols. The seventy pebbles are pelted at the idols, and Satan is defeated.

At this point, the Pilgrim is eligible to stand in Abraham's shoes and sacrifice a lamb for God. This act symbolizes the sacrifice of worldly things that may stand in the way of having a relationship with God, whatever that may be.

Now the person with the title of Hajj before his name (Hajj-khanum if it is a woman) is to return home and live a changed life, following the path of God.

Many Christians believe these practices are evidence that Muslims are trying to work their way to heaven, but they don't look at it like that. These practices are spiritual disciplines that are to position man before God so that a deeper inner working may be accomplished. Some Muslims have admitted to me that their prayers have become routine and meaningless at times, but the faithfulness of a person standing before God every day leaves the witness with a lasting respect. When something is habit, there is always a danger of performing a routine without the person applying his heart to the action. Christians can have the same problem. Unfortunately, there are many people that go to church every Sunday, but their lives show they get little out of it; but the chances that God will speak to their hearts from the worship and Bible reading is more than if they were not ever in church and never heard the reading and prayer. The practice of one's faith is necessary in order to grow in a relationship with God.

As we look at the history of the church, we see it has been difficult for Christians to attain that perfect balance of proclaiming faith and practicing that faith. The church has recently seen a revival of literature on the spiritual disciplines that has been so sorely neglected in this century. The most popular is Richard Foster's *The Celebration of Discipline*. Richard Foster is careful to point out the disciplines are not an end in themselves but are a way to place ourselves before God so that He can transform us.

David Shenk, a lecturer in comparative religion and Church history at the University of Nairobi, says it well:

> ....*many Christians who have Muslim friends are impressed by the sincerity and devotion of Muslim worship. The Muslim discipline of prayer, fasting, or almsgiving is impressive. Christians appreciate that essence of Islamic worship is submission to God. As Christians hear and see the Muslim witness in worship, they are often challenged to also become more disciplined in their own experience of worship. [2]*

Notes:

1. Badru D. Kateregga, David W. Shenk, *Islam and Christianity* (Grand Rapids, Michigan: William B. Erdmans Publishing Company, 1981), p. xx. 2. Ibid., p. 65.

PART II

HISTORICAL ISLAM

THE PROPHET MUHAMMAD

Abraham prayed...Our Lord! And raise up in their midst a messenger from among them who shall recite unto them Thy revelations, and shall instruct them in the Scripture and in wisdom and shall make them grow. Lo! Thou, only Thou, art the Mighty, Wise.   --Surah 2:129, Quran

O People, if you have been worshipping Muhammad, then know that Muhammad is dead, dead, dead. But if you have been worshipping God, then know that God is eternal and never dies. God said in His Holy Book: Muhammad is but a human messenger like other messengers before him. If he died or was killed, would you then forsake your faith that only God is God?   --Abu Bakr, Muhammad's companion

Where did it all begin? In order to understand Islam we must go way back, before Muhammad, into the land of Canaan. It began with a man the Muslims also call Father Abraham. The Muslims are also standing on some promises from the Old Testament. Let's say they have a *piece of the rock.*

Abram and Sarai, knowing that God had promised him descendants as many as the stars in the sky, were perplexed by Sarai's barrenness. They decided to make some effort of their own and Sarai suggested Abram have a child by her own Egyptian handmaid, Hagar. It didn't take Sarai long to regret her decision and she began to mistreat Hagar.

Now Hagar was not just any servant girl. Tradition tells us Hagar was a daughter of the Pharaoh of Egypt, from one of his concubines. During a famine Sarai and Abram traveled to Egypt; Abram feared for his life and said Sarai was his sister. According to Nuzi law, discovered in Iraq in the 1920's, Hurrian wives also had the status of sister. It was within the limits of law, as was substituting a wife's servant for the purpose of procreation. We may recall Paul's words of 1 Corinthians 10:23, that all things may be lawful but not necessarily beneficial. Many Eastern scholars feel these two decisions of

Abraham's were beneficial and directly in God's plan to reach the Arab nation with His word. It was through Hagar and Ishmael that the Arabs become a *People of the Book.*

Pharaoh takes Sarai for his wife but God sends plagues to his court during this time. Abram was reprimanded but was given many gifts. (Gen 12) One of the gifts was Hagar. Two ancient Jewish commentaries, the *Midrash* and the *Soncino Chumash,* and the Palestinian *Targum* are only a few of the sources that confirm Hagar's royal blood. Midrash Rabbah 45:1:

> *And she had a handmaid whose name was Hagar. She had a handmaid of usufruct (Abraham could use her dowry without any accountability) and he was bound to support her and was not permitted to sell her. R. Simeon b. Yohai said: Hagar was the daughter of Pharaoh. When Pharaoh saw what had been done to Sarah in his house he took his daughter and gave her to him (Abraham) saying. "It is better that my daughter be a handmaid in this house than the mistress of a another." Thus it is written "And she had a handmaid named Hagar." he saying "Here is your reward (agar)." [1]*

Another version of tradition is that while Sarah was in the King's court, Hagar became a believer in the God of Sarah. Hagar willingly stepped down from her high position to be a servant in order to be a part of God's people. It was said she was a woman of beauty, piety, and kindness. This information does shed a different light on Hagar and why the Muslims look to her for inspiration.

One day Hagar became very discouraged and decided to run away, but in Genesis 16 she found herself face to face with an angel. God gave her a promise that day by the well of Beer Lahai Roi, meaning *the Living One who sees me.*

The angel asked her where she was going. "I am running away from my mistress," answered Hagar. The angel told her she must return to her mistress and submit to her authority. This is the promise she was given in Gen 16:10-12:

> *...And the angel of the Lord said unto her, I will so greatly multiply your descendants that they cannot be numbered for the multitude.*

*And the Lord said to her "Behold, you are with child and shall bear
a son; you shall call his name Ishmael; because the Lord has heard
your affliction. He shall be a wild man, his hand against every man,
and every man's hand against him.*

This statement about Ishmael has often been misunderstood. The
Hebrew word for wild ass is *pere.* [2] The connotation of that word
was free-spirited and unrestrained. The Ishmaelites had to dwell in
semiarid lands and in deserts and they were a tough people. [3] I
myself grew up in North Dakota and when I graduated and moved to
the big city I found it very easy to find jobs. One interviewer said to
me, "I always hire applicants from North Dakota. I find them to be
tough, honest, hard-working people." The reason for that was North
Dakota was a bit of a barren land itself, and nothing came easy. Harsh
weather, and small towns and cities with a minimum of facilities
developed character. This would be much more pronounced in the
Arabian desert. Ishmael was tough and thrived in the desert despite the
extreme hot and cold temperatures, the winds, and vast landscape of
sand.

Jehan Sadat, former first lady of Egypt tells of visiting Palestinian
refugees living in tents in the desert:

*I shuddered, thinking of the rain that beat so hard on the aluminum
roof of our house some nights that I could barely sleep, of the winter
nights in the desert so cold I could not stand them. I thought, too, of
the scorpions that lived in the desert. One had stung my sister when
she come to visit Anwar and me, and after we had taken her to the
military hospital for treatment we had slept for days with the legs of
our beds set in buckets of water. [3]*

The name Ishmael means *God hears.* Hagar was very impressed by
this visitation from God and she was obedient and returned to Serai
and Abram. It is easy to imagine Hagar going back to Abraham and
Sarah and telling them how she met God at the well, and what he told
her: that she was going to have a son and was to call him Ishmael.
Ishmael was born when Abram was eighty six years old, and Abram
agreed to call him Ishmael.

Thirteen years later God appears to Abram and tells him he is
going to change Abram's and Serai's names to Abraham and Sarah.
The name Abraham means *father of a great multitude,* and Sarah

means *princess*. God then tells Abraham that Sarah is going to be the *mother of nations* and this seems to confuse him. Sarah is ninety years old. In Gen 17:17 it says Abraham fell up on his face, and laughed, and said in his heart, Shall a child be born unto him that is an hundred years old? In verse 18 Abraham said unto God, "O that Ishmael might live before thee!" Abraham receives his answer in verse 19:

> *And God said, Sarah thy wife shall bear thee a son indeed; and thou shalt call his name Isaac: and I will establish my covenant with him for an everlasting covenant, and with his seed after him.*

But God does not ignore Abraham's plea for his first son. In Gen 17:20 God gives another promise for Ishmael:

> *As for Ishmael, I have heard thee: Behold I have blessed him and will make him fruitful and will multiply him exceedingly; twelve princes shall he beget, and I will make him a great nation.*

As the problems in Abraham's household come to a head, Sarah demands that Abraham throw the bondwoman and her son out. Abraham grieves for his son Ishmael, but God tells Abraham to do what Sarah says. He promises that He himself will care for Ishmael in Gen 21:13:

> *And also of the son of the bondwoman will I make a nation, because he is thy seed.*

Hagar and Ishmael are sent away into the desert with bread and a bottle of water and when the water is finished she sets Ishmael under a brush and cries that she cannot watch him die. In Gen 21:17-21(RSV) we find God himself rescuing them:

> *And God heard the voice of the lad; and the angel of God called to Hagar from heaven, and he said to her, "What troubles you Hagar? Fear not; for God has heard the voice of the lad where he is. Arise, lift up the lad, and hold him fast with your hand, for I will make him a great nation." Then God opened her eyes, and she saw a well of water; and she wept, and filled the skin with water and gave the lad a drink. And God was with the lad, and he grew up; he lived in the wilderness, and became an expert with a bow. He lived in the wilderness of Paran, and his mother took a wife for him from the land of Egypt.*

God does not himself will that anyone be thrown out of their home, but he knew these two mothers and their sons rallying for Abraham's affections would be an emotionally unhealthy atmosphere for everyone. We can assume Ishmael became a righteous man because it said God was with him and on the basis of Gen 18:19. God says this about Abraham.

> *For I know him, that he will command his children and his household after him, and they shall keep the way of the Lord, to do justice and judgement; that the Lord may bring upon Abraham that which he hath spoken of him.*

Abraham had more sons by his second wife Keturah. He gave gifts to all his other children and sent them away also. In Gen 25:5 it says he gave all that he had to Isaac.

We don't hear anymore about Ishmael until the death of Abraham where Isaac and Ishmael come to bury him. Then Ishmael himself dies in Gen 25:13-18:

> *These are the names of the sons of Ishmael, named in the order of their birth: Nebajoth; and Kedar, and Adbeel, and Mibsam, and Mishma, and Dumah, and Massa, Hadad, Tema, Jetur, Naphish, and Kedemah. These are the sons of Ishmael and these are their names, by their villages and by their encampments, 12 princes according to their tribes... These are the years of the life of Ishmael, a hundre d and thirty-seven years; he breathed his last and died, and was gathered to his kindred. They dwelt in Havilah to Shur, which is opposite Egypt in the direction of Assyria; he settled over against all his people.*

Havilah is at the southern tip of the Arabian Peninsula and the way to Shur was along the Sinai, and today's northern borders of Arabia. This encompasses the whole Arabian Peninsula which is called the Cradle of Islam and the birth place of Muhammad.

Muhammad was born in the city of Mecca in the year 570 a.d. Muhammad's father died before he was born and he was put in the care of his grandfather. As an infant, he was sent off with a nomadic tribe into the desert where the air was much healthier. His mother and grandfather also died early and at eight years of age he was given to his uncle Abu Talib. Abu Talib was a merchant and Muhammad grew up on the trade routes to Syria and back.

As Muhammad grew he became very responsible and was put in charge of trade journeys. He was about 25 years old when he was given charge of the merchandise of a wealthy woman, Khadijeh. Khadijeh was so taken with Muhammad that she asked him to marry her. She was 40 years old. Muhammad and Khadijeh had been happily married for 24 years when she died in 619 a.d. They had four daughters.

Muhammad's marriage to Khadijeh was a turning point in his life. For the first time he had enough money to participate in merchandising on his own level and also had leisure time which he used to meditate alone in the desert. Muhammad had come in contact with many Jews and Christians on the trade route. Strangely enough, 600 years after Christ there were still no scriptures translated into written Arabic. The Coptic Christians of Egypt had translations in spoken Arabic, but had written them in Greek letters. It is certain Muhammad had heard all the Bible stories because he had intimate friends and family that were Christians.

Another contact Muhammad had that may have influenced him was the Lakmid Arabians. They were in control of many trade routes and were responsible for Arabic being the official language and had fully developed the sixth century pre-Islamic poetry. Parts of southern Arabia, along with the Lakmids had declared monotheism: the Lord of Heaven and Earth.

The Meccans were idol worshippers with shrines around the city, with the Ka'aba being the main shrine. This was grievous for Muhammad. He was also disturbed by the Meccans materialism and neglect of the poor, the widows, and orphans. Mecca was run by clans and anyone outside the protection of the clan was not cared for.

While he was yet married to Khadijeh, Muhammad began to spend much time alone for spiritual meditation in a cave outside of Mecca. One night while meditating, he had a vision in which the angel Gabriel came to him and said, "Recite."

Muhammad said, "What shall I recite?" Muhammad received a revelation from the angel, and continued to have them up to 23 years later. These revelations are what make up the contents of the Quran.

At first Muhammad was disturbed by this experience but his wife

Khadijeh was the first to believe that his revelations were genuinely from God. She was the first woman to become a Muslim. Khadijeh took Muhammad to her cousin Waraqah, who was a Christian, and he believed these identical messages were given to Jews and Christians and the purpose was for Muhammad to share them with his people, the Arabs. Muhammad started having prayer meetings and developed a group of followers.

Muhammad was a threat to the leaders of the clans of Mecca with his call to follow one God. He was distracting some influential people away from their belief of man's achievement and materialism. The Meccans had a number of female gods they worshipped. The selling of idols was a big business. Muhammad and his followers received minor persecution at first; like having garbage dumped at their door. Eventually the persecution became severe and in 622, Muhammad and 70 followers emigrated to Medina. This flight to Medina was the beginning of the Muslim calendar which is still used today in the Middle East. A clan in Medina agreed to bring Muhammad and his followers under their protection.

There was a population of Jews in Medina and it was during this time he received his first rejection from those the Quran calls the *People of the Book.* This group of Jews had been expelled from the Roman empire.

While yet in Medina, Muhammad drew up a constitution for his Islamic State. The Jews were given autonomy and had their own rabbinic court to settle all of their own affairs. The Jews did not accept Muhammad's prophetic position and their loyalty to this Islamic state wavered. This was unacceptable to Muhammad at a time of political unrest. This was not only dangerous to his military planning but was a very big disappointment to him. He felt it necessary and succeeded in expelling some of the Jewish clans from that area.

The years that followed were a time of military conquest. The Muslims planned raids on Meccan caravans on the trade route. They became more and more powerful and with their power came many converts.

After Khadijeh's death, it is estimated Muhammad had about eleven wives. His most controversial marriage was with Zeynab, who had been married to his former slave but now adopted son, Zeyd. Muhammad had arranged the marriage of Zeyd and Zeynab himself but they were not happily married. Muhammad could not talk Zeyd out of the divorce so he took the responsibility and added her to his wives. The Quran's introduction to Surah 33 says this about Muhammad's wives:

...It may be mentioned that from the age of 25 until the age of 50 he had only one wife, Khadijah, 15 years his senior, to whom he was devotedly attached and whose memory he cherished until his dying day. With the exception of Ayisheh, the daughter of his closest friend, Abu Baker...all his later marriages were with widows whose state was pitiable for one reason or another. Some of them were widows of men killed in war. One was a captive, when he made the marriage the excuse for emancipating all the conquered tribe and restoring their property. Two were daughters of his enemies, and his alliance with them was a cause for peace. It is noteworthy that the period of these marriages was also the period of his greatest activity, when he had little rest from campaigning, and was always busy with the problems of a growing empire. [5]

Muhammad has been much criticized for taking so many wives, but yet we know many of the Old Testament characters, like David and Solomon had many wives and we accept it as a custom of that day. Muhammad himself did not condone it for his followers. The Quran, Surah 33:50 calls it... a privilege for thee only, not for the (rest of) believers.

The custom of the Islamic vale for women was implemented at this time. Muhammad's home, with a separate apartment for each wife, was attached to a Mosque. Many visitors and strangers came to the Mosque and on one such instant a stranger insulted the wives of the prophet by referring to them as slaves. It was decided after that they should wear vales, which had been a custom for women among the upper classes, to set them apart. The vale became custom and... "Muhammad's wives found themselves, on the one hand, deprived of personal liberty and, on the other hand, raised to a position of honor and dignity." [6]

During Muhammad's time in Medina his power and popularity increased but through two actions he gained the support of large numbers of Arabs. The Muslims had originally said their prayers toward Jerusalem, the Holy City. After he was rejected by the Jewish population in Medina he proclaimed Mecca the Holy City for Arabs, and instructed them to pray toward Mecca. Secondly, in the year 629 he did his first pilgrimage to Mecca.

In 630, Muhammad marched into Mecca with 10,000 men and took the city with little resistance. Shrines of idols were destroyed and only the empty Ka'aba remained as a shrine to the one and only living God.

Muhammad was a military conqueror as well as a spiritual leader. The Jews of Medina were friendly with him even though they never accepted his claim of prophetship. They did eventually accept his military authority. Muhammad never expected the Jews or Christians to convert to Islam, but he did make them pay a heavier tax than Muslim converts.

Muhammad became seriously ill and retired to the apartment of his favorite wife, Ayisheh. Muhammad died in Ayisheh's arms in 632 a.d. Before he died he prayed, "O Lord, I beseech Thee, assist me in the agonies of death, come close, O Gabriel, to me. Lord grant me pardon; Eternity, in Paradise! Pardon. Thy blessed companionship on high." [7] He was buried beneath Ayisheh's apartment, which is today a Mosque.

This is the legacy of Muhammad, descendant of one of the twelve tribes of Ishmael. He made the Arabs a great nation, worshippers of God. Under Muhammad's leadership, Arabia was united under one state, one law, and one bond of faith, which was the basis of the Great Islamic Empire. The Christian Byzantine Empire to the northwest repeatedly attacked the Persian Empire to the east, weakening it and leaving a power vacuum among many small states. Without Persia to protect them from the Byzantines, those minority states all sent tributes to Muhammad and joined his alliance. By his death, Muhammad had begun the invasion of Syria and Iraq.

After Muhammad's death, the community was ruled by khalifate to act as minister, judge, and spiritual ruler. The first khalif, Ayisheh's father and close friend of Muhammad, Abu Bakr ruled from 632 to 634. Omar was khalif from 634 to 644 a.d. There was rivalry between Uthman, the third khalif and the prophet's son-in-law Ali. In 656 Uthman was murdered and Ali became khalif. Muhammad was only survived by one daughter, Fatimah, from his first wife Khadijeh. Fatimah married Ali. Ali was assassinated in 661, and Uthman's relatives, the Umayyads seized power of the Islamic governments.

The first Khalifs, Abu Bakr and Omar, had started attacks on the weakened Persian Empire. Persia was taken and made an Islamic colony in 640. The Persians were accustomed to the Monarchy system and instituted it into their adaptation of Islam. According to the Persians, Ali was to inherit the position of khalif because he was married to the only descendant of the prophet. They started the Shi'ite party which believed the descendants of Fatimah should be the rightful heirs of the Prophet and his spiritual wisdom. The Shi'ites called their leaders Imams and there were twelve of them. They believed the last Imam, Imam Mehdi, vanished and will come back in the Last Days to establish justice and truth on the earth. The word Mehdi means the same as the word Messiah, the one who will return.

The greatest difference in the religious practice of Shi'ites is that they have a yearly passion play in honor of Ali's son Hossein who was violently martyred. In the 16th century the prosperous Safavid Dynasty in Iran made Shi'ism a state religion.

After the fifth Sunni khalif, Muawiyah (661-668), Sunni khalifs also inherited their positions until 1258. In the early 16th century, because of the military power of the Ottoman Turks, the Khalifite became a Turkish position. In 1924, the Turks terminated the position of Khalif in an attempt to westernize their country. This was a very big loss to the Islamic community and instilled a sense of loss to Muslims worldwide.

The split of Sunni and Shi'ite was basically over succession and is political in nature, rather than doctrinal. Their unity lies in being Muslims, and practicing the five pillars of Islam. [8]

Within a century the Muslims had conquered the area from Spain to India. Muhammad's successors drove the Byzantines out of the Eastern Mediterranean area. Other armies entered Northern Africa and the Berbers all turned to Islam. Christians and Jews were allowed to keep their faith but many Christians traveled North to the Italian borders. The integration of the Arabs and the Berbers in North Africa developed a race called the Moors. The Moors moved into Europe and by 712 a.d. Spain was largely in Muslim hands. They established their capitol at Cordoba. They built the Great Mosque in Cordoba with a thousand pillars. They installed street lighting, built 300 public baths, and dug a sanitation system. A university was founded that taught

Islamic theology, mathematics, medicine and chemistry. They replaced the Roman numerals with the Arabic numbers which we use today. Coming from the desert, the Arabs appreciated gardens and with the influence of the Persian Paradise, they planted beautiful gardens everywhere they went. The Middle Easterners were also very skilled in working with birds. Pigeons were introduced in the European diet. They taught Europeans improved methods of the sport of falconry. The Muslims brought their method of categorizing plants into natural medicines. This was considered the renaissance of Islam while Europe was yet in what was called the Middle Age or Dark Ages. The Islamic State maintained it's rule up until the time of the European crusades.

Muhammad came at a time in history where Christianity was not fulfilling it's mission. There was much disagreement over doctrine. The great power of the day, the Byzantines, were very warring and were said to have carried their cross and various number of icons to war with them. Their relationship with other countries was lacking that blessing that is so inherent to Christian leadership. In the forefront was the endless disagreements about the three persons of the Godhead, along with whether Mary was really the mother of God. How many theologians were excommunicated or executed because of their opinions on the deity of Christ? Even as late as the 16th Century, John Calvin and Martin Luther, men who we uphold in the Christian community today, were instrumental in having other Christians executed because of their theology of Christ and other doctrinal disagreements. [9] Muhammad saw many of these same characteristics in the religious leadership of his day and introduced Islam as an alternative system. The Quran solved the problem of the theology of Christ by saying God is one, and has no partners. Muhammad said, "People will be assembled on the judgement day according to the purposes of their hearts." Muhammad was concerned about the predicament of humanity as is described:

> The plight of humans everywhere distressed him; the status quo of other religions left much to be desired, for these religions had been disfigured by their guardians, the monks, priests, and rabbis. They had long since stopped to inspire and move humanity toward the great goals. And yet, the signs of God in creation were everywhere, arousing wonder and pressing the human mind to break through to its Creator. The patterns of God within the self, in the world of nature

and history, were obvious if humans would only shake off the inherited stereotypes and open themselves to the ever-fresh evidence of the facts of creation. [10]

Today, 44 countries call themselves Muslim countries and 40 countries claim 50 percent Muslim population. Sixty-four other countries claim 10 percent Muslim population. The overall Muslim population in the world is estimated at 800,000,000, making it the second largest religion in the world. [11] Today not all Muslims are Arabs and not all Arabs are Muslims. In fact, the six largest Muslim countries are no longer Arab. They are Indonesia, 145 million; Pakistan, 92 million; Bangladesh, 90 million; the Soviet Union, 50 million; and Turkey, 50 million. Islam is the fastest growing religion in the United States of America. Today America has an estimated 4 million Muslims. [12]

Notes:

1. Louis Bahjat Hamada, *Understanding the Arab World,* (Nashville: Thomas Nelson Publishers, 1990) p. 74, Hamada quotes from Pirke de Rabbi Eliezer, *The Ten Trials of Abraham,* translated by G. Friedlander (New York: Bloch. 1916), p.190-191.

2. Ibid. p. 82.

3. George M. Lamza, *Old Testament Light, The Indispensable Guide to the Customs, Manners, & Idioms of Biblical Times* (San Francisco: Harper & Row, Publishers, 1964) p. 46.

4. Jehan Sadat, A Woman of Egypt, (New York: Simon and Schuster, Inc., 1987) p. 117.

5. Hamada, p. 113.

6. Muhammad Marmaduke Pickthall, trans., *The Glorious Quran,* New York: Muslim World League, 1977) Introduction to Surah 33.

7. Elizabeth Warnock Fernea and Basima Qattan Bezirgan, edited, *Middle Eastern Muslim Women Speak* (Austin: Univ. of Texas Press, 1984) p. 30.

8. Dr. Anis A. Shorrosh, *Islam Revealed* (Nashville: Thomas Nelson Publishers, 1988), p. 71.

9. Phil Parshall, *Beyond the Mosque* (Grand Rapids, Michigan: Baker Book House), Chp 2, Diversity Within Muslim Community, pp. 47-91.

10. Ibid., p. 157. Parshall's references were Roland H. Bainton, *Here I stand: A life of Martin Luther* (New York: Mentor; 1950). p. 297. and Thea B. Van Halsema, *This Was John Calvin* (1959; Grand Rapids: Baker, 1981), p. 199.

11. Encyclopaedia Britannica Instant Research Service, *The Sayings and Deeds of Muhammad (The Sunnah)*, (Chicago, Ill: Britannica Centre), p. 4.

12. Zwemer Institute, *Muslim Awareness Seminar*, (Altadena, Ca: Zwemer Institute of Muslim Studies), p. 45.

13. Julia Cord, World Herald Staff Writer, *Religion Is Fastest-Spreading in U.S., Islam Finds Tiny, Growing Niche in Area*, Omaha World Herald, Living Section, Saturday, October 20, 1990.

THE QURAN AND OTHER ACCEPTED WRITINGS

We were in a state of ignorance and immorality, worshiping idols, eating carrion, committing all sorts of iniquities...The strong among us exploited the weak. Then God sent us a prophet...He called us to worship naught but God...to tell the truth, to hold to trust and promise, to assist the relative or neighbor...to avoid fornication and false witness...We believed and followed him...
--Ja'far ibn Abu Talib, Hadith

Oh my Lord, if I worship Thee from fear of hell, burn me in hell, and if I worship Thee from hope of paradise, exclude me thence, but if I worship Thee for thine own sake then withhold not from me Thine Eternal Beauty.
--Rabia Al-Adawiyya, Sufi poet

There are five different holy writings which are accepted reading for Muslims:

The Suhuf, also called the scrolls of Abraham which are now extinct. The originals have not been found.

The Taurat, also called the Torah, was scripture revealed to Moses.

The Zabur, also called the Psalms of David.

The Injil, also called the Gospels of Jesus.

The Quran, the final revelation to mankind, revealed to the Prophet Muhammad.

Muslims believe these four books (excluding the Suhuf because it is not available), are recorded in heaven; they have a common purpose, to reform mankind. [1] The Quran is the Muslim holy book. It is believed to be the direct word of God given to Muhammad by the angel Gabriel from the seventh heaven. The word Quran means "recite." Muhammad was 40 years old when he gave his first recitation and completed the recitations 23 years later.

The Quran is probably the most widely read book in the world when you consider it is used as a school textbook in Arab speaking countries. It is divided into 114 chapters called Surahs; the longest having 286 verses, and the shortest having only three. It is arranged from the longest chapters to the shortest, rather than in chronological order.

To the Arabs, the Quran is a masterpiece of 7th Century Arabic literature. Muhammad's miracle was that he was not that literate of a person to have written such an advanced work. Some say that he was illiterate, but others claim he must have been able to read and write some to manage the caravans of the trade route. Muhammad was known for his eloquent speech, having been brought up in the camp of Banu Sa'd bin Bakr. Muhammad is quoted to have said, "Literary beauty is a fascinating art." He was a strong advocate of learning. He said, "Acquire knowledge from the cradle to the grave." Muhammad was also known to be successful in convincing people of the truth. His wife Ayisheh reported, "None had touched the strings of the heart and elicited such emotions as did Muhammad." [2]

The Quran loses much of it's beauty when translated into English. Muhammad's close followers memorized the recitations of the Quran, but it was not recorded into a complete work until 20 years after his death. His chief scribe, Zeyd, was given charge of compiling and hand publishing the first copy of the Quran. Some years later Zeyd made one revision and the first copies were all ordered to be burned. That revised version is the Quran still being used today.

The Quran is presented as the speech of God, and God speaks in first person plural, *We.* Biblical stories are referred to as though they were common knowledge of the time. The Quran's message speaks to mankind. Race or color is not even mentioned in the Quran, rather all believers become a part of the Muslim brotherhood. Surah 3:103-105 describes this kinship in God:

> And hold fast, all of you together, to the cable of Allah , and do not separate. And remember Allah's favor unto you: how ye were enemies and He made friendship between your hearts so that ye became as brothers by His grace; and (how) ye were upon the brink of an abyss of fire, and He did save you from it. Thus Allah maketh clear His revelations unto you that haply ye may be guided; and let there be from you a nation who invite to goodness, and enjoin right

conduct and forbid indecency. Such are they who are successful. And be ye not as those who separated and disputed after the clear proofs had come unto them. For such there is an awful doom.

The Hadith is a commentary on the Quran. It is made up of two parts: the Sunnah which are the habitual acts of the Prophet, and the Hadith which are the sayings of the Prophet Muhammad. Because the Quran was their word of God, the people felt a need to record the words and deeds of Muhammad, the messenger of God. At first Muhammad forbid the recording of his own words. He was afraid they would get confused with the words of the Quran. Later, so many of his followers had memorized the Quran that he allowed them to start compiling the Hadith.

The Hadith is not considered to be a holy book, but is second in importance to the Quran. The Hadith has information on judicial, liturgical, ethical, social, economic, and political affairs. When the Muslims say *Islam is a way of life*, the Hadith would give further explanation to that statement.

The Sunnah is the recorded example of Muhammad's life and can be separated into four categories. The first is Muhammad's example of worship. Muhammad felt worship was a full-time occupation, a job never accomplished, never stopped. Secondly, Muhammad was a missionary. Every occasion of Muhammad's life was an opportunity to call men to God. His followers also were witnesses of his teachings. The Islamic Center of Southern California sent a letter in 1987 to their members:

We Muslims know that, besides our individual relationship with God, our duty is to organize ourselves to transform our beliefs into action. It is high time for us to contribute to the Muslim world and American society and face the challenges of our times, particularly, raising a new generation of Muslim Americans. [3]

The third is Muhammad as a family man. He encouraged Muslims to marry and made radical reforms in the area of Arab women. At that time in Arab history, women were just liabilities to be used. Muhammad's own wives were called *mothers of the believers*, and they spoke very highly of his kind and fair treatment. He spent long hours with his children. He urged his followers to have children saying their numbers were, *pleasing to God and His Prophet*. Muhammad's example of strengthening the family replaced some of the old tribal loyalties.

The fourth example was Muhammad as a leader. Muhammad was no doubt an excellent statesman. He felt all men were equal and always tried to do his share of the work, even though he was the leader. He urged Muslims to have their slaves eat at the same table with them and treat them like their own sons. Muhammad said, "The prayer of the Imam (leader) who is hated by the people is unacceptable to God." He reconciled and merged tribes in Medina; he wrote up the constitution of the Islamic State, giving the Jews autonomy. Muhammad was a military leader, and united the Arabs under the umbrella of Islam. [4]

There have been a number of sects that have risen up within Islam. The Sufis, the Ismailis, the Druze, the Wahhbis, and the Ahmadiyyas, are some of the most visible ones, but the Sufis have made the most impressive contribution with their literature.

I became fascinated with Sufi writings when I studied Iranian history and literature in college. The Sufis tried to become as close as possible to God. They were not content simply to follow the rules laid down in the Quran. Many of them believed it contained deeper meanings which could only be understood by in-depth study and thought. They wanted to have an intimate relationship with God. The Sufis are called the Muslim mystics. Through their inspirational writings, Sufis were responsible for much of the spread of Islam.

There were also women Sufis, my favorite being Rabi'a al-Adawiyya. She was born in Basra (today called Basra, Iraq), in year a.d. 712. She renounced this world and all its pleasures and devoted her life to prayer. The sufi's desire was to become one with the beloved and abide in Him forever. Rabi'a is called a saint in Islam today, and many of her prayers are recorded:

> *Would that You are sweet to me even if life is bitter, pleased with me even if all else is angry. Would that what is between You and me is flourishing even if what is between me and all else is desolate. If I secure (can feel) Your love, then all else is insignificant and all on earth is naught but earth.*

Rabi'a lived to be about 90 years old, but never married. She had one proposal, but said marriage was for those who were concerned with the affairs of this material world. "So like her Christian sisters in the life of sanctity, Rabi'a espoused a heavenly Bridegroom and turned her back on earthly marriage even with one of her own intimates and companions on the way." [5]

Jalalu'd-Din Rumi was a 13th century Persian Sufi poet. Many Sufis relied heavily on writings about Jesus because of the intimacy with God He shares. Here is a poem about Jesus from Rumi's third book of the Masnavi; it is carved above the archway of the church in Shiraz, Iran:

Where Jesus dwells, the great of heart forgather. O sufferer! Quit not this door! Come hither! [6]

Rumi started a dance called the Whirling Darvishes. They whirl faster and faster with their arms outstretched, one palm up to receive from heaven and one palm down to transfer heaven to earth. The Sufis have had some criticism of their mystical expression by orthodox Islam, but generally their literature has been well received by the Muslim community. This poem may reveal some of the controversial content:

What is to be done, O Muslims? For I do not recognize myself.
I am neither Christian nor Jew nor Gabr nor Moslem.
I am not of the East, nor of the West, nor of the land, nor of the sea;
One I seek, One I know, One I see, One I call.
He is the first, He is the last, He is the outward, He is the inward.
I know none other except "Ya Hu" (O He!) and "Ya man Hu"
I am intoxicated with Love's cup; the two worlds have passed out of my ken.
I have no business save in carouse and revelry.
If once in my life I spent a moment without Thee,
From that time and from that hour I repent of my life.
If once in this world I win a moment with Thee;
I will trample on both worlds, I will dance in triumph forever,
Up, O ye lovers, and away! Tis time to leave the world for aye.
Hark, loud and clear from heaven the drum of parting calls--Let none delay! [7]

The Muslim writings by Persians have often been misunderstood because they talk about the tavern, wine, and carousing, as in this poem. These words are not literal, but symbolic. The wine is symbolic of the Holy Spirit of God; the tavern has also been called the halls of chastity, or where God dwells. The carousing is what Christians call getting high on the Spirit. Most people will admit that true worship of God can be an emotionally elating experience. In Persian paintings, there is a beautiful young maiden with a flask, or a cup. She is the bearer of eternal joy. Even in early Christian writings, faith was referred to as *she*. The cup was symbolic of man's *portion* or *destiny*, which was poured out by the hand of God. For the believer, it often referred to his capacity to know God, as in Psalms 16 and 23. My cup runneth over meant *my destiny in life is to be filled with eternal joy*. Wine was the symbol of *spiritual joy*. Wine and strong drink were forbidden by Muhammad. [8]

In my readings, I met another person who enjoyed the Sufis. Paul Hunt, chaplain to the Bishop of Iran for six years, was invited to a Sufi prayer house. When he asked them if he could come back again, the Master (the prayer leader) answered, "This is a house of God, your Jesus is ours too; he was the greatest Sufi of all. You are always welcome." Paul Hunt gives a most interesting account of his experiences with the Sufis:

> *This friend was called Hussein. He was a man about my age, with a magnificent Persian moustache. Always he wanted to chat away and practice his English on me. He gave me books on Sufism so that I could learn more about it. He had a great reverence for Christ. One day he asked me why the disciples forsook Christ at his moment of greatest need on the cross. Then he turned to me and asked:*
>
> *"Have you ever forsaken Christ?"*
>
> *It gave me an uncomfortable feeling. He, a Muslim, seemed to be bringing me, a Christian, back to the roots of my faith. [9]*

The last significant group of writings I will mention is the the writings of the Ulama. The Ulama is a group of learned Islamic men. They are the guardians of the Word, as text. They interpret and explain the Quran, the Hadith in context of culture, and the validity of traditions. They define the limits of Muslim practice and belief. There are four administrative and judicial schools: The Hanbali, which is the strictest, the Hanafi, the Shafe'i, and the Maliki.

Membership of the body of Ulama is dependent on ability rather than class distinction. Perspective Alim would be students proficient in memorizing the Quran, as well as those who have superior ability in the field of literature. With the domination of the West, many of these schools experienced a decline. Under colonial regimes, free thinking was not encouraged and many of the schools were supposedly reformed, with the real motive of bringing them under government control. Many students would spend six to eight years memorizing the Quran, but were made to believe understanding the words was another science in itself.

From the very beginning, Muslims have been reluctant to translate the Quran from Arabic, but plans for an improved translation are under way. The president of the Islamic Society of North America has formally announced that an easier to read English Study Quran, with commentaries, is in the process of being translated. Ahmad Zaki Hammad of the Islamic Society in Bridgeview, Ill., is the editor-in-chief. The non-profit Quran Project, which has a $460,000 budget for the first year, has set 1996 as the publication goal. The commentary is necessary, because knowledge of the history of the time is needed to understand much of the Quran. Although Muslims say that the Quran carries a universal message to humanity, the divine admonitions speak often to Muhammad's struggles to establish a monotheistic faith on the Arabian Peninsula. [10]

Notes:

1. Badru D. Kateregga and David W. Shenk, *Islam and Christianity, A Muslim and a Christian in Dialogue.* (Grand Rapids, Mich: William B. Eerdman's Publishing Company, 1981), Chp. 5, The Books of God, p. 34.

2. Britannica Instant Research Service, *The Sayings and Deeds of Muhammad,* (Chicago, Ill: Britannica Centre), p. 4.

3. Kent Hart , *Crescent and Star Rising Across the United States.* (Altadena, CA: The Zwemer Institute Newsletter, Winter, 1987), p. 6.

4. Britannica Instant Research, *The Sayings and Deeds of Muhammad.,* p. 7.

5. Elizabeth Warnock Fernea and Basima Qattan Bezirgan, edited, Middle Eastern Muslim Women Speak, (Austin, TX: University of Texas Press, 1977.

6. Nasekh and Nastaleeq caligraphic scripts. *Rumi, Posters in Persian,* acquired through Iranian Christians International Bookstore, P.O.Box 25607, Colorado Springs, CO 80936., U.S.A.

7. Phil Parshall, *Beyond the Mosque, Christians within Muslim Community,* (Grand Rapids, MI: Baker Book House, 1985), p. 67.

8. George M. Lamsa, *Old Testament Light, The Indispensable Guide to the Customs, Manners, & Idioms of Biblical Times* (San Francisco: Harper & Row, 1964), p. 522.

9. Paul Hunt, *Inside Iran,* (Palm Springs, CA: Ronald N. Haynes Publishers, Inc., 1981), p. 77.

10. *Muslims Seeking a New, More Readable Quran,* Omaha World Herald, Saturday, April 6, 1991, p. 56, originally from Los Angeles Times.

PART III

ENMITY BETWEEN EAST AND WEST

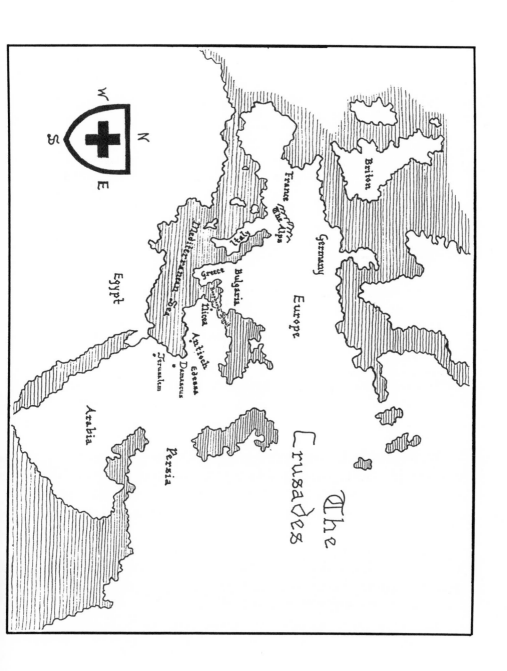

THE CRUSADES

Christ told us to judge by results. When we Christians behave badly, or fail to behave well, we are making Christianity unbelievable to the outside world.   --C. S. Lewis

Ironically, the mission of the Crusaders would not have been so successfully negative had it not involved so high a component of abject Christian commitment. The great lesson of the Crusades is that good will, even sacrificial obedience to God, is no substitute for a clear understanding of His will. It was a devout man, Bernard of Clairvaux, to whom are attributed the words of the hymn "Jesus the Very thought of Thee", who preached the first crusade. In all this period two Franciscans, Francis of Assisi and Raymond Lull, stand out as the only ones whose insight into God's will led them to substitute the gentle words of the evangel for warfare and violence as the proper means of extending the blessings God committed to Abraham and his children of faith.

--Ralph D. Winter
U.S. Center for World Mission

Tenth century Europe was a place of fear and perhaps relief for most common folk. The religious leaders had foretold the end of the world. It had to do with the millennium; one thousand years had past since Christ's birth. That was the predominant prophesy of the time.

It may have been a relief to many because they had lived with famine, self-righteous religious leaders, treacherous kings, and merciless war-lords. A common food during famine was bread baked from ground acorns or bran, and pottage made from grass. Their homes were little better than grass huts.

The kings and barons had quite sophisticated weapons of destruction with quaint and poetic names such as mangonel, tribucket, scorpion, perrior, arblast, and espringale. [1]

Witchcraft, sorcery, and heresy were common charges of the day. Church treaties were written by Archbishops forbidding the association with women who do night rides with Satan. They relied heavily on the passages in Genesis that said the sons of God came in unto the daughters of men. There were stories of men renouncing Christ and making pacts with the devil in order to secure a certain woman's love or to become wealthy. There were instructions on how to satisfy the night goblins with material possessions. The most famous of these documents of the tenth century was the *Corrector*, a collection of canon law written by the Archbishop of Worms between 1008-1012. [2]

Most common people were illiterate; way back in the seventh century Gregory the Great had said, "Woe to us, for the study of letters has disappeared from amongst us." Monasteries were the only institutions of learning.

For devout Christians it was very popular to do their pilgrimage to Jerusalem, the Holy Land. There were monasteries that served as stopping off places for pilgrims along the way to Jerusalem. By the 11th century, thousands of pilgrims were making their way to Jerusalem. One pilgrimage from Germany in 1064-1065 is said to have numbered more than ten thousand people.

There were two major developments which led to the Crusades. The Seljuk Turks (also called *Saracens*, which literally meant *Easterner*) had come to power in the Middle East, and had attacked Constantinople, the Eastern frontier of the Christian Empire. Constantinople had requested help from the Western Christians. Secondly, Jerusalem had been in the hands of Muslims over 300 years by this time. The traveling European pilgrims had been welcomed by Muslim merchants because of the business they brought, but stories of pilgrims being mistreated in the holy lands was reaching European ears.

At the Council of Clermont, Southern France, in 1095, Pope Urban II called for European Christians to rise up against the infidel and regain the holy land. His reasoning was that on Christ's return, He would not find any Christians in the Holy Land to stand with him against the anti-christ.

The Pope made promises that appealed to every class of men in one way or another. For all Crusaders he promised forgiveness of sins, canceled debts, suspended taxes while away at war, and prisoners and serfs set free. Men had a variety of motives for going to the crusades. The Western religious leaders had dreams of enlarging their Christian

Empire, and improving their relationship with Eastern Christians. Feudal warfare in Europe had been rampant, and church leaders saw an opportunity to busy the troublemakers elsewhere. Kings, feudal lords and barons had heard about the wealth beyond imagination in the Middle East. The Italians were thinking about enlarging their foreign markets. Of course, there were always the adventure seekers who found this a way to see the world.

The first group that started out in the First Crusade consisted of European peasants who were discouraged by famine and oppressive feudal lords. They were led by a wild-eyed, fiery preacher, Peter the Hermit, and his knight, Walter the Penniless. Peter had gone through France recruiting volunteers with his stories of horror from the Holy Lands. He himself had been mistreated on a pilgrimage and was forced to turn back.

The peasants sold all their belongings and many brought their families with them. They wore a cross sewn on their shirts. Most of them were on foot. They started out from France, Briton, Germany and Italy but picked up volunteers along the way and eventually became quite an impressive group. They expected cities along the way to supply them with food and lodging. When they reached Germany they decided to take care of local infidels first so they attacked and killed 10,000 people in the Jewish quarters. They looted, rioted, and raped women as they went and Peter the Hermit could no longer control them. Thousands of Crusaders were killed by angry Hungarians and Bulgarians in retaliation for their own ill treatment.

When the Crusaders reached Constantinople, the Byzantine Emperor was anxious to move this ragged, violent group on and sent them across the Bosphorus strait and there they were attacked and killed by Muslim Saracen fighters. From the estimated 300,000 of the First Crusade, just a handful returned home and among them was Peter the Hermit.

A second group of Crusaders organized in a.d. 1097 and was called the Crusade of Princes. Historians categorize this as the second group in the First Crusade. It was organized by more learned fighting men; they had 1300 trained knights in shining armour. The European aristocracy, with the exception of Germany and Spain, organized their own Crusade, not wanting to be associated with the first disaster. Only Peter the Hermit was with them again. The four separate armies that started out from Europe finally met in Constantinople. Alexis, the Byzantine Emperor did what he could to supply this enormous army with food and guides while traveling through a dense jungle on the way to Nicea.

Capturing the Muslim Principality of Antioch (Southern Turkey) was one of the greatest trials of the Crusaders. It was a nine month siege and many of the Crusaders starved to death. After seven months one of the Turkish Amirs named Firus, became tired and after being promised his life would be spared, betrayed the city. He opened the city gates one night and the Crusaders entered and massacred everyone in sight. Whoever could, escaped into the mountains with their lives. The Crusaders raped women and burned nearly 2000 buildings, churches, and houses.

Next, Mara, the town south of Antioch was taken. The leader of these Crusaders, Prince Bohemand of Tarentum, had promised Turkish leaders that if they went to the inner court of the palace with their families and belongings he would spare their lives. The Crusaders killed everyone in the town and Bohemand broke his promise to the leaders. He killed some of them and sold the others into slavery, but only after relieving them of all their gold and silver jewelry. There was one Crusader who grieved at this barbaric behavior:

> *The Franks rested at Mara for a month, during which time the Bishop of Orange, "who had done so much to exhort us to piety," died. The cynical might attribute this prelate's death to sheer despair after Bohemond's lapse, and especially in view of what the indestructible Peter the Hermit is alleged to have told his comrades: "Do you not see these dead Turks? That is excellent food." This is recorded in Chanson d' Antioch of 1130, which adds of the Franks that "they loved Turk flesh better than spiced peacock." [3]*

The Crusaders traveled down the eastern Mediterranean coast on to their destination, Jerusalem. The Seljuk Turks had poisoned all the wells around Jerusalem so water was scarce, and many of the knights' horses died. But the crusaders penetrated the walls of Jerusalem and brutally massacred every Jew or Muslim they could find. Arab history tells us Christian Arabs didn't fare much better. The Mosques and Synagogues were filled with frightened civilians; the Crusaders barricaded them and burned them down. Ten thousand men, women, and children were beheaded in the Temple of Solomon. Crusaders told of blood everywhere up to the ankle of their boots.

The Crusaders captured the Middle Eastern lands bordering the Mediterranean Sea, and called it the Latin Kingdom. Four states were set up between Constantinople and Egypt; ruled by European noblemen. Many Crusaders had brought their families with the intention of acquiring estates in the Middle East. One of the Crusaders castles, Krak des Chevaliers, is still standing today in Syria.

The Crusaders were awe-struck by the splendor and beauty of the life style of the Middle Easterners. Their first fascination was with the huge water-wheel irrigation system. David Attenborough describes the new life style:

> *...the Crusaders, settling down in castles where they might well spend most of their lives, began to adopt the customs of the people around them...They developed a taste for the foods...dishes were flavored with spices that few of the Europeans had tasted before— cloves and nutmeg and cinnamon. Cane sugar..sticky sweetmeats... drinks flavored with orange and lime—both "sherbert" and "sorbet" are Arab words...some of the Christian ladies not only perfumed themselves with attar of roses, a fragrant oil made by boiling rose petals, but also patronized the public bath. They even dusted their skin with "talcum" ...the women adopted the Islamic style of long clinging garments, and occasionally the veil; and the men started to wear silk cloaks embroidered with thread of silver and gold and white tunics over their armour which kept them cool...the Crusaders were also growing their beards. [4]*

The Crusaders ruled the Latin Kingdom for 45 years and then in 1144, the northern city of Edessa was retaken by the Seljuk Turks. This prompted the Second Crusade led by King Louis VII of France and the Emperor Conrad III. St. Bernard, founder of the Cistercian Order at Clairvaux, gave a plea for volunteers, although he himself was not totally convinced that war was the way to deal with the Muslims. Peasants were no longer volunteering because they knew it was only noblemen that returned from the Crusades. They had heard the tales of peasants being beheaded or sold into slavery rather than take the trouble to return them to Europe.

This Crusade failed due to mistrust that had developed between Christian Constantinople and the Crusaders that were now ruling the

Holy Lands. The first Crusaders in Constantinople had promised to conquer the Holy Lands in the name of Emperor Alexius of Byzantine. In the end, the only conquered land the Emperor received was Nicea; the Crusaders decided to keep the rest for themselves. This added to the mistrust between the Eastern and Western Christian Empires. Also, an unlikely business relationship had developed. The Italians had long been selling supplies to the Muslims, while Constantinople had been supplying the Crusaders. This deeply angered the Byzantine Empire.

In 1187, Jerusalem fell to the Muslims under the leadership of the Kurdish Saladin. Saladin was the vizier of Egypt and once again united the Muslim world. This prompted a call for a Third Crusade which was launched by three monarchs: Frederick Barbarossa of Germany and Holy Roman Emperor, Richard the lion-hearted of England, and Philip Augustus of France. Richard the Lion-hearted did manage to draw up a treaty with Saladin that Christian pilgrims could have free access to the Holy City, Jerusalem. Ten years later a fourth Crusade was called up by Pope Innocent III. The Italians alone took up this Crusade and never even made it to the Holy Lands. The trade competition between Venice and Constantinople came to a head and under the orders of Henry Dandolo, known as the business dog of Venice, Crusaders attacked the Hungarian port of Zara. They then went on to sack and burn the weakened Constantinople. The Crusaders tried to establish a Latin government in the Eastern Christian territory. At last the very Christian people that had asked for help were destroyed by the Crusaders for economic reasons.

After all, European Crusaders caught up in war with some unknown enemy had no knowledge of who was who. Henry Treece puts it well:

> *Many scores of thousands "took the Cross," hardly knowing that it signified anything more spiritual than that their past sins would be forgiven them as long as they kept on the move. To them, the men who lived beyond the boundaries of Germany or Italy were all "Saracens," to be slaughtered wherever they were found. To them, Constantinople herself was a vast, rich treasure-chest meant for their picking, its guardians exotic and strange, deserving a slaughter for which there need be no atonement. [5]*

Constantinople had been a city of splendor. Back in the sixth century they had a drainage system, an impressive collection of churches, with the cathedral of St. Sophia being the masterpiece. There were large palaces with elaborate decorations, mansions for the upper class, and apartments for the workers. The Palace of Water had 420 pillars. The destruction of this empire put a permanent wedge between the Western and Eastern Churches. When Pope Innocent III heard that the crusaders had sacked and pillaged the Greek churches, he was furious and realized they were completely out of his control. His reply was stern:

> *The Latins have given an example only of iniquity and of works of darkness, He wrote. The Greeks may well detest us as dogs. These defenders of Christ [the Franks], who should have turned their swords only against the infidel, have waded through Christian blood...They have presumed to lay hands on the Church's wealth...They have been seen tearing away the silver plating of the altars, breaking them into fragments which they have disputed with each other, violating sanctuaries, and plundering icons, crosses, and relics. [6]*

In the year 1212, a shepherd boy, Stephen of Cloyes, came to King Philip of France and said he had a letter from Christ telling him to take a group of children to the Mediterranean Sea and that Jesus had shown him in a vision that they would walk across on dry ground. Philip told the boy to go back to his sheep, but Stephen stayed on and preached in the streets to the children. He himself was only 12 years old. Thirty thousand children gathered in Vendome, France to march to the Holy Land to convert the Muslims. Many local clerics were calling Stephen a blasphemer but Pope Innocent III made a public statement saying, "The very children put us to shame."

Stephen and the children started off on foot with no supplies. Many of the children died on the way and when they reached the sea it did not open up, as Stephen had expected it to. Two rouges called Hugh the Iron and William the Pig offered to take the children over the Mediterranean in their ships. Stephen took this for divine intervention and all the French children boarded the ships. Two of the ships sunk at sea, but the other five ships sailed to Algeria and Hugh the Iron and William the Pig sold the children to Muslim slave traders. Some of the children were sent to Egypt and the Governor, al-Kamil bought 700 of them and used them for secretaries and interpreters. As the story goes, al-Kamil was an enlightened person who spoke many foreign languages and did not insist that the children convert to Islam if they did not choose. One child returned after 18 years of slavery to tell the story.

There were nine crusades in all, They started in a.d. 1095, and ended in 1291 with the last battle between the European Christians and the Egyptian Muslim army. The relations between Roman and Greek churches never recovered, and the weakened Byzantines were easily conquered by the Muslim Ottoman Turks in the early 1400's. There was no positive outcome accredited to the Crusades except for a more peaceful Europe while thousands of warriors were distracted away from their local feudal wars.

Europe learned science and mathematics from the Arabs, plus a knowledge of Geography through all their travels. Economic development by expanded trade, improved banking methods, and adaptation of a luxury lifestyle were all influences from the East. But these were all processes that had begun before the Crusades and they may have even developed faster in peacetime. The end of the Crusades coincided with the Mongol invasion of the Middle East. The Europeans stayed on the good side of the Mongol leader, Ghengis Khan, which helped open the way for Marco Polo and his travels. Marco Polo had a much more pleasant learning experience through friendship with the Eastern people.

The Crusaders slowly trickled back to Europe during the last 20 years of the 13th century, bringing the Orient to the West. They brought steel blades patterned with inlaid gold and silver, damask silk, and muslin cotton fabric from Damascus. They rebuilt their European homes or castles to imitate their Eastern lifestyle: rooms for bathing, platforms for a sofa, and arched windows. The women brought back mirrors, hand-woven carpets, bronze lamps, and exotic spices. Many artifacts were given as gifts to the church despite the fact they were engraved with Arabic scriptures from the Quran.

One thing they brought back in their carts and trading sea vessels that would change the face of Europe, was the black rat. This rat was from China by way of India, and had always lived outdoors in the warmer weather. When the black rat resettled in Europe, it could not stand the harsh weather and found places inside the building to make its home. The brown rat had always been around and was content to stay in basements or holes in the ground, but the black rat liked to be up high, and one of its favorite nesting places was on the roofs of buildings. It was this crisis that obviously inspired the writer of *The Pied Piper of Hamelin*. This fairy tale was a combination of the Children's Crusades and the black rat.

These rats began to multiply; they carried a deadly bacillus in their blood, and they were infested with fleas. As the rats died, their infected fleas would find another host. The black rats became so numerous that their fleas found their way to domestic animals and humans. The disease they spread was called the Black Plague or more commonly, the Black Death, and it quickly reached epidemic proportions. Many times it struck so swiftly that the patient died without even one symptom.

The epidemic started in Italy, spread to France, and then England and Scandinavia between the years of 1347 and 1350. One monastery lost 46 monks in just a few days. Doctors nursed patients and then died themselves. While the universities were working on trying to find the source of the plague, they were being emptied of professors by the disease itself. No one was willing to come to a home and record and bury the dead. In some homes, the whole family along with their dogs and cats died. Corpses were buried in large pits to try and prevent the spread of the disease.

Emotionally, the population did not fare well. In 1338 England had entered into the "100 Year War" with France. With the Black plague striking ten years later, people were convinced God had forsaken them completely. Cults of Satan were formed, many practiced religious excess, others joined a group that flagellated themselves in hopes of purging the sin that was bringing on such punishment. Peasants revolted against their land owners and governments. Cities completely shut themselves off from the world by quarantine. The plague had devastated Europe. Ralph Winter, director of Center for World Missions, describes:

> *By the time it had run its course 40 years later, one third to one half of the population of Europe was dead. Especially stricken were the Friars and the truly spiritual leaders. They were the only ones who stayed behind to tend the sick and to bury the dead. Europe was absolutely in ruins. The result? There were three Popes at one point, the humanist elements turned menacingly humanistic, peasant turmoil (often based in justice and even justified by the Bible itself)*

ended up in orgies and excesses of violence. The poverty, confusion and lengthy travail led to the new birth of the greatest reform yet seen. [7]

Did the Muslim Saracens hear about the devastating disease that took so many Europeans lives? We can be sure they did, and probably said, "They got what they deserved after what they did to us." One thing I do know is that the Crusades left a lasting impression of militant Christianity with the Middle Eastern Muslims that lingers to this day. An underlying mistrust of the Christians motives comes from a deep wound that has never healed. Henry Treece concludes:

> The historian, as he gazes across the centuries at the Crusaders gallant story, must find his admiration overcast by sorrow at the witness that it bears to the limitations of human nature. There was so much courage and so little honor, so much devotion and so little understanding. High ideals were besmirched by cruelty and greed, enterprise and endurance by a blind and narrow self-righteousness; and the Holy War itself was nothing more than a long act of intolerance in the name of God, which is the sin against the Holy Ghost. [8]

Notes:

1. Henry Treece, *The Crusades,* (New York: Random House, 1963), p. 79.
2. Jeffrey Burton Russell, *Witchcraft in the Middle Ages,* (Ithaca, New York: Cornell University Press, 1972), pp. 80, 86.
3. Treece, p. 136.
4. David Attenborough, *The First Eden, The Mediterranean World and Man,* (Boston: Little, Brown and Company, 1987), p. 158.
5. Treece, p. ix.
6. Treece, p. 229.
7. Ralph D. Winter and Steven C. Hawthorne, Ed. *Perspectives on the World Christian Movement,* A Reader, (Pasadena, California: William Carey Library, 1981), Ralph D. Winter, chp. 16., The Kingdom Strikes Back, The Ten Epochs of Redemptive History, p. 152.
8. Treece, p. vii.

DOMINANCE OF
THE WEST

The American people are satisfied that the worst native government in the world is better for its people than the best government which any foreign power can supply; that governmental interference upon the part of a so-called civilized power, in the affairs of the most barbarian tribe upon earth, is injurious to that tribe, and never under any circumstances whatever can it prove beneficial, either for the undeveloped race or for the intruder. They are further satisfied that, in the end, more speed is made in developing and improving backward races by proving to them through example the advantages of Democratic institutions than is possible through violent interference. The man in America who should preach that the nation should interfere with distant races for their civilization, and for their good, would be voted either a fool or a hypocrite.   --Andrew Carnegie

One was, and one wasn't. Other than God, there was no one. That is the way Persian fairy tales begin. There were times I had wished I was living a fairy tale; maybe in the end I will find out it is.

Once upon a time I was sleeping on a mattress on the floor in our extra bedroom. I had the sensation I was sinking down, down. "I must pull myself up," I thought. "Oh, there's that song again; that droning music, the helicopters, the machine gun fire. It's the sound of gunning down innocent people. I feel like I'm sinking, sinking."

"I must get a hold of myself," I thought, "I must not be consumed by this grief." It was times like this that I wondered if it was an advantage to understand so much of the Farsi language. All of the sad poems about the people who had died and suffered during the revolution were really starting to depress me.

That is what set off my sinking feeling that day; the song about Black Friday. The poems about the hundreds of people slaughtered by the Shah's police. "I must get up and turn off the radio," I thought, "my family needs me." It was so quiet.

"Where is everyone?" I got up and looked out the window. Bahram was coming up the lane with a newspaper. Newspapers were sold out by ten o'clock in the morning. Since the Shah left and the people took over the radio and television there was a free press I had never seen. It was fascinating. Anyone whose motives were not completely pure was susceptible to relentless criticism by some talented Persian writer.

Bahram said, "Look here, Imam Khomeini has said that all women have to wear the veil and the women are angry. Ayatollah Teleghani has come on television to smooth things over, as usual. Now the journalists are even criticizing Khomeini, in rhyme and verse yet. I can't believe this!"

"Bahram where are the children?"

"Oh, they are outside playing army behind those big piles of sand the workers keep moving back and forth."

"Oh dear," I thought, "that's all our children are going to learn is war." The other day our little son, Javad, asked me why they were saying "down with America" on television. I told him that the American government and the Iranian government were having an argument but hopefully they would talk it over and decide to be friends again very soon. I couldn't blame a five year old for being preoccupied with the military. The Iranian government had assigned revolutionary guards to the entrance of our paper mill. We had to pass an inspection to get to the housing area we lived in. Sometimes they searched the car, and other times they would wave and flag you on. Of course, the less attention you received from them the better.

One incident with the guards I will never quite forget. I had traveled to Teheran with my two children on the TBT bus service. It was an eight hour ride. I stayed for one week at my sister-in-law's home and was returning to our northern province of Gilan. One of our neighbor's sisters, Shahin, and I coordinated our return trip. Three hours north of Teheran the bus started to climb the steep road through the Alborz mountains. Into the mountains there was a city called Rudbar. It was famous for its olive trees, and we would always stop and buy olives and olive oil. The Alborz mountains are very high mountains. The highest peak, Mount Damavand, is 18,386 feet. All of the clouds from the Caspian Sea sit in the mountains, unable to pass over. The trapped clouds create a tropical climate around the seashore.

As the bus drove down the mountain, rice paddies came into the landscape and the smell of garlic filled the air. Northern Iranians eat lots of garlic to ward off rheumatism in the humid climate. Many women work planting rice in the paddies, and must wrap their legs in rags and stand knee deep in water all day. The rice must be planted under what looks like small lakes. When the rice begins to grow above the water, the landscape turns bright lime green and it thrills your heart.

The TBT Bus stopped at the entrance of the government facility and dropped us off. I breathed deep the fresh sea air of the Caspian and caught sight of our Paper Mill in the distance. I stood by the country road with our suitcases while Shahin went to call her brother-in-law to pick us up at the entrance door. I stood a way off because we never wanted to stand too close to the revolutionary guards that had been posted at the gate. One never knew what kind of questions they would ask you and what kind of possible trouble you would be in after you answered them.

But this fellow kept looking my way and finally edged over to where I was standing. "Are you an American?" he asked me.

"Yes I am," I answered, even though as the wife of an Iranian I automatically held an Iranian passport. The rest of our conversation was quite unexpected for me. He went on to tell me about his brother who lived in America and his dream was someday to visit him.

"My brother told me that I had to go and see that beautiful country before I died. Someday I hope I can go."

I looked at this fellow with his camouflage suit, his machine gun and the childlike look on his face as he was talking about America. That moment, the reality of the Middle Eastern dilemma hit me. The beginning of America, after all the hard work, and the 150 year struggle to free ourselves from the British, did seem kind of like a fairy tale to Middle Easterners. Americans said beautiful words about virtue, and freedom of all people. I was 22 when I first saw the Statue of Liberty and it really brought tears to my eyes. I remembered the music room in my elementary school where we sang my favorite words, "Give me your tired and your poor, your masses yearning to be free." Middle Easterners expected Americans to understand their struggles for freedom, and they were disappointed when we didn't.

When we first went to the Middle East, Bahram had been so proud to have an American wife. But after all the terrible stories had been told about what America had done there, it was no longer an honor to have an American wife. To Middle Easterners, the American fairy tale has been reduced to a hard reality.

During the 1991 Gulf War, Americans seemed surprised that Iranians condemned the attack of their former enemy, Iraq. But all Middle Easterners resent the treatment Middle Eastern countries have received from the West. Some countries over there seem especially angry, like Libya, and Syria, and Iran. Why are they so angry? Why do they call America the *Great Satan*? We cannot excuse bad behavior, but we can take a more objective look at these countries and their angry leaders. Let us try to understand how they feel and if there is anything America can do to repair the broken relationships.

The easiest way to understand America's present day problem with the Arabs is to watch the movie "Lawrence of Arabia." That is where this present day situation started. Most of the Arab countries were under the domination of the Ottoman Turkish empire for about 400 years. During World War I (1914-1918) the Ottomans allied with Germany and the British appealed to the Arabs to help defeat Turkey. For this formidable task a special man was called upon, the British T. E. Lawrence. Lawrence was educated in archaeology at Jesus college of Oxford, England. D. G. Hogarth, a leading archaeologist at the time, educated Lawrence in enlightened Imperialism which he felt would propel the British empire into a new era.

Lawrence was especially interested in the Middle East and he walked across Syria during his college years. Just before the war Lawrence did a secret mapping survey of the Sinai Desert for British military intelligence, working under the cover of an historical group called the *Palestine Exploration Fund*. The rest is in the movie: how he made friends with the Arabs, how they trusted him, how they made him their leader, how they planned and carried out a victorious Arab revolt and defeated the Ottoman Turks. Lawrence escorted Emir Faisal to the Paris conference after the War. Emir Faisal was the third son of Sharif Hossein, ruler of the Hejaz, direct descendant of Muhammad and guardian of the holy places in Mecca and Medina. Lawrence was dressed in the white robes his Arab tributes had presented him, with a gold dagger across his chest. Everyone was wondering who Lawrence really represented at the conference. Emir Faisal thought Lawrence was there to make certain the Allies kept their promise to give the Arabs freedom and self-government because they had helped the

British defeat the Turks. The British officers thought Lawrence was there to calm the Amir down when he heard the bitter truth--that the British and French were going to divide the Arab countries up as spoils of war, and establish a Jewish state in Palestine. The British India office thought Lawrence was there to frustrate their plans of making Iraq a province of India. Another one of their plans was to make Kuwait a fueling station for British ships traveling to and from India.

Lawrence tried to justify his own actions by clinging to the illusion that somehow things would turn out alright, and that everyone would go home happy. He didn't realize how painful it would be when Emir Faisal looked at him with the realization that the Arabs had been tricked by the British, and that the great Lawrence of Arabia had helped them. The reality became more gruesome when the British began burning Arab villages of protesters. Lawrence sarcastically remarked, "By gas attacks the whole population of offending districts could be wiped out neatly; and as a method of government it would be no more immoral than the present system."

Actually, Winston Churchill suggested that if the Royal Air Force took the job they would use some sort of asphyxiating bombs which would cause disablement rather than death. That would take care of turbulent tribes.

Lawrence of Arabia died a broken-hearted, emotionally disturbed man. Many people feel Lawrence purposely took his own life in a motorcycle accident. One sympathetic American biographer called him *a prince of our disorder*. The tragedy of the Middle East is largely due to these servants in the imperial mold. [1]

After World War I, the Sykes-Picot Agreement divided the former Ottoman province of Syria into three parts. The French received Syria and Lebanon, and the British received Palestine. Iraq, which had been called Mesopotamia, also went to the British. The Arab states were to be mandates of the newly established League of Nations, an almost meaningless designation to the majority of the Arab inhabitants. [2] At the same time the Europeans were carving up Arab land and preventing Arab self-rule; the British started to discuss giving part of Arab land to a free, independent Jewish state. Had the British kept their promises and given independence to the Arabs, perhaps Arabs may have been more accommodating toward the formation of a Jewish state.

Sharif Hossein was to be left to rule the Hejaz, the land in Arabia bordering the Red Sea. Sharif Hossein had four sons who had led armies in the ousting of the Turks; of course they were heros to the Arabs. Sharif Hossein's third son, Emir Feisal I, was appointed King of Syria. But the French threw him out, infuriating the entire Arab world. In consolation for being rejected in Syria, the British offered him the throne of Iraq. Winston Churchill offered Abdullah, Sharif's second son, the kingdom of Transjordan. Churchill knew the British needed help in ruling the Arabs and T.E. Lawrence convinced Churchill that Sharif Hossein's family was the most influential. On the other hand, neither Sharif Hossein, nor the Arabs were happy with the little consolations they received, but had decided anything they could get was better than nothing. Emir Feisal wrote to his younger brother Zeid on January 25, 1921, "We cannot compel England to fulfill her pledges to the letter; we cannot abandon our heritage; we cannot fight England and take what we want by the sword. This is the bitter reality." [3]

Sharif Hossein abdicated his rule of the Hejez in favor of his oldest son, Ali. But the house of Saud drove King Ali out of the Hejaz and the Saudis ruled what is now called Saudi Arabia. Let us look at the development of a number of these Arab countries.

LIBYA

Libya has a population of 4 million. Most of Libya's people live along the Mediterranean coastline because the vast bulk of the country lies within the Sahara desert. Ninety-seven percent of Libyans are Sunni Muslims.

Libya is a socialist Republic and Colonel Muammar Qaddafi is the head of state. Qaddafi is very angry with the West and has been given negative and one-sided coverage in American media. Let's see what he's so angry about.

Colonel Qaddafi was born in a tent in the Sirte desert. His parents were uneducated Bedouin desert dwellers. Bedouin people submit to no one except their own sheiks. Desert dwellers live the ultimate life of simplicity and have a contempt for the civilized world. One story told is that if they travel through settled areas they stuff their noses with rags to keep the smell of civilization out.

Qaddafi has pitched a large tent beside his home which is a

combination of the Sirte desert and high technology. There are mats on the floor with pillows and a coffee table. He has color television, a stereo system, tapes of popular Egyptian music, and a small globe of the world inside his tent. But visitors may be distracted by camels bellowing and belching outside of his tent. [4]

The Arabs are great story tellers and Qaddafi learned the stories of his tribe's history and the foreign villains at a very early age. He claims to have watched foreign tank battles from World War II raging across his desert. Libya was a sought after country because of its strategic location.

The Ottoman Turks ruled Libya from 1711 to 1911 and set a puppet King on the throne. In 1911, the Italians invaded Libya and maintained a cruel and oppressive colonization. They saw Libya as a convenient entry into Africa. The Libyan nationals revolted and in 1922 Italian Mussolini sent his toughest General, Rudolfo Graziani. David Blundy describes Graziani's brutal efficiency:

The chronicle of war crimes laid against the Italian general is lengthy. It is claimed that the Italians bombed civilians, killing larg e numbers of women, children, and old people. They raped and disemboweled women, they trampled on copies of the Koran, and they forced men into airplanes and threw them out from a height of 400 meters....12,000 Libyans were executed every year and nomads were moved to concentration camps where they died in their tens of thousands. A 200-mile barbed-wire fence was built to stop Libyans escaping. [5]

You can be sure this is a story Arab Libyans are still telling their children today. Colonel Qaddafi's grandfather was killed about this time. The movie *Lion of the Desert* with Anthony Quinn, tells the story of one of the more successful Libyan revolts. But by 1943, Libya was destitute. The oil reserves had not been tapped, and the country had an illiteracy rate of 90 percent.

During World War II, Libya was occupied by British and French military forces and the Italians were defeated. After the second world war, when the Allied nations were dividing up the Middle Eastern countries between themselves, the United Nations General Assembly decided Libya should become a sovereign state. In 1951 Libya became independent under a hereditary Monarchy, headed by King Idris. The only income Libya had at that time was three million pounds a year for rent on British and American military bases. The United States pledged $42 million aid over a ten year period if they could keep their air base in Libya. Besides using it as a rest-stop for the army and airforce, the Americans tested bombs and missiles there.

Much anti-American sentiment developed during the Suez crisis in 1956. The Libyan Prime Minister announced they would not allow the Americans, British, French, or Israelis to use their bases in the attack on Egypt. Libya supported the nationalization of the Suez Canal. Libyans were beginning to identify with Arab nationalization.

Qaddafi was a school boy then and his teacher described him as gifted, conscientious and solitary, with a sobriety bordering on asceticism. The Middle Easterners are big on radio programming and Qaddafi memorized Nasser of Egypt's speeches from Egypt. He loved Nasser's book *Philosophy of the Revolution*. Qaddafi and many of his fellow countrymen thought King Idris was a weak man who was responsible for Libya's dependence on the West.

Qaddafi joined the army. With the revolutionary ideas he learned from Nasser of Egypt, among others, he set about to rally troops against King Idris. The British colonel in charge of Libyan troops in the 1960s said, "I noticed a wind blowing from the East." A lot of the cadets were pro-Nasser, anti-Western and particularly anti-American. In the military Qaddafi organized a group of free officers and they began plotting to overthrow King Idris. There were four different groups trying to overthrow the king. Abdul Hamid Bakoush, former prime minister of Libya, claimed that the Americans not only knew about Qaddafi's coup ahead of time, but helped him. Bakoush claimed that he talked it over with the American Embassy in Paris himself while he was the Libyan Ambassador to France. He said either the British and Americans did not take him seriously or they thought Qaddafi's group would make a good puppet government. King Idris, now old and tired, left the country and did not come back.

In September, 1969, Colonel Qaddafi told the British ambassador that there had been a rearrangement in Libyan government and his committee was taking over the country. He said commitments to foreign businesses would be honored; foreign people and property would be safe, but all foreign military bases would have to leave. Qaddafi has made a vow that no foreign government would ever again occupy or control Libya.

The Western countries have never given up trying to get rid of Qaddafi. Bob Woodward, editor of the investigating staff for the Washington Post gives a picture of an out of proportion paranoia with Muammar Qaddafi during the Reagan administration. Along with William Casey, the CIA director, President Reagan had an all out campaign to harass Libya's Colonel Qaddafi. The story about the five-man Libyan hit team entering America to assassinate Reagan turned out to be a fluke. The CIA's secret informer was Manucher Ghorbanifar, the Iranian arms dealer whom we saw regularly on the television screen during the Iran-Contra scandal. Ghorbanifar was working with the Iranian and Israeli intelligence in the Middle East, and the CIA had received wrong information from him one too many times. The CIA officially and secretly declared Ghorbanifar a "fabricator," and never trusted him again. But the damage had been done to Qaddafi's already shaky reputation in the West.

Qaddafi appeared on the David Brinkley show on December 6, 1981, and heatedly denied that he had sent any hit team. Qaddafi said:

This is not my kind of behavior. This is the behavior of America, preparing to assassinate me, to poison my food. They tried many times to do this. Reagan..and his administration is practicing terrorism against Libya militarily, economically, and psychologically. [6]

Was Qaddafi right? Well according to CIA records Qaddafi wasn't completely wrong. In the fall of 1985 the Reagan Administration declared all-out psychological warfare on Qaddafi:

William Casey felt that they had Qaddafi on the ropes, that the United States had to keep up the pressure, and jar him, cause him to lose confidence in himself, create a centrifugal force so that his regime would fly apart and he with it. The Pentagon could send planes just off the Libyan coast to break the sound barrier, generating sonic booms. 'Humiliate him,' Casey said. [7]

Casey did not trust people with many of his covert actions. Secretary of State, George Shultz, did not have any problem with a misinformation campaign on a foreign leader. He quoted Winston Churchill, "In time of war, the truth is so precious, it must be attended by a bodyguard of lies." [8]

The Reagan Administration made the decision to bomb Libya April 15, 1986. The American CIA had advised against bombing Qaddafi because the motivation was all wrong. After the bombing of the marine base in Lebanon, the Reagan Administration had looked helpless in the face of terrorism so they needed a show of force. The CIA reports showed Syria as a worse threat to terrorism but Washington was afraid an attack on Syria would upset the Soviet Union. No one really cared what happened to Qaddafi, so they chose to make him a scapegoat instead.

The CIA was afraid the attack would make the Arab world more sympathetic to Qaddafi. They felt that the attack might lead to further terrorism; if not from Libya, from other angry Arab groups. Qaddafi survived the 1986 attack but 50 other Libyans and Qaddafi's 15 month old daughter Hanna, were killed in the bombing.

Again in 1992, America with the help of the United Nations, put an economic blockade on Libya. They said Libya must turn over two men who they felt were responsible for a 1988 terrorist incident. Again, the American government was giving Libya negative attention rather than rewarding them for their good behavior during the 1992 Gulf war. Qaddafi was quiet during the war and has tried to portray a better image with the world. Again, the Middle Eastern countries questioned the underlying motives of the 1992 blockade.

JORDAN

The Hashemite Kingdom of Jordan has about four million people, 93 percent being Muslim. The remaining seven percent are Christians and other minorities. The Jordanian boundaries were set up by the British after World War I (1914-1918). The British put Abdullah, the second son of Sharif Hussein, on the throne and called it Transjordan. In 1928 the British recognized Transjordan as independent but maintained control of the country. In 1946 Transjordan gained complete independence. England continued giving financial aid to the country and commanded their Arab Legion.

In 1949, during the Arab and Israeli fighting, the West Bank became part of Transjordan and the country's name was changed to Jordan. In 1950 Jordan officially annexed the West Bank.

Jordan would have probably been the most stable and tranquil of all the Arab countries except for two things. First of all, it has no oil, and its economy is dependent on other countries, particularly Iraq. Secondly, Jordan's population has doubled in a few short years solely because of the heavy influx of Palestinian refugees.

King Hossein inherited the throne in 1952, at 17 years of age. Jordan sided with Egypt during the six-day war of 1967. Many more Palestinian refugees fled to Jordan, and the West Bank has been occupied by the Israelis who have been building new Jewish settlements ever since.

Jordan funded Palestinian government agencies, public service workers, and facilities such as hospitals and schools. Israel claimed the territory for their own, and was building new settlements on it, but the financial responsibility for its people was an extra drain on the Jordanian economy. Palestinian guerrilla groups formed within Jordan, and the country became even more vulnerable to Israeli attacks. It was a no win situation for King Hossein because Arabs from all Middle Eastern countries were sympathetic to the Palestinian plight. In 1974 King Hossein, in agreement with the other Arab states, gave up his claim to the West Bank. He said the West Bank should be a part of an independent Palestinian state. He turned over all responsibility to the Palestinian Liberation Organization. But Jordan continued to finance the West Bank government facilities. After continued protest by the West Bank Palestinians and bloody reprisals by the Israeli soldiers, King Hossein ended Jordan's role completely in the West Bank. In 1988 he called upon the PLO to take complete responsibility of what would hopefully become a Palestinian state.

King Hossein is one of the few surviving Monarchies from the post World War I era. He was Western enough in his ways that the British felt they trusted him, but yet he cared about his people enough that they never gave up on him. The Jordanian Monarch has weathered many storms by speaking his mind, visiting army troops, and giving parties to establish personal repertoire.

King Hossein married a young American architect Lisa Halaby, daughter of Najeeb H. Halaby, one time President of Pan Am airlines. She went to Jordan in 1976 to work on plans for the Arab Air University. Lisa was of Syrian-Swedish ancestry and is a lovely and charming queen. King Hossein renamed her Lisa Noor Al-Hossein, which means "light of Hossein." They now have four children, two boys and two girls. Queen Noor has traveled extensively and done public speaking on the problems facing Jordan in the complicated world of the Middle East.

Jordan is wary of the American CIA because of unpleasant past experiences. In 1977, it was leaked that King Hossein had been on the American CIA payroll for 22 years. President Carter, embarrassed that a Middle Eastern leader was exposed and humiliated in this way, stopped payments. However, this involvement discredited King Hossein in the Arab world. [9]

Middle Easterners felt very bad about the treatment King Hossein received during the 1991 Gulf War. About one half of Jordan's population is made up of Palestinians and King Hossein is obligated to please his people. King Hossein is a survivor; he has matured and gained the respect of his Arab people and should not be publicly humiliated because he does not feel he can always go along with American policy in the gulf. Arab leaders deserve the luxury of having principles to live by, and they also have national interests to protect. I have heard Middle Easterners call King Hossein the most honest leader in the Middle East.

LEBANON

Lebanon has a population of about three and a half million people: 75 percent Muslim and 25 percent Christian and other minorities. Lebanon has the largest population of Christians in the Middle East. There are also 400,000 Palestinian refugees.

After World War I, when the allied forces divided the spoils of war, Lebanon ended up with a French military government. The Maronite Christians trusted the French and were favored under the French government. But the Muslim population, including the Druze, wanted to be either a part of Syria or of the Arab world. To ease tensions, in 1926 a constitution was written supposedly giving the Christians, Shi'ite and Sunni Muslims equal rule. By French convention, the president (the most powerful) would be a Christian, the prime minister a Shi'ite Muslim, and the speaker of the chamber a Sunni Muslim. For a time Lebanon prospered as a center of trade.

In 1943, Lebanon had elections and the nationalists were voted into power. Bishara al-Khuri was elected president. The Lebanese rewrote their constitution, eliminating all French control. Of course, the French opposed this action, and on November 11, 1943 they arrested the President and all key members of his government.

In 1945, the French and British withdrew from Lebanon and in 1946 Lebanon became an independent state. By this time they had become members of the Arab League and the League of Nations.

The Christian Presidents have not been popular for a number of reasons. They have shown partiality to the minority Christian population, have made secret agreements with Israel and have fallen into corruption.

There were a number of reasons for the outbreak of civil war of Lebanon in 1974. The rule that the president must be a Christian has been a continual insult to the Muslim majority. They feel it was manipulation by the Western powers to dominate them and the convention has been held until this very day. Also, the ratio in Parliament must be six Christians to five Muslims, with the same kind of representation in all administrative appointments for public office. It is clearly prejudice against the majority population.

Many Syrians and Lebanese felt is was a big mistake for the French to separate Lebanon from greater Syria after World War I. The Lebanese-Israeli cooperation through the Christian Phalangist group has permanently alienated Lebanese Muslims.

As a result of the formation of Israel and the expulsion of Palestinians, a large population of Palestinians settled in southern Lebanon. Guerrilla groups developed in the refugee camps and they would attack Israel's northern border and Israel would retaliate by attacking southern Lebanon. Eventually the deprived Shi'ite Muslims of the Bekaa valley, who were sympathetic toward Palestinians, also became victims of the Israeli raids. The Christian right, particularly the Phalangist Christian party began attacking the Palestinians with their well-organized militia. The Lebanese army was discreetly assisting the Phalangist. This led to an all out civil war.

By 1974, it was obvious the Christians were losing the war. Syria foresaw either a Palestinian-Muslim government or a partitioned Lebanon. Syria feared that Israel would invade and occupy Lebanon, and that no Arab country would ever be able to expel the well-armed and trained Israelis. Syria figured the less of two evils would be the same old Christian dominated Lebanon; so they started helping the Christians. With Syrian help the Christians won the civil war, but Syria was so disillusioned with the Christian Phalangist behavior that they switched their support back to the Muslim- Palestinian groups in 1978.

Israel invaded southern Lebanon in 1978 and destroyed Palestinian bases and United Nations troops came to restore order. Israel continued to supply arms, money, and troops to the Christians in southern Lebanon. The Civil war left Lebanon in ruins, and the people were embittered from all the death and destruction. Israel came out the winner and the Christian Phalangist party became even more indebted to Israel.

Where does America fit into all this? American (CIA) and Israeli intelligence (Mossad) work very closely, and the CIA is very involved in activities in Lebanon. Bob Woodward from the Washington Post tells:

The CIA man, Phalangist militia leader Bashir Gemayel, was playing an increasingly important role in Lebanon, and over the years Bashir had developed close relations with Sharon and the Israeli Mossad. The CIA had played matchmaker, putting the Christians and the Israelis in touch with each other, making Bashir a shared CIA-Mossad intelligence asset...There was an inclination in the CIA to side with the Christians over the Muslims in Lebanon. But old CIA hands who had served in Lebanon knew that the Christians, particularly Bashir and his Phalangists, were as brutal as anyone. The relationship was hazardous. [10]

On June 6, 1982, Israel again sent 60,000 troops to invade Lebanon. Their excuse was the assassination of their ambassador to London three days earlier. The CIA knew this was just an excuse because intelligence reports showed that their ambassador had been assassinated by renegade Palestinians that had no connection with southern Lebanon.

The United States intervened. United Nations troops evacuated 11,000 PLO fighters from Lebanon. The United States had promised Yassar Arafat that they would protect their women, children, and elderly.

Bashir Gemayel, the Christian Phalangist, was appointed president and the CIA took him off the payroll so no one would find out how much help he had been in organizing Israel's invasion of Lebanon. But nine days before he was to take office someone planted a bomb in the local Phalangist's eastern-Beirut office where he was giving a speech, and he was killed. CIA and Mossad intelligence traced responsibility for the assassination to the Syrians.

Two days later, the Phalangist Christian party took revenge on Palestinian refugees. Israeli soldiers had been in charge of guarding the refugee camps. Seven hundred to eight hundred Palestinian women, children, and elderly were massacred at the Sabra and Shatila camps. Pregnant women had their wombs cut open, diapered babies, and even horses, dogs, and cats were killed. The Christian cross was carved into the flesh of some victims. [11]

In two weeks a peace-keeping force from America had been sent, but they eventually got pulled into the fighting also. The battleship New Jersey was sending cannon-balls into the Muslim section and killing civilians. Then a truck with explosives, driven by an Arab, entered the marine compound and killed 275 American marines.

The Americans withdrew from Lebanon but William Casey carried on covert operations. Casey could not get the cooperation of his own CIA men, but with the help of Israeli and Saudi intelligence, they carried out a plan to kill fundamentalist Muslim leader Sheikh Fadlallah. President Reagan signed the formal finding and issued $1 million and King Fahd of Saudi Arabia contributed $3 million. An Englishman was hired to do the assassination. Bob Woodward gives an account:

On March 8, 1985, a car packed with explosives was driven into a Beirut suburb about 50 yards from Fadlallah's high-rise residence. The car exploded, killing 80 people and wounding 200, leaving devastation, fires and collapsed buildings. Anyone who had happened to be in the immediate neighborhood was killed, hurt or terrorized, but Fadlallah escaped without injury. His followers strung a huge "MADE IN USA" banner in front of a building that had been blown out.

Of course, the Saudi Ambassador, Prince Bandar, was horrified. Information was planted that the Israelis did it. The way they took care of Fadlallah was to offer him money to prevent future terrorist attacks on Saudi and American installations. Sheikh Fadlallah agreed to accept payment in food, medicine and educational expenses for some of his people. Ambassador Bandar remarked, "It was easier to bribe him than to kill him." [12]

The militia groups have the real power in Lebanon, and the central government controls very little of the country. The government is looked upon as an instrument of Western domination.

SYRIA

Syria has a population of about 12 million people who are 90 percent Muslim and 10 percent Christian and other minorities. After World War I the British installed a military rule under Sharif Hossein's son Feisal.

The Syrians had their own Congress meeting in Damascus and elected Feisal king of a united Syria including Lebanon, Transjordan and Palestine. But two years later Syria was given to the French and in June of 1920, the French troops occupied Syria and demanded that Syria recognize the French mandate. The French threw King Feisal out of the country.

The French set up a number of local governments within Syria and began building roads, encouraging agriculture, planning urban areas, and set up the University of Damascus. But the Syrians never accepted French rule and after continuous revolts, in 1936, the French made a show of giving Syria its independence. A treaty was signed that the new government under Hashim al-Atasi would accept French advisors and maintain two French military bases. But the French never ratified the treaty.

Syria went through a series of coups and military governments until Egypt's revolution in 1958. With the Ba'ath Party in government, Syria merged with Egypt in the United Arab Republic. But the Syrians were not happy with this arrangement, and in 1961, there was another coup and Syria again became independent.

The Ba'ath Party had branches in Iraq, Lebanon, and Jordan. The Syrian Ba'ath party became independent of the pan-Arab central committee in 1966 through another coup. They now called themselves the Syrian Ba'ath. Hafez al-Assad was sworn in as President on March 14, 1971. Assad has survived as a leader in Syria when many others didn't but the cost has been great. Assad has a reputation for being a cruel dictator. In 1982, Syrian government troops of Hafez al-Assad mowed down some 20,000 Sunni Muslim fundamentalists who challenged his rule in the city of Hamah.

Syria has had an insurmountable number of problems to overcome. There is much religious and cultural diversity within the country. Their diverse culture has three kinds of Muslims and a large population of Christians with twelve denominations. Israel has been a continuous threat, and took the Golan heights from them. Syria has been preoccupied with what to do about Israel's repeated invasions of Lebanon. With these continuous pressures from outside the country it is difficult for these countries to put their resources into domestic issues.

The American CIA has an endless amount of information on the Syrian government's involvement in so called terrorist activities. But the CIA is reluctant to start any confrontations with Assad. They call him the most cunning of the Middle Eastern leaders.

EGYPT

Egypt is another Arab speaking country with a population of about 55 million. Most Egyptians are Muslims but there is a large population of Coptic Christians and other minorities. During the Ottoman rule, the Egyptian economy suffered from European control of the Indian Ocean trade routes that by-passed Egypt.

Egypt has always been a sought after country because of the Isthmus of Suez. In 1863 the French were contracted to rebuild the Suez Canal. The Suez Canal was originally excavated by Darius I, King of Persia in 400 B.C. During Construction of the present canal, a large gold plaque was found that had cuneiform writings on it which began, "I, Darius I, King of Kings of Persia..." The Suez canal links the Mediterranean Sea and the Indian Ocean by way of the Red Sea.

By 1875 Egypt's ruler, Ismail, had created such a large national debt that he sold Egypt's shares in the Suez Canal to England. Because of the Suez canal, the Ottomans did not have as strong of a hold on Egypt as they did the rest of the Middle Eastern countries. The French and British had Dual Control for a time but the British managed to win out by 1882. The Egyptians tired of the British occupation and Egyptian government officials were constantly in a power struggle with the British agents.

Former Egyptian President Anwar Sadat recalled sitting on his grandmother's knee in the village and hearing stories about their foreign enemies, the British. The most impressive story he recalled was the Ballad of Zahran, the hero of Denshaway. Denshaway was a village only three miles from Sadat's village. In 1906 a party of British officers were pigeon hunting and one of the officers was killed in a scuffle with the village farmers. The village men were arrested and scaffolds were built right on the spot. Many villagers were whipped and others were hanged. Zahran was the hero of the story and the first to be hanged. Sadat's grandmother would spend much time describing how brave Zahran was and how he held his head high, proud that he had stood up to the foreign aggressors. Sadat said:

I often saw Zahran and lived his heroism in dream and reverie--I wished I were Zahran....Lying on the rustic oven in our home in the village, I realized then that something was wrong with our life. Even before I saw the British, I had learned to hate the aggressors who whipped and killed our people. [13]

British control plagued Egypt well into the 20th century. During World War I Egypt was declared a protectorate of England, and this led to heightened anti-British sentiment among the Egyptian population. Any Egyptian ruler that tried to minimize British control was removed from power. After much political turmoil and revolt, the British granted Egypt independence in 1922. But the Egyptian Monarch was a puppet of England.

During World War II, the Egyptians were made to fight for the British and they declared this a violation of their sovereignty. Egyptians claimed the war had nothing to do with them. Actually, they considered Britain their worst enemy.

In July of 1952, a group of army officers including Anwar Sadat, and Gamal Abdel Nasser, called themselves the Free Officers and overthrew the Monarchy. At that point in history, Americans still had a reputation for championing the cause of freedom and supporting liberation movements. Before even announcing their revolution, the Free Officers got in contact with the American Embassy. The U.S. Ambassador thought this was a nice gesture and invited them all to dinner. So while the British were trying to figure out who the revolutionary council was, the American Ambassador was having them all to dinner. [14]

In 1954, Nasser became Prime Minister with ultimate power and began massive reform in Egypt. More money was allocated for education; and the government took over all foreign-run schools. The Aswan High dam on the Nile River was eventually constructed for irrigation and electric power. This improved Egypt's agriculture. The Egyptians figured the greatest reform was the evacuation of all British troops from their country. Camelia Sadat, Anwar Sadat's daughter said, "The British were like a self-proclaimed friend who moves into one's household but refuses to leave even when it becomes clear that their welcome has expired." [15]

The good relationship the Egyptians thought they had with the United States soon deteriorated. Egypt refused to join the Bagdad Pact, and discouraged other Arabs from joining it. This angered the U.S. and Britain, and they instigated an Israeli raid on Gaza in February, 1955. That action became a great political defeat for the Western countries because it made Egypt and other Middle Eastern countries realize they needed arms to protect themselves. By this time Israel was being supported by the United States, with the cooperation of the British. For the first time, Egypt went to the Soviet Union for help. Anwar Sadat expressed this feeling:

That deal...effectively raised the morale of the Third World countries, whose members began to feel that there was somebody they could resort to in their effort to liberate their national will fro m the colonial hegemony under which they had lived for centuries... [16]

That same year, the first Asian-African Bandung Non-Alignment Conference was held and President Nasser gained badly needed credibility by being photographed alongside great world leaders like India's Jawaharlal Nehru.

Nasser was the most beloved of all Arab leaders. He gave birth to Arab nationalism. To his own people, he was the first native Egyptian leader they had had in 400 years, and they loved and trusted him.

Egypt had counted on help from America in building the Aswan Dam project but in 1956, John Foster Dulles, the American Secretary of State under President Eisenhower declared Egypt bankrupt. No money would be lent to Egypt. Nasser decided the only thing to do was to Nationalize the Suez Canal, which was owned by the French and the British. France and Britain gave Egyptians 12 hours to change its mind or they would attack. Nasser had no intention of changing his mind, and the French and British with the help of Israel, attacked Egypt. The Nasser government appealed to the U.S. Ambassador and to the Soviet Union, and these two countries insisted on a ceasefire. The Israelis withdrew four months later.

In 1970, President Nasser of Egypt died of a heart attack. Nasser stood up to the Western powers and the Arab people loved him for it. After Nasser died, Egyptian people wandered in the streets crying and calling, "Good-bye Nasser. Good-bye our leader." Nasser is still the hero of the Arab world. He had given them hope for the future.

After Nassar's death, Anwar Sadat became President of Egypt. Sadat's relationship with the United States was very confrontational. Egypt, out of a desperate need for economic and military assistance, turned more than ever to the Soviets for help. In reality, the Soviets did very little for Egypt. But America was in its Soviet paranoia days and was calling Egypt a Soviet-backed regime. Anwar Sadat said, "All we ever receive from foreign countries is abuse."

The United States did not take President Sadat seriously and ignored his pleas for help to expel Israel from Egyptian land they had taken in the 1967 war. The American Secretary of State, William Rogers pledged that the United States would maintain Israel's military superiority over not only Egypt but all the combined Arab states. [17] Sadat, in partnership with Syria, prepared to go to war with Israel. It was the 1973 Yom Kipper War.

Israelis had been boasting that they would crush the bones of Egyptians. But the Israelis were performing badly in the Yom Kipper war, and the new American Secretary of State, Henry Kissinger, became nervous. The United States sent the latest weapons that were still in testing stages to defeat the Egyptians. President Sadat was not going to fight the United States because his weapons were no match for America's latest technology. Sadat knew that if his air defense was destroyed they would be vulnerable to more Israeli attacks like what they had experienced in 1967. Sadat informed Syria, Egypt's partner in war, that he would be accepting a cease-fire. But the Egyptians felt they had regained some of their honor by being a formidable foe to the West. Anwar Sadat felt if America or Israel had shown some interest in their problems the Yom Kipper War should never have taken place, and they could have had peace in 1973. But the United States and Israel assumed the Arabs just wanted to get rid of Israel, so they did not make a sincere effort to find out how the Egyptians really felt. Sadat wanted peace and in the years that followed he proved it by his actions.

In 1974, Egypt declared it was reopening the Suez Canal and Sadat reluctantly approached Henry Kissinger for help. The United States had the only equipment that was able to do the heavy digging that was needed. This seemed like a turning point for Egyptian-American relations. Kissinger picked up on this opportunity and this venture started a warmer relationship between the two countries. Henry Kissinger is very unpopular in the Middle East but his shuttle diplomacy between Egypt and Israel did much to prepare the stage for peace. President Sadat felt that Kissinger was his friend because of a few personal gestures. Kissinger retrieved the remains of Sadat's brother's body from the Israelis after the Yom Kipper war.

In September of 1978 President Sadat of Egypt and Prime Minister Begin of Israel signed the Camp David peace accords under the direction of American President, Jimmy Carter. Sadat recognized Israel's right to exist and in return Israel returned the Sinai to Egypt. Sadat traveled to Israel and spoke at the Israeli Knesset:

Why don't we repeat together the Psalms of David the Prophet: "Unto thee will I cry, O Lord. Hear the voice of my supplications. When I cry unto thee, when I lift up my hands towards thy holy oracle. Count me not with the wicked, and with the workers of iniquity, who speak peace with their neighbors, but mischief is in their hearts. Give them according to their deeds and according to the wickedness of their endeavors." Ladies and gentlemen, to tell you the truth, peace cannot be worth its name unless it is based on justice and not on the occupation of the land of others. It would not be right for you to demand for yourselves what you deny to others. With all frankness and in the spirit that has prompted me to come to you today, I tell you to give up once and for all the dreams of conquest and give up the belief that force is the best method for dealing with the Arabs. [18]

After the Camp David accord, the United States began giving Egypt economic aid, but peace with Israel and America was not without a cost. Egypt lost it's financial support from the Arab states. They felt Sadat had sold out the Palestinians, and the Arabs as a whole. In 1977 Egypt suffered from economic hardships, and the masses of people were demonstrating. Seventy people were killed, and thousands wounded and imprisoned. Helping to keep Sadat in power after the peace treaty was a monumental task for the CIA, which provided security and intelligence reports. Sadat had been given detailed information on the threats to his life from Libya, Ethiopia, Syria, and Iran.

On October 6, 1981, President Anwar Sadat was assassinated by an Egyptian fundamentalist group. Hosni Mubarak became President of Egypt and kept his commitments to Israel and the United States, but has taken a much more moderate tone. Mubarak's cautious leadership has done much to reassure Egyptians and integrate Egypt back into the Arab community.

IRAQ

Iraq has a population of about 18 million. Iraqis are 97 percent Muslim, and 3 percent Christian and other religions. After World War I, the British determined the boundaries of Iraq. Then in 1920 the Iraqi people revolted. The Iraqi nationalists had voted Abdullah king of Iraq but the British gave it to Emir Feisal I. With the establishment of this monarchy, a treaty of alliance was signed with Great Britain and a constitution was drafted.

It soon became apparent that full independence had not been achieved. Iraqi nationals claimed there were two governments in Iraq, one national and one foreign. Iraqis suffered repressive rule under the British installed government. Some sources say the Monarch, Emir Feisal was really quite moderate, but while he was out of the country Assyrian demonstrators were brutally put down. The government fell and was replaced by a more moderate one. Emir Feisal died that same year of heart disease and was succeeded by his young and inexperienced son, King Ghazi. King Ghazi was killed in a car accident in 1939 and four year old King Feisal II was put on the throne with an uncle as regent. The Iraqi people were continually plotting against them. During World War II Iraq became increasingly hostile toward the British because of their control over Arab countries. In the spring of 1941 British troops returned to Iraq and there was an armed conflict. Iraqi leaders fled from Iraq and the British hanged four Iraqi officers.

In the early 1950's, the Iraqis witnessed the nationalization of Iranian and Arabian oil. Iraqis had renewed hopes of breaking unsatisfactory alliances with the British.

Within the military a group of young officers formed the Free Officers, and planned their own revolution. On July 14, 1958, under the leadership of Colonel Abdul Karim Qassem, the monarchy was overthrown. King Feisal was assassinated and Iraq was declared an Islamic republic.

The assassination of King Feisal was traumatic to all the monarchies in the region but especially to King Hossein of Jordan. King Feisal was King Hossein's cousin.

The Iraqi coup was very threatening to England and the United States. They were afraid that other Arab peoples, seeing a successful Iraqi revolution, would all think the time was ripe to throw off their own cumbersome foreign rule.

Of course, Premier Qassem received no cooperation from the West. Britain continued to pump less oil from Iraq, and eventually boycotted Iraq's oil on the international market. Qassem was a simple man with a life-long goal to deliver Iraq from oppression. He never married, and dedicated his younger years to his military career. While Premier of Iraq he slept about four hours a night, lived in the defense ministry and would drive to a simple home once a day to take a shower. Qassem was a teetotaler who never smoked. He had eight dogs, all of which he called Lassie.

Qassem's dream was for Iraq to become a democracy. But no one was going to let that happen. Nasser of Egypt wanted Iraq to become a part of the United Arab Republic, and make the Palestinian plight their main agenda. Qassem's main concerns were domestic; he wanted to raise the standard of living for the Iraqi people. He thought the oil revenues should first benefit the people of Iraq.

The Iraqi people loved him, and even the Kurds liked him. On his way home to take his daily shower Qassem would tour the city and stop at the gate so the people could see him and thrust petitions—for jobs, for property, claims, or simply for money into his open car window. Then the crowds would chant, "Qassem is our jewel!"

The United States and Britain called Qassem a Soviet communist. In reality they were pushing him into Soviet arms by refusing to help him organize a democratic government. Time magazine of April 13, 1959 had this to say about Qassem: "So long as Qassem, lifelong conspirator and dissembler, keeps any of the keys of power in Iraq, there is always the chance that he may yet teach Russia a lesson that the West has learned to its sorrow—the lesson that events in the Middle East have their own momentum."

But in the end, no amount of personal dedication or hard work from Qassem could overcome Iraqi internal political divisions, especially since they were constantly being fueled by outside influences. In 1961, Qassem became extremely angry by the Western countries' rejection and threatened to invade Kuwait. He claimed it was Iraqi territory that had been taken by the British. The United States stationed troops in Lebanon and the British brought troops to Jordan. Premier Qassem did not carry out his threat but in the end the only country he remained friendly with was the Soviet Union. In 1963 Qassem's regime collapsed and he was executed.

There was a tragic recurrence of military coups until 1968, when Saddam Hossein lead a coup and emerged unrivaled leader of the Ba'ath party and Iraq. The Ba'ath party leaders accomplished what Qassem couldn't, the nationalization of Iraqi oil.

America had a rocky relation with Saddam Hossein until the Reagan-Bush administration. The Carter administration listed Iraq among terrorist nations and in 1980 barred sales of U.S. made commercial jets and turbines to Iraq. In 1982 the Reagan administration became friendly with Saddam, and in 1984 removed Iraq from the list of terrorist nations. The U.S. sold Saddam helicopters, and granted him $210 million worth of food credits. In 1986, during the Iran-Iraq War, the American CIA shared satellite photo data with Iraq that aided in air strikes against Iran.

The U.S. Senate moved to impose sanctions against Iraq for using chemical weapons against the Kurds in 1988, but the Reagan Administration defeated the bill. Even as late as May, 1990, when Congress wanted to impose sanctions against Saddam for using chemical weapons, President Bush threatened to veto the bill. In July of 1990 Iraqi troops were massing on the Kuwaiti border and again, both houses of congress wanted to pass sanctions. President Bush was still threatening to veto any sanctions. The Bush administration claimed the Iraq-Kuwait dispute was regional and America had no interest in getting involved. However, one month later when Iraqi troops invaded Kuwait, the Bush administration started giving Saddam Hossein ultimatums. The United States began massive air lifting of troops to the gulf, and in January of 1991, started the bombardment of Iraq. [20]

According to President Bush's war rhetoric, Saddam Hossein was the modern day Hitler. If this was true, why had the Reagan-Bush administration been so supportive of him? Hossein had served a purpose. The Western nations were worried about Khomeini exporting his revolution to other oil-exporting countries. Saddam Hossein was distracting the Iranians with the war efforts, as well as keeping their power in check. But this created a number of problems for Saddam Hossein as well. Iraq, with its 18 million population, had plenty of soldiers but was short on money. Kuwait, with only 2 million population, was able to contribute money. After Iran and Iraq signed their ceasefire, the Kuwaitis wanted their $17 billion loan repaid. If that wasn't bad enough, Kuwait was also flooding the international market with oil so the price of a barrel was down from $28 to about $11. This caused Iraq to lose billions in revenues. Saddam Hossein felt as though he had been used for 8 years by the more powerful countries to keep Khomeini occupied.

The borders in the Middle East had been drawn up by the British in the 1920's and Iraq ended up with almost no access to the Persian Gulf for shipping. This was the main dispute between Iraq and Iran, and was also a contention between Iraq and Kuwait. Saddam Hossein claimed the two islands, Bubiyan and Warba, were of little use to Kuwait, but Iraq needed them for access to the Gulf. Iraq also charged that Kuwait was pumping oil from their border well, Rumaila Field. None of these problems were addressed before the fighting started.

We Americans did not see the war, but we saw only reports on the war. Eighty-eight thousand five hundred tons of bombs were dropped. We were made to believe these bombs only hit military installations but in reality only seven percent of these bombs were the so called precision-guided smart bombs. Seventy percent of the bombs missed their targets. President Bush said he had nothing against the Iraqi people but virtually all of Iraq's main infrastructure and public utilities were destroyed. Richard Reed, the regional director of UNICEF said children in Iraq have become malnourished because of the food shortages. Maramus and kwashiorkor, vitamin deficiency illnesses, have become common. In many demolished cities, six months after the war, Iraqi people were still walking knee deep in sewage. A Harvard University team predicted tens of thousands of deaths from cholera, typhoid, and gastritis. [21]

Christianity Today told of all the many Christians in Iraq and how they find themselves caught between a *jihad* and a *just war*. They have been made to look like they are embracing the Western religion, and are held in suspect by their Muslim countrymen.

Ahmad Chalabi of the Iraqi Democratic Resistance said before the fighting started they came to Washington, D.C. to rally for support and discuss setting up a democracy in Iraq, but they were laughed at by the Bush Administration. the opposition was ignored by Bush, although Saudi Arabia kept very close contact with them. The thing that really angered the opposition the most was that America let Saddam Hossein and his republican guard go with all their weaponry. What the American bombings did not accomplish in Iraq, the republican guard did. They went through Kurdish and Shiite towns and demolished everything.

President Bush had called on the Iraqi people to rise up against Saddam Hossein. Hazir Temourian, journalist with the Times in London, said an American financed radio program was broadcast in the Kurdish language calling for Kurds to revolt. It said, "Rise, this is your moment, this time the Allies will not let you down." The reason they said "this time" is because the Kurds have been used before to harass Saddam Hossein.

Between 1972 and 1975, against the advice of the CIA, Kissinger and Nixon funnelled $16 million in CIA funds to the Kurds. The Shah of Iran and Israel also gave military funding for the Kurds to fight Saddam Hossein. Neither the U.S. nor Iran wanted the Kurds to win. They needed them to pressure Saddam Hossein. In the words of Henry Kissinger, "Covert action should not be confused with missionary work." In March, 1975, the Shah and Saddam Hossein signed the Algiers Agreement giving Iran sovereignty over the Shatt al-Arab waterway. In return, the Shah promised to stop funding the Kurds. The Shah then gave America and Israel the word that the funding was no longer necessary.

In the American government's Pike Report the CIA chief of the Middle Eastern region called Washington and said he felt that this betrayal of the Kurds was endangering thousands of lives. He was also uncomfortable with the ethical implications. At one point, Mulla Mustafa Barazani, leader of the Kurdish people, sent three valuable Persian carpets and a gold and pearl necklace to Henry Kissinger's wedding, to try and get in his good graces again. But Kissinger chose to cooperate with the Shah of Iran, and ignored the leader of the Kurds. People have said the present leader of the Kurds should have remembered how his father was betrayed, and not listened to the enticing words of the Western Allies. [22]

Bill Moyers summed up the situation nicely on his program, *After the War:*

The United States said we couldn't impose democracy but we did precisely that in Germany and Japan after defeating them in World War II. No, what guided the White House this time was not concern for Democracy, but for stability and access to oil. The argument was that if the rebellion in Iraq succeeded, the country might split apart and Iran, Turkey, and Syria might fight over the pieces. If the Shi'ites and Kurds struggle for autonomy it might insight rebellion in neighboring countries. Better let the rebels lose than to risk upheaval in Baghdad. This is not the first time the Kurds have been betrayed to power politics by an American government.

America has left a bitter and angry Saddam Hossein in power. It will only be a matter of time until the West hears from him again.

In conclusion, by the time the United States entered the role of world power, the Middle Easterners had suffered abuse from the Turks, and the Europeans. The United States cooperated with the Europeans, and most often took their side whenever a conflict arose. Middle Eastern Muslims, for the most part, look at Israel as the remnants of Western domination in the area. Indeed, Israel has been a useful tool for keeping the Western agenda on track. Whenever it isn't politically expedient for America to directly involve itself, they send Israel to do the job, or blame Israel. When Washington gets backed into a corner, government spokesmen say Israel did it. The Reagan Administration claimed Israel was responsible for the Iran-Contra scandal. Recent evidence has shown that the Reagan administration not only knew of all arms sales to Iran, but planned and approved of arms shipments. This was particularly unfair to American allies, who through great sacrifice cooperated with the economic blockade on Iran.

If American news media do not tell people the truth, journalists from other countries will tell the story. Journalist, Tom Fox, asked, "Could it be that inside the United States—blanketed in U.S. war hysteria and dependent on a press so seemingly submissive and committed to the establishment's view that it does not even need to be government-controlled, we are blind to reality?" [23]

The British have made a documentary on Desert Storm called *The Information War*. Dead bodies everywhere, charred soldiers on their demolished tanks, and grieving people are compared to Hiroshima.

The Ziggarat of Ur is shown and compared to the beginning and end of civilization. The BBC is famous for its excellent documentaries and they are shown world-wide. [24]

There is a Persian poem that gives a little lesson:

From a dried-up branch of an old tree...

in a drought-stricken land....

a tear from an eye of a swallow....

a very tired swallow....

played the role of a rain drop....

A fish in a dried-up spring saw the reflection of the tear drop, and
*   unknowingly boiled over and screamed....*

Rain! Rain!

And all the other fish....rain!...rain!

The name of rain was pouring everywhere...

How do we Americans feel about ourselves after we have gone home from all the victory parties? These little animals calling rain remind me of Americans calling victory!...peace... But saying it does not actually make it so. When the Gulf War of 1991 was over, the situation was more problematic than ever. The original problems were never addressed, and now they have a new set of problems as a result of the war. Two years after the end of the Persian Gulf War, a report by the Arab Monetary Fund released in Damascus, Syria estimates that the conflict cost the region $676 billion in 1990 and 1991, not counting vast damage to the environment and a continuing suppression of the rate of economic growth in the region. [25] The Gulf War was carried out with disregard to the masses of people in that region and it has created even more anger and alienation.

As long as Middle Easterner's problems are not being addressed, the West will have to live with terrorism. The Middle Eastern governments know they cannot win a war with the West so they funnel money into existing Muslim groups. This money may be used for social services, humanitarian aid, military training, or religious classes. [26] Throughout history, this has been a common tactic for weak countries trying to get out of under the control of more powerful countries.

In the 1950's, the Nationalists came into power in a number of the Middle Eastern countries. The Western countries called these leaders communists, and somehow were instrumental in their downfall. Iraq's Qassem was executed; Egyptians feel Nassar died of a broken heart; Iran's leader Musaddiq, of whom we will look at next, was put on house arrest for the rest of his life. The Middle Eastern people now feel that Nationalists are too vulnerable and it is necessary to turn to Muslim religious leaders. There are a few moderate religious leaders, but the revolutionaries look upon any compromise as weakness because the Western diplomats push as far as they are allowed. What the West will have to deal with next is the fanatical Muslim elements. These groups may not be interested in peace with America; they may only settle for victory. The people in these groups are dedicated, self-sacrificing, and zealous. This bombing of the World Trade Center is a taste of what comes next. It is not going to help for us to retaliate against innocent people in these countries, because as we have seen with Saddam Hossein; their leaders are willing to sacrifice all their people. The Western countries have a last chance to deal with the moderate elements in the Middle East, before they are forced out by hardliners. Our governments must deal with the Middle Eastern peoples grievances and give them a fair hearing. Leon T. Hadar, author and teacher at the American University School of International Service, comments:

> *The political clout the Islamists now have is due not to the desire of Arabs and others to live under strict Islamic rule, but to the perceived failure of Western models of political and economic order, including nationalism and socialism, to solve the Middle East's problems. [27]*

Whatever happened to the old adage you must be a friend to have a friend. All countries have national interests, and Middle Eastern countries are no different. Is it fair that those countries with oil reserves have received so little benefit from this valuable resource? Now as the scientists predict the depletion of oil reserves, Middle Easterners grieve for a lost blessing, usurped by the Western world. Dr. Saed Hassan Nassar, professor of Islamic studies, philosophy, and sociology at George Washington University comments:

> *In the West, a kind of historiography grew up which is very deeply Eurocentric. It is the idea that other cultures are important provided they are in the long past, and sort of contribute to Western*

civilization. The fact that one cannot accept full legitimate existence
of other civilizations which are still living today is a very powerful
mental and intellectual force in contemporary America and Europe.
Other societies only have value in as much as they contribute to
Western society. If Islam is an accepted civilization standing on its
own, as an independent civilization, which is still around, which still
has a right to do things, much as Western civilization, as much as
any other civilization has a right to do things in its own way, this
would challenge this totalitarian view of history which is very
prevalent with many people in America without they themselves
realizing it. This is why everything in the Islamic world keeps
getting judged according to current Western standards. No one
asked the Islamic world if they wanted to be a part of President
Bush's New World order. [28]

I have heard Christians say the peace in the Bible does not mean
peace between people but rather, peace in our hearts. Is it possible for
us American Christians to have peace in our hearts if we support
exploitation and the long list of wars with other countries?
Psychologist Agnes Sanford, author of *The Healing Light* says we
don't:

The people of this nation are riddled with fear. Of those who come
to me for help in mental difficulties, ninety-nine hundredths are
tormented by fear. Fear of what? They do not know...It is a safe
guess that everyone in the United States is afraid of the destructive
force that we have released through the splitting of the atom. Our
very excuses expose our fear...But I wonder whether those excuses
will hold good before the throne of God. [29]

Some American leaders say we need another war victory to feel
good about ourselves. We as Americans, will feel good about
ourselves when we start taking the words of Jesus literally. Jesus said,
"Overcome evil with good! He who lives by the sword dies by the
sword!" The arms dealers and many of our government leaders have
tried to convince us that the only way we will be secure is to have
massive weapon systems. But we feel more insecure than ever. Deep
down we know that uncontrollable forces have been released and
building bigger and better bombs are not going to protect us. We need
leaders that have more knowledge about personal relations.

The week after I finished this book, we went to Disney World with our children. Walt Disney used his knowledge of technology and management for the betterment of men. Disney World has a theme of international love and brotherhood. At least one-third of the people at Disney were foreigners. I myself, in the locker room of River Country, made friends with a little British girl.

As I walked along the boulevard of International Village at Epcot Center; I grieved for the Iraqis that received death and destruction from us when we have such wonderful things to share with the world. I remembered the Iranian revolutionary guard with the childlike look on his face when he said, "My brother told me that one day before I die I must see America." Our government would have been better to take Saddam Hossein on a tour of Disney World than a chemical weapons factory. [30] What makes us think our enemies will be any more convinced by threats of death than by rewards for cooperation. I prayed that day, "O Lord, I repent of what my nation has done to Iraq. Lord help us to change our ways of dealing with the Middle Eastern people. Give us your compassion."

We need leaders that are willing to take new initiatives to help Middle Easterners solve their problems. President Bush's efforts toward an Israeli-Palestinian peace conference was a step in the right direction. While Secretary of State James Baker was on one of his 1992 diplomatic missions to Israel, his wife, Susan, met with Palestinian religious leaders and peace activists at St. George's Anglican Cathedral in East Jerusalem. They ended their time together with an inter-faith prayer service. The world rejoiced at the signing of the 1993 Peace Agreement between Israeli Prime Minister Yitzhak Rabin and PLO Chairman Yasser Arafat. We need this new point of reference. [31]

As Christians, we should be encouraging our government leaders to pursue peaceful means of settlement in the Middle East. Gary McSpadden, host of a Christian program, had British Graham Lacey on his show. Lacey is a world financier and Christian. He was staying with a New York family one Thanksgiving and suggested they invite the loneliest man in town for dinner. They came to the conclusion this would probably be the Libyan Ambassador, because America had just bombed Libya. To make a long story short, the Libyan Ambassador not only came to dinner and but was moved to tears that someone had shown him this kindness. Through this encounter, Graham Lacey got an opportunity to visit with Colonel Qaddafi himself in Libya. Graham Lacey asked Qaddafi if he could pray with him, and Colonel Qaddafi was so pleased with this gesture that he aired Lacey's prayer on Libyan radio and television. Colonel Qaddafi told Graham Lacey, "This is the first time a Christian is praying with me."

Patriotism is not condoning cruel treatment of other peoples of the world. Patriotism is living a Godly life that reaches out to others so God can bless us as a nation, and through our blessing, other nations will be blessed. We can make all the excuses we want, but deep down in our hearts we know that if we do not have peace with other men, we will not have peace in our own hearts either.

Notes:

1. Phillip Knightley, Legacy of Lawrence of Arabia Clouds Chances for Mideast Peace, *Sunday World Herald,* Omaha, Nebraska. This is an excerpt from his book "The Secret Lives of Lawrence of Arabia"

2. James Lunt, *Hossein of Jordan, Searching for a Just and Lasting Peace* (New York: William Morrow and Company, Inc., 1989) pp. xxi, xxii.

3. Lunt, p. xxiv.

4. David Blundy & Andrew Lycett, *Qaddafi and the Libyan Revolution* (Boston: Little, Brown and Company, 1987) p. 2.

5. Blundy, p. 37.

6. Bob Woodward, *Veil: The Secret Wars of the CIA* (New York: Simon and Schuster, 1987) p. 185.

7. Woodward, p. 471.

8. Woodward, p. 473.

9. Woodward, pp. 218, 381.

10. Woodward, pp. 217.

11. Woodward, p. 219.

12. Woodward, pp. 395-397.

13. Anwar el-Sadat, *In Search of Identity, an autobiography* (New York: Harper & Row, Publishers, 1978) p. 7.

14. el-Sadat, p. 108.

15. Camelia Sadat, *My Father and I*, (New York: Macmillan Publishing Company, 1985) p. 27.

16. el-Sadat, p. 135.

17. Camelia Sadat, p. 110.

18. el-Sadat, p. 337.

19. Woodward, p. 414.

20. Timeline: U.S.-Iraq relations, *Minneapolis Star and Tribune,* Jan 15, 1991.

21. Bill Moyers National Public Television Special, *After the War,* June 18, 1991.

22. James Bill, *The Eagle and the Lion, The Tragedy of American-Iranian Relations* (New Haven: Yale University Press, 1988) p. 207.

23. Thomas C. Fox, *Iraq: Military Victory, Moral Defeat* (Kansas City, MO: Sheed & Ward, 1991) p. 111.

24. Moyers.

25. Report: Gulf war cost region $676 billion, Mercury News wire services, San Jose, CA, Sun, April 23.

26. Robin Wright, Iran spending millions to aid Muslim groups, experts say, *Los Angeles Times,* April 7, 1993.

27. Leon T. Hadar, "Why West should not fear Islam," reprinted for *San Jose Mercury News* April 11, 1993

28. Dr. Saed Hossein Nassar, Professor of Islamic studies at George Washington University spoke to the National Public Radio noon forum at Minneapolis Westminster Presbyterian Church.

29. Agnes Sanford, *Behold Your God* (St. Paul, Minnesota: Macalester Park Pub. Co., 1958) p. 173.

30. Hodding Carter, The Arming of Iraq, *Frontline* Public Television, Sept 11, 1990. Neil Livingston tells how Saddam Hossein, along with a group of young Iraqi soldiers toured a series of American chemical weapons factories. They were informed about design, manufacturing, and employment on the battlefield.

31. Signs of Hope and Concern, *Christianity Today* May 27, 1991, p. 48.

IRAN –
AN OFFENDED PEOPLE

Pray as much as you like; it is your oil they are after—why should they worry about your prayers? They are after our minerals, and want to turn our country into a market for their goods. That is the reason the puppet governments they have installed prevent us from industrializing, and instead, establish only assembly plants and industry that is dependent on the outside world.　　　　　　　　　　　　　　　--Ayatollah Khomeini
　　　　　　　　　　　　　　　　　　　　　　　　　Beyond the Mosque

We were slowly beginning to realize that we were surrounded by millions of Iranians who saw their country through very different eyes from ours. They felt exploited by the extravagances of the regime—so obviously backed by Western interests.　　　　--Paul Hunt, Chaplain to the Bishop of Iran
　　　　　　　　　　　　　　　　　　　　　　　　　　　　Inside Iran

The social life in Iran was wonderful. We had so many relatives that we didn't even have time to think about making outside friends. But life was not all having a good time. Bahram needed to find a job.

We were in no way prepared for the maze of bureaucracy we were to be faced with. The first incident was three days after we arrived in Tehran. We had a call that our airfreight packages were in. We had airfreighted my childhood cedar chest and two other large boxes. We took the taxi to the airport. In Tehran you just walk out to the closest busy street and shout out your destination as the taxis pass. If the taxi driver is going in your direction, he stops. Once in the taxi it is better not to watch the road because it is similar to riding the mad mouse at the fair. One day I saw a taxi run over a man's toes. The man's face turned dark red, but he walked off as if nothing had happened. The taxi driver didn't even look up.

The taxi let us off in front of the customs center of the airport. Bahram said, "You wait over here on the grass and I'll go get our things and be right out." I waited for two hours. He came out with a worried look on his face. "They say we have to pay a $5000 custom tax to get our things, we're going to have to leave it all."

"You must be out of your mind," I exclaimed, "Those are things I have been saving since I was a child." A young Iranian fellow named Parviz overheard our conversation.

"I can help you; I know how to deal with these people. How much money do you have?"

Bahram had only about $25 on him. "That will do," said Parviz. In the mean time we called a college friend of ours who worked in the main airport.

She called the customs office and said, "Why are you bothering these students like this, eh? They have come back to their country and were promised they would not have to pay customs for their things."

Well, Parviz knew why they were bothering us. He showed Bahram how you slip a bill in your passport and show it to the officer. Bahram did not approve of this method of dealing with authorities, but he knew how much my hope chest meant to me. He could not believe what had happened to his country in the ten years he had been gone.

I waited on the grass another five hours before Bahram and Parviz came wheeling a large cart out with our monstrous air freight packages. Bahram thanked Parviz for his help but secretly vowed he would never stoop to this method of bribery ever again, not for any reason. That turned out to be a very hard promise to keep.

Bahram decided to check into a few job leads before we left for Isfahan the next week. The Iranian Oil Company was his first stop; he had heard they were accommodating returning college graduates. He was hoping his Master's Degree in chemical engineering with emphasis in radioactive waste management would give him an edge on the job market. He had heard the Shah was interested in building seven nuclear power plants in various parts of Iran.

This time I thought I would sit across the street in a coffee house and sip some of their strong French coffee while I waited. He was gone for about an hour and a half but didn't come out looking very happy.

Bahram had not served in the army, and this was not an obligation they were going to overlook. If they hired him, they said they could shorten his military time to basic training. He could either go six months right away or break it into two three months periods. The starting salary was 8000 tumans a month which was only about $1150. In Teheran apartments rented for about $1000 a month; that would leave $150 to cover all other expenses. It did not look like a hopeful situation to a 28-year-old engineer with four years of experience. He was worried about leaving me for even three months at this point. It was a new culture for me and I couldn't speak much Farsi. It would put a big responsibility on the rest of the family.

The other problem was that we were out of money. We had spent what money we had on household items and shipped them to Iran. We had bought a GE refrigerator, a gas stove, an Electrolux vacuum cleaner and a bicentennial rocking chair. The rocking chair had a lovely eagle with 1776-1976 on it. We had felt it would be a nice reminder of our time in America, even though it looked like it may be awhile before we would have a home to put it in.

"Well," Bahram said, "let's wait until we get to Isfahan and see how things go there." Isfahan was my favorite city in Iran. It was the old capitol during the reign of Shah Abbas (a.d. 1588-1629). Isfahan had the largest square in the world. It was there that the game of polo originated. The Shah would sit up on his palace terrace and watch the polo games. There was also the beautiful Shah's Mosque beside the king's palace, Ali Qapu. These buildings were over 400 years old and were now museums.

At the other end of the square was the bazaar, miles of tunnels lined with shops. There were venders that sold everything from Persian carpets to kitchen utensils to water pipes. Whatever you wanted, they had. Shoppers haggled for their prices. I thought that was great fun, and Bahram taught me how to get the best price. I loved going there and shopkeepers really liked me too. They would call to the neighboring shop keepers, "Hey, come and meet this American Isfahanian. She haggles just like one of us." They were so amused by me that they would give me a real good bargain.

My sisters-in-law would say, "Send Judith to buy it for you, she gets better prices than we do."

Isfahan is home to the beautiful Zayandehrud River with two ancient stone bridges crossing over it. All along the river were parks with families out strolling in the evenings. I had a special feeling for this lovely city.

We never got to live in Isfahan, although we made every effort.

Bahram heard Dupont was opening a company with Iranian businessmen. He went to see them, but they could not hire him until his military obligation was fulfilled. Later I talked with an American Dupont executive who told me they were building company housing in Isfahan. "It's going to be the most modern housing in Isfahan; you won't see one veil there," he boasted. I suppose he was confiding in me as a Westerner, not realizing that my mother-in-law wore a veil. I wondered what they would do to keep her out of the housing if we lived there. During the Shah's reign, there was an unwritten rule that women with the veil could not go into certain restaurants or hotels. I used to buy my Time magazine at Hotel Kourosh (Sheraton Hotel) and Maman would have to wait outside for me while I went in to buy it.

In Isfahan our relatives assured us Bahram wouldn't have to go to the military. As the oldest son, he was legally exempt because his mother was a widow. But with the bloated bureaucracy in Iran, we would need numerous signatures before he would see an exemption in his hand.

It took us eleven months in all. In Isfahan we waited from Tuesday to Tuesday for military court to convene. I accompanied Bahram, and we would wait on the sidewalk in front of the office. We would take our lunch with us and eat standing in that crisp fall weather. We would sometimes hold our feet in our hands for awhile to thaw them out. Our pride and the evidence of what happened to others prevented us from asking for assistance. I learned all the swear words in Farsi while I stood there watching that sergeant throw village men out of his office. He knew we were there, but he wasn't pulling our file for court that particular day.

By this time I was pregnant with our second child. I didn't mind standing those Tuesdays with my husband because it was the first time I had felt able to help him. It is difficult to explain how helpless one can feel without cultural knowledge and without the ability to communicate.

The rest of my days were spent redecorating the second story of the family homestead. It was a gorgeous old home with high decorative plaster ceilings. The floors were all stone mosaic and I stripped the old wax off them. I wanted to paint but I had to scrape the old finish off the walls first. After the scrapping was completed, I painted the walls white. I had always had a dream of having a black and white room, and I thought the sitting room would do nicely.

The day came when the walls were painted white, and we were ready to pick out wall paper. We went to a shop and looked through all their sample books. I wanted black and white but at the same time I knew there was a possibility that my mother-in-law would be living in the house and she liked spring flowers.

"Oh, look Maman, wallpaper with lovely spring flowers." Maman seemed willing to go along with anything that made me happy.

After about an hour and a half of looking through books Bahram said, "You better decide, we are supposed to be at Aunt Hamdam's house for dinner right now." We picked out four or five patterns just in case one was out of stock.

We called the two fellows drinking tea behind the counter and said, "We have decided on some patterns for wallpaper."

The fellow said, "Oh, we don't have any of those wallpapers; the only ones we have are in this book." Bahram gave me a look that could kill.

"Now, we mustn't be ugly Americans; things move more slowly in the Middle East. Let's look through this book."

Needless to say, we were late for dinner, and we ended up with a beige and dark brown floral design. The next day a worker came and put the wallpaper up for us.

That evening my sister-in-law stopped by and said, "Don't you think it would have matched better if you had painted the walls beige?"

Maman and I became great friends. From her I received my most beautiful wedding gift. She had been Isfahan's Mother of the Year in 1971. That year coincided with the 2500 year celebration of Persian monarchy. Empress Farah came to Isfahan and in a televised ceremony presented Maman with a commemorative gold coin. Maman had never worked outside the home and this coin represented what she had really accomplished in her life. I was very honored when she gave me that coin for a wedding gift.

She taught me how to cook Iranian food and how to speak Farsi. If Bahram and I had a fuss over something she would come to me and say, "He didn't mean it; you can see how much he loves you. His father was the same way, always saying things to me he didn't mean when he was distressed." Then we would both feel ashamed of the way we had acted. Because of her I have wonderful memories of that difficult transition time.

Four months passed. One Tuesday, as we were standing out in front of the military office, the sergeant called our name. We were taken in to a group of men, and they asked us many questions and they signed Bahram's papers. That sergeant said he finally got embarrassed watching that faithful American girl stand out in the cold beside her husband. Bahram was so happy on the way home he swung me around and gave me a big kiss right on the sidewalk. This was not a usual sight for the local people and one car almost ran off the road.

What we didn't realize was that our troubles had actually just begun. Now we had to get the final approval for his army exemption in Teheran. It was very difficult for me. In my sister-in-law's home in Teheran they were very kind to me, but there was nothing for me to do. With my limited Farsi, I dared not venture past the corner store. Our evenings were spent watching television I couldn't understand.

My only daily companion was Javaheir, their servant girl. We became very close. She was very intelligent, but her mother had died when she was three years old and she was not given an education. She was put to weaving carpets until she came to my sister-in-law's home at thirteen. Javaheir would tell me her sad stories and we would cry together. She became very protective of me.

I taught her how to make pizza and some other American foods. She was a very quick learner. She became a valuable asset to the extended family; they called her the servant girl who made delicious pizza. They would borrow her for the evening when they had a party. I still think about Javaheir and wonder how she's doing. She married and has lived in southern Tehran through all the Iraqi bombings. I have prayed for her safety. No one seems to have any information about her.

Another three or four months passed, and we were getting very discouraged. Maman had come from Isfahan, and we were discussing the military situation. There was one last colonel that had to sign Bahram's papers, and Maman and I decided to go talk to him ourselves.

The colonel's office was very intimidating. There were six different parties sitting around on couches and we were obligated to state our business in front of everyone. When it came to my turn, I started explaining in my limited Farsi that my husband was a graduate returned from studying in America. He interrupted, "Oh I see, you have gone to America and had all your fun and now you want to shirk your responsibilities to the Iranian government." Then he coldly flagged me out without even asking my name. I became very angry.

"Do you call spending ten years of weeknights in the library and weekends at work fun? We have worked our younger years away, just dreaming to come back here for this kind of treatment!"

I said many other things and in my distress had reverted back to English, burst into tears and rushed from the room. Two very kind soldiers out in the hall tried to comfort me and one brought me a glass of water. I thanked them and left.

Maman had been waiting downstairs and I rushed down to her and admitted the horrible mess I had made of things. I was convinced after seeing what a hysterical wife Bahram had they would never sign his papers. I asked myself a hundred times on the way home in the taxi how I could have attempted such a venture.

Fortunately for me that colonel never even asked what my name was, and had signed Bahram's papers that very morning at the request of an old family friend. Bahram was now officially free to pursue his career. But that experience remained in my mind and I thought, "God forbid we end up at the mercy of these government people ever again."

Bahram accepted a job at Iran's first paper mill on the Caspian Sea coast. They had company housing for employees so that solved the problem of the high rent. The homes were Finnish style villas and were large and spacious. The kitchen had a gray floor, pink cupboards, yellow counter tops, blue ceramic tiles and beige paint on the walls. "They must have let the workers do the color coordinating," Bahram said. I took a can of blue paint to the kitchen.

There was a Canadian company working with us. They had a combination of Canadians, Americans, and some European expatriates working for them and living in a trailer court. If any of them had four or more children, they were given a villa. We had all been promised furnishings for our homes, but only the expatriates received them. I didn't mind; I was full of hope. We had eight sliding glass doors, and I sewed my own drapes for them.

I had a unique position in that townsite. Being raised an American with all the privileges that involves, I found myself an Iranian with the Westerners on the other side. Technically, I had the rights of an Iranian wife.

Everything was separate. The expatriates had their own school, restaurant, and housing areas, except for the larger families living in the villas. The Canadian restaurant had everything imported from the West, right on down to their milk and matches. The first day the Iranian cafeteria opened 400 workers got food poisoning. It was not surprising that all the Iranians wanted to go to the Canadian cafeteria. The expatriates soon made the rule that Iranians were not allowed to use their facility. If a Canadian engineer invited an Iranian engineer to lunch there would be nothing said.

The Canadian school was a much better quality building with imported furnishings from the West but the Iranian school was a sorry situation. Many of the people in charge of the Iranian school were locals, and their standards were not up to the standards of the group of educated Iranians that had moved from the city. I became very close friends with a lovely British girl, Rosana, who also had an Iranian husband, and we drove over to the school the day before it was to open. It was unbelievable. Some men had come to sweep with brooms and the chairs were not even in place. It was very discouraging.

In all fairness, the Westerners were better organizers, but the fact remained that they ended up with good facilities and we had to make do.

The unfair situation became reality for me before the Christmas of 1977. We heard that the Canadian school had put on the play Hanzel and Gretel. I had Canadian neighbors and their children played with my children and spent many hours in my home. I looked at my children and realized the only entertainment they had was to play out in the piles of dirt and sand the workers kept moving from one side of the street to the other. Not that they were unhappy; they weren't. They were well-adjusted, happy children, but I grieved for some of the cultural arts they could have had living in America.

At the mill, my husband shared with the Canadian men how I had felt and they said, "Gee, that's too bad. Tell her there is going to be a Christmas party the 23rd of December and to just come. Tell her to bring a gift for the children and put it behind the podium. Santa will come and call out each child's name and give them their gift."

I thought I would test my Canadian neighbor. I went and complained to her about not being invited to the play. I wanted to see if she would tell me about the Christmas party, but she didn't say a word.

I talked to my friend Rosana and asked her why she thought they were like that.

She said, "Because they will never associate with us."

"Rosana, is it possible it is not in their company budget or there wasn't room for everyone?"

"Why did they invite the Europeans then? When are you going to wake up, Judith? They despise us because we married Iranians."

"Well... I'm going to show up at that Christmas party whether they want me or not."

I didn't tell anyone about my plans and I just showed up at the party with my two children. There were some embarrassed faces but the children got to see Santa Claus. After that I decided to forget about the Westerners and their culture. At least the Iranians wanted me and were nice to me. Every year after that I would invite Iranians over to my home for Christmas. There were some Jewish Iranians, some Muslims, and Rosana would bring her guitar and we would sing Christmas carols. The technicians would bring us a pine tree and we decorated it the way the pioneers did, with popcorn and berries. One Christmas a worker dropped off a 15 foot pine tree in our front yard. Bahram had to saw the top off for our tree that year. We put one present for each child under the tree for our Christmas party.

It didn't look as though the expatriates would be around much longer anyway. From the time we first arrived in Iran there had been rumors of revolt. The college students said there were groups called Mujahadeen, which meant *soldiers of God.* They would rob banks to finance their political activities. They said the Iranian people couldn't stand the corrupt and repressive Shah who had been forced upon them by the Western countries from the very beginning.

I knew some of the history of Iran. Back in college I had done a research paper on the oil industry of Iran. The Industrial Revolution in the West gave much of the Western world a strong appetite for new sources of fuel and other natural resources. The less developed countries like Iran with abundant sources of energy became the target of domination by outside powers. In the late 1800's the British went to Iran and saw that there was so much oil, it was sitting around in puddles on the ground. The Iranians were unaware of the value of their resource and signed contracts with the British, allowing them to take their oil with a minimal of charge. In 1909 the Anglo-Iranian Oil Co. officially came into being.

In 1925, Reza Shah Pahlavi, the Shah's father, crowned himself King of Persia. He had been an officer in the Persian Cossack Brigade; had usurped the throne from the Qajar dynasty and started the Pahlavi dynasty. He ruled until 1941 when the British and Soviets drove him into exile for allying with Hitler. Reza Shah had turned to Nazi Germany for help in freeing Iran from British and Soviet exploitation. The Iranians were an Aryan race and therefore acceptable to Hitler. In 1935 the government officially changed their name to Iran (land of the Aryans). Iran is called the *gateway to the west* because it geographically is the easiest route from Asia to Europe. In every major war Iran has been occupied by foreign troops because of its geographic location.

The Iranians trusted and welcomed Americans in the early part of the century. They had every reason to. America had not yet shown interest in their oil fields.

The American missionary-teachers that went in were not there just to evangelize, but to meet physical needs. They went in to educate and improve health conditions. Louis Dreyfus, Jr., the American diplomat to Iran during the war years of 1940-44, was well liked in Iran. He and his wife, Grace, associated with all levels of society and Grace volunteered her nursing abilities to the slums in southern Teheran. The Iranian people trusted Americans and looked to them for help in freeing themselves from the abuse of the British and the Soviets.

But in the 1940's the problems started and James Bill in *The Eagle and the Lion* says it well:

> *The growing American presence in Iran in the early 1940's sharply increased tension between the United States and Britain. In response to Winston Churchill's questions about America's interest in Iranian oil, Franklin Roosevelt wrote in March 1944 that "I am having the oil question studied by the Department of State and my oil experts, but please do accept my assurances that we are not making sheep's eyes at your oil fields in Iran and Iraq." Churchill*

responded: "Thank you very much for your assurance about sheep's
eyes at our oil fields in Iran and Iraq. Let me reciprocate by giving
you the fullest assurance that we have no thought of trying to horn
in upon your interests or property in Saudi Arabia." [1]

One British diplomat described Iran as a *victim* in the hands of
America, and the British were aware that American involvement in
Iran could end their monopoly on Iranian oil.

During World War II, Iran was occupied by the British, the Soviets,
and the Americans. In 1941 Reza Shah's son, Muhammad Reza
Pahlavi, was placed on the throne by the Allied powers at 22 years of
age. From the very beginning this made the young Shah very insecure.
He was afraid the Western powers were going to break up his country.
The Iranians were especially paranoid of the British because of their
self-serving attitude with complete disregard for the needs of the
Iranian citizens. The Russians were a large power to the North to
always be aware of.

In the meantime, both Britain and America severely under-
estimated Iranian political forces. The Americans have never been able
to recognize the Iranians' talent and ability to determine their own
policies. Over the years, Iran has had a series of brilliant politicians
who have been forcefully removed but managed to protect Iran's
independence. America has often been responsible for the ousting of
Iranian prime ministers. The most important of these was Prime
Minister Muhammad Musaddiq. James Bill describes Musaddiq:

Musaddiq was a beloved figure of enormous charisma to Iranians of
all social classes. His wry sense of humor was infectious, although
it was not understood in the West. His very emotionalism and
physical frailty (he was in constant poor health) endeared him to his
people, who saw in him the embodiment of a weak and embattled
Iran. [2]

Musaddiq was a staunch supporter of democracy and dreamed for
Iran to be a democratic country. But Musaddiq knew the first job that
had to be done was to nationalize Iranian oil from the hands of the
British. It is not surprising that Iranians were horrified by foreign
powers coming in and not only controlling, but getting all the profits
from their natural resource.

In 1951, Musaddiq introduced, and the Iranian Parliament passed, an act to nationalize Iranian oil. But the British would not negotiate. Then Musaddiq, representing the Iranian Parliament, went to the World Court in The Hague, The Netherlands and won his case. This was the court of International Law set up by the United Nations.

But the Western countries effectively boycotted Iranian oil on the world market. Two years of boycott left Iran with a devastated economy, and the people poured into the streets demonstrating against the Shah's rule. The Shah fled the country on August 16, 1953.

In that same month, the British under Winston Churchill and the American CIA during the Eisenhower Administration overthrew the Iranian Musaddiq government in a project called "Operation Ajax." The CIA went to villages and hired people to beat Musaddiq supporters with clubs in the streets of Teheran. They executed 60 leaders of the Musaddiq government, returned the Shah, and put him back on the throne. Muhammad Musaddiq was put under house arrest and died March 6, 1967, twelve years before the 1979 revolution. His only request had been that he be buried along the men that died for the nationalization of Iranian oil. Iranians say he was buried in his own back yard.

Musaddiq's name was secretly revered and he became a hero to the Iranian people. His efforts were not in vain. Iranian oil was nationalized as an outcome of that 1953 Revolution. Iran then received 50 percent of oil profits. The Iranians never forgave America for preventing what they believe would have been a stable, friendly democracy under the leadership of Mussadiq. Many Iranians feel Khomeini's triumph over Iranian politics was a direct consequence of decades of social, political and economic manipulation and interference in Iran's affairs by the outside powers. They think they would not have the Khomeini government today if they had been allowed to continue under the leadership of Dr. Musaddiq.

The Americans were rewarded for their help to the British; they were given 40 percent of British interests in Iranian oil. The CIA then helped the Iranian government establish and train an internal security organization to protect the Shah. SAVAK, the terrored organization was developed to suppress and oppress its own people. James Bill reports:

Over the years the United States, Iran, Israel, and Turkey were to cooperate closely in intelligence matters. Domestically, SAVAK was

*viewed as a police-state monster, and as its tactics became more
extreme and ruthless over time, it acquired an unsavory reputation
not only in Iran but throughout the world. [3]*

Iranians' anger fumed beneath the surface from 1953 to 1979. The
Shah, on the other hand was more insecure than ever. Anyone within
the country that became too influential he got rid of, and at the same
time constantly manipulated America like an insecure lover to test its
loyalty to him.

The one American President that had the Shah figured out was
John Fitzgerald Kennedy. He saw the Shah as an egotistical, corrupt
tyrant. Equally, the Shah was jealous of the Iranian masses' affection
for President Kennedy. In 1962, Kennedy pressured the Shah to make
economic and social reforms. It had been obvious for many years that
the biggest threat to the Shah was from his unhappy people within.
Kennedy sent the American Peace Corp which gave the United States
some needed credibility.

The Kennedy Administration came up with a land reform program
which took the land from the large land owners and gave it to the
peasants. It was a part of a larger social and economic reform named
the *White Revolution.* This reform was developed with pure motives
on the part of Kennedy and his staff but failed for a number of reasons.
Mainly, its purpose was not to serve the masses as much as protect the
Shah's political system. Ironically, the Shah did not even trust
Kennedy's White Revolution and did only a half-hearted follow up of
the land reform. The poor, uneducated peasants were unable to work
the land themselves. Without efficient back up programs the peasants
all got discouraged, sold their lands and moved to the cities. This
ruined Iranian agriculture and the country was even more dependent
on America for food imports.

We have an Iranian friend whose father owned a farm implement
company and he went bankrupt after the White Revolution. He said the
peasants didn't have money to buy farm machinery; that they were
trying to farm by primitive means. Unfortunately, this well-intended
program became looked upon as one more trick to make Iran
dependent on America. In the past, there had always been three
sources of power that ran the country; the government, the bazaar, and
the religious establishment. The foreign businessmen began to
compete with the bazaar for domination of trade. Foreigners

increasingly replaced the clergy as advisors to the Shah. [4] Another revolutionary seed was planted because the Shi'ite religious establishment was one of the large land owners whose land was taken away.

Secondly, it set the masses of Iranians up for disappointment because they expected some real transformation of their political and social system which was never to come. This not only awakened old anger but gave more credibility to revolutionary leaders.

In 1963, Ayatollah Ruhollah Khomeini came on the scene of Iranian politics. A popular uprising calling for a better life in Iran instigated riots and demonstrations. The participants were from every segment of society. The Shah's police were called out and thousands of Iranians were killed. Ayatollah Khomeini was arrested and put in prison but later released.

There were two final factors that led to the revolution that ultimately toppled the Shah. One was the law passed by the Iranian Parliament that American military and their dependents were immune to Iranian law. Ayatollah Khomeini became very involved in the angry backlash from Iranian nationals. Khomeini called it a *document of enslavement.* He gave his most impressive speech of which this is a part:

> *Our dignity has been trampled on; the dignity of Iran has been destroyed. A law....states that all American military advisors, together with their families, technical and administrative officials, and servants—in brief, anyone in any way connected with them—are to possess legal immunity concerning any crime they may commit in Iran....The files must be sent to America so that our masters over there can decide what is to be done....The previous government approved this measure without telling anyone....They have reduced the Iranian people to a level lower than that of an American dog. [5]*

Khomeini was exiled to Turkey on November 4, 1964 for giving that speech.

The second factor was the fact that the Shah was spending much of the oil income on weapons and military machinery while even large cities like Teheran didn't have gas lines to their homes. In 1967-68 the

Shah purchased $96 million in military equipment and in 1969-70;
$289 million. By the mid-70's Iran was spending an average of $5
billion a year on the military. [6]

Obviously, the Shah of Iran had lost touch with reality. American
President Nixon and his Secretary of State, Henry Kissinger, gave the
Shah unlimited access to purchase American arms. Most of the oil
money was going right back to the American economy. A group of
Iranian elites rallying around the Shah were becoming rich and living
lavish lifestyles while the needs of the masses were going unmet. Paul
Hunt, chaplain to the Bishop of Iran describes the Iranian peoples'
feelings:

> *People began openly to question where all the wealth was going.*
> *Why was it that less than a tenth was reaching the industry of the*
> *country and the pockets of the people? Food prices rose alarmingly.*
> *The poor were particularly affected. Frequent price commissions*
> *were quoted in the press, but they didn't seem to do any good.*
> *Suddenly the electricity would be cut off and we were plunged into*
> *evenings of darkness. There wasn't enough power for domestic use*
> *because so much was being used by the newly-installed industrial*
> *plants. [7]*

The final insult was the lavish 2500 year celebration of Persian
monarchy the Shah held in Persepolis in 1971. Dignitaries from all
over the world were invited and an estimated $200 million was spent
on the occasion. [8] The Iranian people had not been invited. Messages
from Khomeini in Iraq sent college students out demonstrating in the
streets and they were again attacked and beaten by the Shah's police.

In 1978, we were going to have an opportunity to see the Shah in
person. He was coming to initiate our paper mill in the province of
Gilan. Each employee was personally interviewed weeks ahead. For
various security reasons, many people had been confined to their
homes for the day. There were soldiers with machine guns posted all
along the road the Shah would be coming on. He was to make his
appearance in front of the Canadian school.

A group of us walked down from the housing area. I wanted my
children to be able to say they had seen the Shah of Iran. But he came
so fast and had a police wagon and an ambulance following him.

There was a group of men with him that came running among us shouting, "Long live the Shah." He brought his own admiration society with him. My four year old son Javad kept asking, "Where is he Mommy?"

I said, "There he is; now he's sitting; now he's standing. Did you see him?" I was thankful he said yes because the Shah had been driven away as fast as he came in.

During the walk back home there were many comments made. One neighbor whispered, "He doesn't look well; his coloring is bad."

Another answered, "They say he's sick, maybe cancer, and he's got people that are out to get him."

That was the last factory the Shah was able to visit. A month later on August 19, 1978, an Abadan movie theater called Cinema Rex was set on fire, and more than 400 people burned to death inside it. No group claimed responsibility but someone had locked all the exit routes, trapping people inside. That started riots in every city. On September 8, over 400 peaceful demonstrators were machine gunned to death in Zaleh Square in Teheran. They named that day *Black Friday.*

The government had a system during the demonstrations of 1978. They would open fire on the people, then bring an ambulance and take the ones that looked alive to the hospital, throw all the ones who looked dead in the back of a truck, and then a fire truck would hose down the area. This continued through February of 1979. An estimated 10 to 12,000 persons were killed and another 45 to 50,000 were injured. [8]

The army was not doing well. Soldiers can only shoot down so many of their own people. There were stories of soldiers turning and shooting their superior officers and then shooting themselves. Thousands of soldiers defected and joined the people. There were rumors that they had brought Israeli soldiers to help shoot demonstrators.

The Canadians with our company were evacuated out during the fall of 1978. A few of them came to visit us before they left. One couple told us that they had suggested that I might want to evacuate with them, since I was an American. But the fellow in charge of evacuation said, "She's made her bed, let her sleep in it." I told them not to feel bad because I would never want to leave my husband anyway.

Some of the expatriates were unwilling to haggle or compromise on the price of their garage sale cast-offs, and smashed them in their front yards. A few of the expatriates did feel very bad about the way things had turned out. The Canadian neighbor that didn't invite me to the Christmas party cried for one week, and brought us bicycles for our children and many other things they had to leave. Many people, like us, felt caught in between two government's policies.

After the expatriates left, the Iranians took over running the paper mill themselves. The mill was down for a while but they did start making paper eventually. The biggest problem for them was the economic blockade. If any of the equipment broke down, the Western countries would not sell them parts. A letter would come back with a big *SORRY* written on it. This experience impressed upon the Iranian people the importance of encouraging Iranian inventors to make their own parts. During the Shah's regime, any initiative to make Iran self-sufficient was looked upon as a threat to the Shah's power. Blind obedience was the accepted behavior if one wanted to further one's career.

Living in a townsite which was dependent on a paper and pulp mill which was no longer functioning was a bit frightening for me. Also, the national workers were striking to wear down the Shah's government. We are very thankful that our needs were met that year, but we certainly learned the practice of simplicity. Once when we didn't have water for four days, a large semi-truck would come around and we would fill up every container we had. Gas capsules were another problem. We had two capsules but with no assurance we'd ever get another. I used my American electric frying pan a lot. Bahram had wired a 110 volt electric outlet for me in the kitchen so I could use my American appliances. Ironically, we had electricity but there was a shortage of gas. Once a week we would hook a gas capsule up to the hot water heater and all take a very quick shower. Bahram finally built us our own electric hot water heater. That's when I learned how creative people can be when they have to do without.

The electric company would go on strike from eight to ten every evening because that's when the national news was on. The workers said they did not want the people to hear the government's propaganda. This did cause some inconvenience for us, but we learned to cope. The Christmas of 1978 we had about 40 guests. By 8 o'clock we had all the food on the table buffet style and our candles set all around the room. Our neighbor, a Jewish Iranian lady had gone to town and bought a gift for each of the children and wrapped them and put them under the tree. Right before the electricity went out I heard our son Javad crying very loudly and ran to see what was the matter. It seemed Parvine had misunderstood and thought I had already gotten Javad a gift. Consequently, there was no gift for him under the tree. At that very moment the electric workers went on strike and we were in complete darkness. By the time my husband got all the candles lit, I had managed to find something to wrap for Javad and was back by the Christmas tree. I said, "Oh, here is your gift Javad." By his beaming face I could tell he hadn't even noticed I'd been out of the room. We went on to have a lovely Christmas meal by candlelight.

Ten days after Christmas of that year, all of Iran had heard that General Huyser, deputy commander-in-chief of the U.S. European Command under Alexander Haig, was in Iran. We all thought that Huyser had come to take the Shah out of Iran because the Shah left January 16 while the General was still there. But that was just like the Iranians to think that America was still controlling their circumstances. In reality, General Huyser had come to stabilize the Iranian military and see that it supported the Prime Minister Shapour Bakhtiar government. Should the Bakhtiar government fall, Huyser was supposed to help the Iranian generals carry out another coup d'etat. Huyser also intended to see about two CIA listening posts on the Soviet border. But General Huyser did not have success in either of these matters, and a tearful Shah left Iran for the last time. The Iranian people celebrated in the streets, showering the military with flowers and candy.

We have heard a variety of conversations that supposedly led to the Shah's decision to flee, but I personally believe he himself realized there was no longer any way to force himself on a people that never wanted him.

When the Shah was permitted into the United States, the Iranians took the American hostages. The Iranians thought America was going to do a repeat "Operation Ajax." They believed Musaddiq's fatal mistake was that he was too kind-hearted. This time they were going to be tough, so no one could ever overthrow their government again. But once the Iranians took the hostages they didn't know how to let them go without losing face.

I used to take a taxi around Teheran during the hostage crisis and people were very kind to me. They would apologize to me and wouldn't take my money. They would ask me why I was staying there. I would tell them I was the last of the Mohegans. Speaking their language and having a sense of humor did help. They would say, "Take your husband and go to America until all this terrible trouble is over." The Iranian people had once loved the Americans but felt it was time to face the fact that their good will had not been returned. They realized I was just a person caught in-between the policies of two governments.

Ayatollah Khomeini is a very curious figure to the West but the Middle Eastern people are familiar with his type of person and dress. Khomeini, from the very beginning stood up for Iranian rights. Even the women in Iran were willing to go back to the veil if it meant recapturing their national dignity. One Iranian said, "He's a dictator, but at least he's our dictator." Unfortunately, it took someone as tough as Khomeini to convince the Western countries that Iranians were a people to be contended with. His message was that Iranians would decide for themselves what kind of government they would have and what they would do with their own natural resources.

The Iranian Revolution was very frightening, but at the same time the process of revolution was interesting to witness. It really is the complete turning around of policies. In Isfahan under the Shah's regime, Mamon had to wait outside for me while I went in to the Sheraton Hotel to buy my Time magazine. In 1979, the first year of the revolution I held out my arm to Mamon and said, "Come on Mamon, we are free now." We held arms and walked in together. One year later, we traveled to Isfahan for the Iranian New Year in March, and I had to wait outside while Mamon went in to buy my Time magazine for me. Then I was the one not allowed in because I was not wearing a veil.

During the political upheaval in Iran, one American missionary was trying to decide what to do. After praying, she opened her Bible.

The light fell on Jeremiah 49:36(TJB):

Yahweh Sabaoth says this:

I am going to break the bow of Elam,
 the source of all his might.
I will bring four winds down on Elam
from the four corners of the sky,
and I will scatter the Elamites to the winds:
there will not be a single nation into which the Elamites
have not been driven for refuge.
I will make the Elamites tremble before their enemies,
before those determined to kill them.
I will bring down disaster on them,
my own fierce anger....
I will set up my throne in Elam,
and purge it of king and nobles.
It is Yahweh who speaks.
But in the days to come I will restore the fortunes of Elam....

This was most likely a prophesy for the ancient country of Elam which later became a part of Persia. These missionaries also discovered the Bible was full of Persian history. The Persians have a very favorable rating in the Bible. Starting with Cyrus, they were the nice guys that sent the Judeans back to rebuild their temple in Jerusalem. As much as the Jews were persecuted under the rule of Nebuchadnezzar, they were living comfortably under Persian rule. The Persian kings ruled with great tolerance. They envisioned an empire with self-governing colonies. Cyrus is credited with the original thoughts of democracy by many historians. The Jews were so comfortable under Persian rule that most of them did not return to Judah, and many of them named their children Persian names. This was obviously the case with the prophet, Daniel.

The Persians were Zorostrians, and the religion had evolved to a monotheistic faith with the flame as a symbol of eternity. Elam is the ancient name for the area in Iran that was ravaged by the ten year Iran-Iraq war. The Elamites were a power to be contended with as far back as 2700 B.C. Their power struggle was often with the great city of Ur that Abraham grew up in. But with the creation of the Persian Empire

in 550 B.C., Elam was assimilated. The ancient capitol for the
Elamites, and later the Persians, was Susa. Susa is where even today a
magnificent mausoleum for the Prophet Daniel stands.

During much of the ancient history of Persia, Susa was their main
capitol. In A.D. 1598, Isfahan was made the capitol by Shah Abbas the
Great, who once again united Persia under a vast empire. Since Shah
Abbas of the Safavid dynasty, the borders of the country have stayed
pretty much the same. The name Persia was Greek, named after the
area of Parsa, but the Iranians had always used the name Iran which
means *land of the Aryans*. In 1935, the government officially changed
the name of the country from Persia to Iran. The present capital of Iran
is in Teheran.

The missionaries held a great respect for the impressive history of
this ancient nation. They knew the Persian church from the sixth to the
tenth century started churches as far as India and China. The church
had legal protection under Islam and the Nestorian scholars had a
viable influence on Arab culture. In the 14th century the Eastern
church was almost entirely wiped out by the Turkic leader from
Central Asia, Timur. Pockets of the church remained; a good number
in the Kurdish provinces of Iran, Iraq, and Turkey. In 1551, some
Nestorians reunited with Rome. In 1599, the Nestorians in India united
with Rome and were called the Christians of St. Thomas. In 1898, a
group of Persian Nestorians united with the Russian Orthodox Church.
The original Nestorians are now called Assyrian Christians. Today we
attend an Iranian Christian church in San Jose, California which is
literally bursting at the seams. The American missionaries did not
know what the future would hold for this historic country. They did
know that from the time of the writing of Jeremiah, this was the first
time in the history of Persia that it had not had a king. My husband
Bahram said, "We have 3000 years of history, and we are having
another one of our growing pains."

The cost for Iran has been high. The wealthy friends of the Shah
either fled to America or were executed, stripped of their wealth, or
humiliated in other ways. During the revolution there were thousands
of casualties; during the American economic blockade there was
suffering because of shortages of food and heating fuel. By far the
worst was that while the country was weakened by revolution, a dozen
Iranian airfields were attacked by Iraqi bombers. Mehrabad Airport in

Tehran was the most serious, as it closed down all international travel. James Bill reports:

> *As the longest Middle East war in recent history, the Iran-Iraq conflict has resulted in an estimated 400,000 deaths and 1 million wounded on the Iranian side....By 1987 Iran had suffered more battle deaths than the United States in World War II, and Iran had only one-third the population that America had in 1945. [9]*

The largest group of Iranian Americans have congregated in California. The climate in California is very similar to the dry, arid air of the Middle East. They have organized restaurants, movie theaters, night clubs, and radio stations for themselves and feel quite at home. But it is not Iran, and the past haunts many of them. One of their famous singers, who died of a heart ailment in California, sang a song reminiscent of the grief many still feel over the devastation of their native land:

> *Days of light, good-bye; my homeland, good-bye.*
> *Tell me where the good days have gone,*
> *did they join the story books or just leave.*
> *No one is living here,*
> *it is time for crying, not laughing,*
> *it's fall in our hearts.*
> *Famine stricken rain throws down anger,*
> *everyone is mourning with hanging heads.*
> *Men have been hung, and women are in prison,*
> *it is night, and the day is gone,*
> *from every home a loved one has vanished.*
> *Everyone has become distant and are not speaking,*
> *days are like nights and they are dead silent.*
> *We are neither in heaven, nor on earth,*
> *it seems we are having a nightmare.*
> *We are far from our land and separated from time.*
> *We have wandered from our faith in God.*
> *Days of light, good-bye; my homeland, good-bye,*
> *We wait our turn with no direction or purpose,*
> *even to die we must wait in line until our turn.*

Our days and nights pass in this way.
Time takes us wherever it wants.
How long can we sit motionless and weep in despair,
and wish there was something we could do.
Oh lonely woman, oh vagabond man,
get up and do something, think of a solution,
think about this fragmented heart. [10]

Notes:

1. James Bill, *The Eagle and the Lion, The Tragedy of American-Iranian Relations,* (New Haven and London: Yale University Press, 1988), p. 28. I personally feel Bill's book is the most objective and completely correct study of Iran-American relations.

2. *Ibid.*, p. 55.

3. *Ibid.*, p.78

4. Robin Wright, *In the Name of God, The Khomeini Decade,* (New York, New York: Simon and Schuster, 1989), p. 52.

5. Bill, *The Eagle and the Lion,* p. 159.

6. *Ibid.*, p.173

7. *Ibid.*, p.183

8. *Ibid.*, p.236

9. *Ibid.*, p.305

10. Translated by my husband Bahram and me.

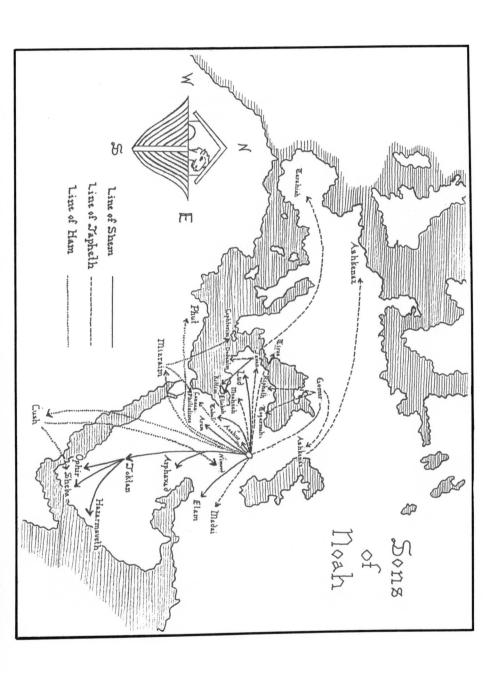

THE PALESTINIAN
ISSUE

This is what the Lord says: "Maintain justice and do what is right, for my salvation is close at hand and my righteousness will soon be revealed..." Let no foreigner who has joined himself to the Lord say, "The Lord will surely exclude me from his people." And foreigners who bind themselves to the Lord to serve him, to love the name of the Lord, and to worship him, all who keep the Sabbath without desecrating it and who hold fast to my covenant--these I will bring to my holy mountain and give them joy in my house of prayer. Their burnt offerings and sacrifices will be accepted on my altar; for my house will be called a house of prayer for all nations. The Sovereign Lord declares--he who gathers the exiles of Israel: "I will gather still others to them besides those already gathered." --Isaiah 56:1,3,6-8

Every year, Minneapolis has a celebration of its 10,000 lakes. It is an exciting event. They have milk-carton boat races, aqua shows with swimming beauties doing ballet in the water, and water sports. It lasts for a whole two weeks. It is called the Aquatennial Celebrations. The week begins with the Aquatennial Parade. Thousands of people line up along Nicollett Avenue downtown and it starts out about noon and goes until way after dark.

I was only 18, and it was my second summer in Minneapolis. I was getting a little more adventurous than I had been, so when my roommate said, "Let's jog over to the parade," I thought it sounded like fun. We were standing on Nicollett Avenue watching the parade, waving at all the beautiful girls sitting on top of flower covered floats, and two guys walked up to us. The older one had olive skin, but the younger one was quite fair. I looked at him and took him for one of the Jewish boys from St. Louis Park. "They were usually quite stuck on themselves," I thought. But this boy had a very heavy accent, and asked me, "Could you tell me how to get to Nicollett Ave?"

"Poor fellow," I thought, "He doesn't even know where he's at." Well, I found out it was a good opening line anyway. We went and had coffee at a little shop there on Nicollett Avenue. His name was Bahram, and he was from Iran. I had never heard of Iran.

"Have you ever heard of Persia?"

"I've heard of Persian cats and Persian carpets."

"Close enough," he said.

He was working at Charlie's Cafe Exceptionale. It was one of the ten best restaurants in America. All the movie stars went there when they visited Minneapolis. He had seen Natalie Wood, and Liberache had played the piano for them one night. We said good-bye and parted ways. Later that night on the way home I told my roommate, "I'm going to see this fellow again, I don't know where, maybe at a bus stop or something. I just know it."

Three months passed and the summer was about over. I was working as a long distance telephone operator at the downtown Minneapolis Bell Telephone. It was a gigantic building one block square with at least a thousand girls working there. I had graduated from a transportation and airline school but decided I didn't like the airlines afterall. I wasn't so sure I liked being a telephone operator either. The night before there had been a terrible storm in Minneapolis, and it was a busy day for the operators. That was before they had the 911 number for emergencies. All at once, my whole switchboard lit up and I didn't know which hole to plug into first. One lady's house was on fire, one little girl was home alone, and a tree had fallen on an old man's house. I was really proud of myself; I reassured each one of them, and got them connected to the right emergency service. But we had a bunch of little old ladies for supervisors, and the next day all they could think about was the little circles I didn't get filled in on my call cards. Not one word of praise. I was getting fed up. After work, I caught a bus and found a place to sit. I leaned back and started thinking about what I would do if I quit my job. I looked out the window and there he was. It was that boy from Persia, standing at the bus stop waving at me to come off the bus. I asked the driver, "Would you please let me off at the next stop?"

Bahram said, "Where have you been? One day I took a taxi to the address you gave me and they said you had moved."

"Yes, we moved."

"Then," he said, "I have waited out side of the Bell Telephone building so many times but I never saw you."

"That's interesting," I thought, "it's funny he didn't meet someone else."

"Why didn't you come to Charlie's Cafe, you knew I was there?"

I looked at him and said, "It crossed my mind, but I thought you might lose respect for me. Where I grew up girls don't go looking for boys."

"But we may have never found each other again!"

"I guess that was just a chance I had to take, but we did find each other, at this bus stop."

The next week Bahram was leaving for college in Mankato, Minnesota which was an hour's drive. We wrote letters and visited each other and then I decided to go back to college. He said, "Why don't you come to Mankato, then we could be together everyday."

When I moved to Mankato I met all of Bahram's friends and immediately joined the International Club. There weren't that many Iranians so they became quite close to all of the foreigners there at the college. We had a very interesting group of friends. There were two brothers from Iran named Ali and Mamadee (short for Muhammad). They were as different as day and night. Ali was a tall husky fellow and Mamadee was short and very slim. The only thing they had in common was their soft brown eyes. We also had Turkeman Iranians from the Northern parts of Iran, Sean, his wife A'aishe, and her sister Sarah. They were Mongol descendants and looked very Asian. Many people would ask Sarah if she was from Japan, and we would all chuckle because we knew how mad that made her. "I am Iranian!" she would answer.

Another Iranian boy named Reza told everyone he was the Prince of Persia. He ordered pencils that had *Prince of Persia* printed on them and he was even invited to many small towns in the area to speak. He always passed out his pencils to everyone. He played the guitar and sang. Once in awhile he would come to the student union with his Muslim warrior costume. It was a head-dress made out of flexible chain mail. We used to say, "Good evening Prince Reza, you're looking exceptionally fine this evening." He would bow and say, "Thank you."

Reza also had Einstein's equations of relativity written all over his wall. He had two fluffy Persian cats, and an American girlfriend named Gail. She really believed he was the prince of Iran and never seemed to question why he asked her to bring him potato salad sandwiches from the cafeteria. The staff never seemed to mind if the students took an after supper snack. It never occurred to Gail that a prince would never need left over sandwiches from the cafeteria.

Reza had a roommate from Kuwait, whose name was Moe (short for Muhammad). Moe never did run short of money because his government provided him with a generous monthly allowance. It was a regular sight to see Muhammad tooling main street with his red convertible full of American girls. Reza and Muhammad had really fun parties, and all the international students knew they were always welcome at their apartment. It was a fun place to go; the stereo was always on the same time as the television and they kept switching channels every few minutes. Everyone was mostly interested in good conversation between friends. But with the multiple languages, it was possible you couldn't understand the conversation, so you could always listen to music, watch television, play with the cats, or try and figure out Einstein's equations.

I shared an apartment with a beautiful Iranian girl named Lili. They used to call Lili Farah for fun, because she looked so much like the Shah of Iran's third wife. Lili and her boyfriend Masoud, and Bahram and I were a foursome. Masoud and Bahram were both studying engineering so we spent the majority of our courtship in the library. I was studying nutrition and did not have as many studies as Bahram did in engineering. If I finished studying before he did I would go to up to the third floor in the library and find books on Iranian history. We all ate supper together in the cafeteria and would go to the student union for a coffee break. Those were really fun times.

Lili taught me many things. I helped her with her English and she helped me learn Farsi. She taught me to cook. She would cook Iranian food and I would help her. We would buy fresh tomatoes and put them in the sink, pour boiling water over them, and I would peel them. Then we would make delicious lamb stews with eggplant, zucchini, greenbeans, lots of fresh chopped parsley, green onion, and mint. We would always make a side dish of fried spinach and yogurt. One day Lili came home and said, "Thanks a lot! Why didn't you tell me?"

"Tell you what?" I asked.

"That they have cooked tomatoes in a can!"

"I didn't know you wanted them," I replied, "I thought you liked peeling fresh tomatoes." Lili's parents were originally from Lebanon so she also taught me delicious Lebanese dishes like *Taboli*, and *Kibbe*.

The four of us have been fast friends over the years. We got married about the same time, had our first babies, moved to Iran, and moved back to America together.

Masoud and Bahram both had to transfer to the University of Minnesota to finish their engineering degrees. Bahram and I got married and rented an apartment in an old house close to the University campus. One day the doorbell rang and I opened the door and there stood Muhammad, the Kuwaiti. "Hi, I thought I'd come and stay with you for awhile."

Muhammad and Bahram and I were all sitting around one evening after supper and Muhammad said, "Isn't it terrible what is happening to the Palestinians, the Jews are taking away all their land." Being the typical American, I knew very little about world affairs. I had not been to church for quite a few years but somehow I knew enough to say, "You see Moe, people here think God gave that land to the Jews; that's what it says in the Bible." "But what about all those Palestinian people who have lived there for two thousand years?" demanded Moe.

I gave Moe a long look, and said, "I guess no one has ever thought about them." After that, I did start to think about them, but back in 1971 there was literally nothing written about the Palestinians. So I started reading about the Jews. I read about the formation of Israel, Ben Gurion, the graveyard in Russia called Baba Yar, and the life story of Moshe Dayan. As a child, I had been taught a thorough Biblical history of the Jews in church. The information I received from books about them was quite predictable, although the holocaust was a tragedy beyond all imagination.

Over the years I have tried to gather what bits and pieces of information I could about the Palestinians. The real picture of the Palestinians is quite different from what I was taught as a child. Only we Americans call them Palestinians; the rest of the world still calls them the Philistines. Americans have not followed the historical development of the Palestinians. In order to understand either the Jews or the Palestinians we must go back to the Bible:

After Adam and Eve's fall in the Garden of Eden, they were expelled from the Garden and relinquished their close communion with God. It seems they still had knowledge of God because they taught their sons Cain and Abel to be obedient to certain kinds of worship, although they had little success with Cain. The scriptures seem to show a slow deterioration in the relationship between God and man because other than Enoch, whom according to Genesis 5:24 walked with God, there weren't many godly men left. By the time we get to Noah in Genesis 6:9, he was the only one left that was righteous. The earth was corrupt and full of violence and God was sorry he had ever created man. God's heart was full of pain.

According to the Bible, the ark landed on Mount Ararat which is about half way between the Black Sea and the Caspian Sea. The only humans left on the earth were Noah, his wife, his three sons Japheth, Ham, Shem, and their wives. The descendants of Japheth are named in Genesis 10:2; they are the Indo-European or Aryan people who mostly went Northwest and into Europe except for one tribe called the Madai. It is generally accepted that the Madai were the Medes living West of the Caspian Sea and then moved down toward the Persian Gulf, more commonly called Persians.

The descendants of Ham moved southward. They were Cush, Misram, Phut, and Canaan. The sons of Cush, in Genesis 10:7, moved down into the area now called Ethiopia, of whom the Queen of Sheba was a descendant. Some of them returned North and among them was Nimrod who started the empire of Babylonia. Misraim sired the Egyptians and the Philistines, Phut's descendants became the Libyans and the Canaanites. The Canaanites stayed in the area we still call Palestine.

There is some differences of opinion about the original location of the Philistines but they were once known as the *sea people*. Some historians believe they had settled on the island of Crete and in about the 12th Century B.C. they invaded Egypt and eventually settled in the areas between Egypt and Canaan. More careful study shows that there were two different groups of Philistines and the tribe of Gerar in Genesis 26 was very friendly with Abraham and Isaac. Even later on when Israel became a strong nation, the more war-faring Philistine cities paid tribute to Israel. The Philistines had learned the manufacturing of iron weapons, and were skilled goldsmiths. Ancient Israel was more bothered by the Philistines because of their superior weapon systems.

The descendants of Shem stayed in the Middle East. They were Elam, Asshur, Arpachshad, Lud and Aram. The Elamites settled along the Persian Gulf. Assurs descendants were the Assyrians. Arpachshad is assumed to be the Chaldeans. Lud's people became the inhabitants of Asia Minor, and Aram's people became the Arameans of Syria and Mesopotamia, generally called Syrians. Abraham was a descendant of Aram. Abraham was the sixth generation of Eber through Peleg who stayed in greater Syria. Scholars feel the term Hebrew was derived from Eber's name. Eber's other son Joktan traveled south into the Arabian Peninsula and became the father of the southern Arabs.

Therefore, the Hebrews of the Bible days were Syrians. In Deuteronomy 26 the Israelites were told to bring their first fruits to the priests, and as they approached the alter were instructed:

5. And thou shalt speak and say before the Lord thy God, A Syrian ready to perish was my father, and he went down into Egypt, and sojourned there with a few, and became there a nation, great, mighty, and populous.

The NIV Bible uses Aramean in place of Syrian because these names were used interchangeably. George Lamsa, an Assyrian Christian scholar says Aramia is the ancient name for Syria. [1]

By going over the genealogy of man from the time of Adam to the development of these different tribes we see how related all these people are. The Jews, the Southern tribes of Arabia, the Chaldeans and Assyrians (modern day Iraqis and Syrians) all descended from Aram. And even the Philistines were descended from the sons of Cush, which would have made them distant cousins of Abraham. Then there were the different groups that migrated and then returned or intermarried. The Arabs and the Jews really are blood brothers.

Arthur Koestler, a Jew born in Budapest in 1905, has written a well-documented book, *The Thirteenth Tribe.* He proves the majority of the world's Jews today are not descendants of the Orient at all, but are of Russian Caucasian blood. In a.d. 740, the King of Khazar was caught in a political situation. Rather than align with the Christian Byzantines or the Muslim Arabs, he declared Judaism the state religion. A. N. Poliak, Tel Aviv University professor of medieval Jewish history, says those Khazar Jews who stayed where they were, those who emigrated to the United States and to other countries, and those who went to Israel—constitute the large majority of world Jewry. [2]

We are often confronted with the question "Is Judaism a race or a religion?" Now we also can ask "Are today's Jews with their mixed nationalities, even Semites?" What is the Semite race, and what is anti-Semitism?

It seems mankind again lost its personal knowledge of God after Noah, because it was a long time before God revealed himself in a completely new way and with a new character. That character was Abram. God had a plan for Abram. He wanted to make him a nation based on his strong faith, a nation of priests. This was God's plan for communicating with mankind. As the generations pass, the heirs were carefully hand-picked by God: Jacob over his brother Esau, Joseph over his older brothers. According to Genesis 15, the Israelites spent 400 years as slaves in Egypt to strengthen them.

After the ancient Israelites were led out of the land of Egypt, and their children reached the promised land, God gave specific instructions on what to do with the inhabitants. Deuteronomy 20:16,17 (NIV):

> *...in the cities of the nations the Lord your God is giving you as an inheritance, do not leave alive anything that breathes. Completely destroy them--the Hittites, Amorites, Canaanites, Perizzites, Hivites and Jebusites--as the Lord your God has commanded you.*

In Numbers 33, God told Moses to destroy all of their idolatrous worship places.

At this point, we may ask how a loving God could give the Israelites permission to so violently massacre another group of people. Was it because the Israelites were God's chosen people and they were more special to God? Was this other group sacrificed in order for God to keep his promise to Israelites? Was it because God gave the Israelites this land and the Canaanites were just in the way? Could it have been God's permission to declare war on Canaanites in Israel's national interests? It was absolutely not any of these reasons. In fact, God was worried about the Israelites coming to these very same conclusions and He warns them in Deuteronomy 9:5, 6 (NIV):

> *It is not because of your righteousness or your integrity that you are going in to take possession of their land; but on account of the*

wickedness of these nations, the Lord your God will drive them out before you, to accomplish what He swore to your fathers, to Abraham, Isaac and Jacob. Understand, then that it is not because of your righteousness that the Lord your God is giving you this good land to possess, for you are a stiff-necked people.

Moses goes on to tell them if he hadn't fell on his face and fasted and prayed for forty days on their behalf, the Lord would have destroyed them too when they built the golden calf in the wilderness. In Deuteronomy 18 God says it is because of these nations detestable practices that he is destroying them.

In the novel, *The Source,* James Michener presents a scenario of how one pagan city remained, and a tribe of Hebrew people made their home near by. One of the Hebrew girls fell in love with the pagan mayor's son, and they were married. That was the beginning of the Hebrews worshipping the pagan gods. [3]

That was the very fear God had for his people and He warned them time and time again that they must not get pulled into this evil pagan worship. In Deuteronomy 11:16, 17 Moses tells the people, "Take care your heart is not seduced, that you do not go astray, serving other gods and worshiping them, or the anger of Yahweh will blaze out against you, he will shut up the heavens and there will be no rain, the land will not yield its produce and you will quickly die in the prosperous land that Yahweh is giving you." In other words, they were God's chosen people, but not so special that they could live in sin. The blessings of God were conditional. Deuteronomy 11:26(NJB) says "See, I set before you today a blessing and a curse: a blessing, if you obey the commandments of Yahweh your God that I enjoin on you today; a curse, marked out for you today, by going after other gods you have not known." Deuteronomy, chapters 12 through 27 gives the law that the Israelites must obey in order to receive the blessing, and keep their land. Some of the laws and customs are very interesting. Caring for the strangers in your land is mentioned at least nine times. Duet 14:29 says during the third-year tithe the strangers must be invited to the feast, and eat until they are full. Deuteronomy 16 instructs Israelites to invite the strangers among them to the feast of Weeks, and for seven weeks for the feast of the Tabernacles. In verse 24:17 it says "You must not pervert justice in dealing with a stranger or an orphan, nor take a widow's garment in pledge." It keeps reminding the Israelites that they were once strangers themselves in Egypt.

In verse 20 and 22 it says they must not beat the olive branches twice, or pick your vineyard twice but to leave some for the strangers in the land. Again in chapter 26 it mentions to share the first fruit and third year tithe feasts with the Levites and the strangers who live among them. In Deuteronomy 27 the Levites spoke loudly and cursed those who displace his neighbor's boundary mark, tamper with the rights of the stranger, the orphan, and the widow, or on him who strikes down his neighbor in secret.

In Deuteronomy 20:19 it says never to cut down fruit trees during an attack, "Is the tree in the fields human that you should besiege it too?" In Deuteronomy 28:12 says Israel must lend to many nations but it should not borrow. Deuteronomy 17:20 (NJB) says "Strict justice must be your ideal, so that you may live in rightful possession of the land that Yahweh your God is giving you."

Israel did become a great nation during the years of 1020 and 922 B.C. But from 922 to 587 B.C. Israel became a kingdom in the process of decay. During the reign of Saul, David, and part of the reign of Solomon the Israelites lived in obedience to God and his Law. It was King David's dream to build a temple for God, but in I Chronicles 22:7,8 (NJB) David tells Solomon that God did not give him permission:

My son, David said to Solomon, my heart was set on building a house for the name of Yahweh my God, But the word of Yahweh came to me, You have shed much blood and fought great battles; it is not for you to build a house for my name, since you have shed so much blood on the earth in my presence. But now a son is born to you...for Solomon is his name, and in his days I will give Israel peace and quiet.

Solomon's reign was a time of peace and he built a beautiful temple for all people to worship in. Solomon started out with a rich blessing from God. He carried on extensive business with other countries even so far as what today is the south of England. He had a fleet of vessels, and carried on transports by land with camel caravans. But somewhere along the way Solomon began to lose touch with God. Solomon built up his national defense even during peace time. In

Megiddo, archaeologists have unearthed 450 horse stalls in one site. I Kings 10 says Solomon had 1400 chariots and 15,000 horses. He made friends with far away kingdoms by marrying their princesses and making compromises for these women who did not believe the same as he did. Many of these marriages were political arrangements. I Kings 11:3-8 tells that in the end Solomon had seven hundred wives and three hundred concubines.

Even the riches God blessed Solomon with were not enough to cover the expenses of such an entourage. The people were heavily taxed. The common people were bitter from having labor forced on 30,000 of them during the building of the temple. Solomon established *Corvee*, which was like drafting the common farmers to come and work without wage one month out of three, and it took seven years to build the temple. [4] It seems this was a heavy burden the common Israelites never forgot. The Law, in Deuteronomy 17:17 had said "Nor must he increase the number of his wives, for that could lead his heart astray. Nor must he increase his gold and silver excessively."

God was angry with Solomon and in I Kings 11:11 tells Solomon, "Since you have behaved like this and do not keep my covenant or the laws I laid down for you, I will most surely tear the kingdom away from you..."

The kingdom of Israel split and the northern ten tribes took Jeroboam as their king and called themselves Israel. Their capitol was Samaria. The two southern tribes of David and Benjamen were called Judah and accepted Rehoboam to rule over them. Their capitol was Jerusalem.

The northern kingdom only lasted for 200 years and in 721 B.C., they were conquered by the Assyrians. The Kingdom of Judah survived another 134 years because of the righteousness of two kings, King Hezekiah and King Josiah. Unfortunately, King Hezekiah's son Manasseh was so evil and did so much damage to the kingdom that Josiah, with all his religious reforms, could not save the country. According to II Kings 23:25, it was too late:

...the Lord said, "I will remove Judah also from my presence as I removed Israel, and I will reject Jerusalem, the city I chose, and this temple, about which I said, 'There shall My Name be.'"

What was it that could have been so unforgivable that good King Josiah could not turn it around with his righteous leadership. II Kings

24:3,4 (NIV) says Manasseh had killed too many innocent people in Jerusalem and the Lord was not willing to forgive.

The prophet Jeremiah was about 18 years old when King Josiah had all of the temple prostitutes, priests of pagan practice, and sorcerers put to death. Even after Josiah's reforms it seems the remnants of pagan worship still lingered. Jeremiah continued to receive messages of prophesy from God. Jeremiah 22:1-5:

> *Go down to the palace of the king of Judah and there deliver this message, Listen to the word of Yahweh, king of Judah sitting on the throne of David, you, your servants too, and your people who go through these gates. Yahweh says this: Practice honesty and integrity; rescue the man who has been wronged from the hands of his oppressor; do not exploit the stranger, the orphan, the widow; do no violence; shed no innocent blood in this place. For if you are scrupulous in obeying this command, then kings occupying the throne of David will continue to make their entry through the gates of this palace mounted on chariots and horses, they, their servants and their people. But if your do not listen to these words, them I swear by myself--this palace shall become a ruin!*

Jeremiah continually told his people to surrender to the powerful kingdom of the day, Babylon, and they would live. But King Zedekiah would not listen. Instead he threw Jeremiah in prison, hung him down a well to die, and humiliated him. He also came and asked Jeremiah to pray for him, and when things weren't going right he would ask Jeremiah what message the Lord had for him. The problem was, the Judeans did not want to hear that they should be submissive to any other power and continued to rebel against the government. Rebels from the Judean military commanders murdered Judah's last governor and fled to Egypt, taking the broken-hearted Jeremiah with them. Jeremiah is believed to have died in Egypt, far from his beloved Judah. Babylon decided there was no alternative except to destroy them completely.

The Judeans taken to Babylon were stunned by its magnificence. The famous palace of the hanging gardens, the restored tower of Babel, and the Ishtar Gate with its colorful bas-relief tiles, were world renowned. Although some may have received harsh treatment, the Judeans were treated very well. It was in Babylon that the Judeans were first called Jews, a term which later included all Israelites. The Jews found a variety of professions open to them and many became wealthy businessmen. Jeremiah, while still in Judah, sent them a message to build homes, plant gardens, give children in marriage and make themselves at home, because they would be there 70 years. The boy Daniel, with others, was put through the royal school and became a great statesman in both Babylon, and later, what became Persia.

Ezekial was another prophet of Judah who had disagreed with Judah's foreign policy. He was taken to Babylon with the first group in 597 B.C., and accomplished great things in exile. In the beginning of the book of Ezekial, he was warning the Judeans before Jerusalem was captured in 587. They did not heed his advice to submit to the leadership of Babylon. The last parts of Ezekial were to help the Jews understand that they must live for God even though they were not in their own country. The Jews experienced a religious awakening in Babylon and retained their identity. Synagogues came into being, and the books of the Old Testament were compiled and written by Ezekial and his scribes. Ezekial helped to keep the faith alive; he wrote passages like Ezekial 16, about the intimate love of God. Ezekial promised that God would give them a new heart and a new spirit. Let us take a look at present day Israel to see if that promise has yet been fulfilled.

THE PRESENT DAY ISRAEL

In 1947, there was another son of Abraham. His name was Elias Chacour and he was an eight year old child in elementary school. Elias lived in a peaceful world of fig and olive groves with countless cousins, aunts and uncles in the village of Biram. Biram was one of a series of Christian villages in Galilee. Elias and his family were Melkite Christians. They claimed after James and the other apostles died, the early church nearly split over a sect called the Gnostics, who claimed Jesus was a mystical being and not a man at all. Melkite meant *king's men* because these Christians sided with the king against the Gnostics. The Melkite Christians take great pride in helping unite the early Christian church.

This particular day held excitement in the village of Biram, and Elias was trying to find out what it was. His mother was still in the fig groves working, and from the elders in the town square Elias found out his father had gone to the neighboring Jewish village to barter for a lamb. Elias did not find out until supper when his five brothers and one sister were all gathered around. His father made the announcement; they were going to kill the fatted lamb and have their Easter celebration two weeks early. His father said, "In Europe there was a man called Hitler. A satan. For a long time he was killing Jewish people. Men and women, grandparents—even boys and girls like you. He killed them just because they were Jews."

Elias's father said their own people, the Palestinian Christians, had lived in Galilee, tilled the land and worshiped here longer than anyone could remember. He said their lives were bound together with the other people who inhabited Palestine—the Jews. The Palestinians and Jews had suffered together under the Romans, Crusaders and Turks, and had learned to share the simple elements of human existence—faith, reverence for life, and hospitality. He said these were the things that caused people to live happily together.

Elias's father said some Jewish soldiers would be coming through Biram and they would be staying for awhile, maybe a week. They would be wearing guns but he assured them no one would be hurt. Then the soldiers would be moving on.

His father told them they should do their best to make the soldiers feel welcome and then he said this prayer:

Father in heaven, he began softly, help us to show love to our Jewish brothers. Help us to show them peace to quiet their troubled hearts.

The soldiers came and Elias and his brothers and sister were nervous because the soldiers were not very friendly. The soldiers ate with them, but it did not feel like a celebration. After a week the military commander told the men of Biram they had urgent business with them. The commander said the village of Biram was in grave danger but they would protect them. They said the people must stay out in the hillside for a couple of days; that they should lock up their doors, and give the keys to the soldiers.

The men of Biram thought there was going to be a confrontation between the British and the Zionists so it would be better to keep their families safely out in the olive groves. Elias's father locked their house, gave the key to the Jewish soldier and said, "I know that God will protect our house, and you will be safe too."

The soldier said, "Yes," and smiled.

They had been told to take nothing with them. For two weeks hundreds of the Palestinian villagers slept in the olive grove and had no word from the Jewish soldiers and finally a group of men decided to go ask the military commander why he hadn't signaled them to come back to their village.

A group of men walked up the hill to Biram and what they found were smashed and ransacked homes. The armed soldiers hollered at them to get out! The men of Biram stood their ground and demanded to know why they had wrecked their homes. The soldiers pointed their machine guns at them and said, "This land is ours now, get out!"

When the men returned to the olive grove and told the people that the European Jews had tricked them out of their homes, they were bewildered. These Palestinian villagers were no match for a battalion of soldiers with machine guns. They knew they could no longer stand sleeping out in the cold and rain with no blankets or shelter. They decided to climb the hill to the neighboring village of Gish, but there they found a worse situation than their own. Only a few old people were left; the rest had been run out by Israeli soldiers. Gish had been a smaller village, but the people of Biram crowded into the damaged and abandoned houses of Gish. Elias and a few other boys were playing soccer on the hill and found dozens of people buried in the sand.

There in their cramped quarters, Elias's family learned that Palestinians all over Palestine had been run out of their homes, many killed, some drowned in the Mediterranean Sea fleeing from Israeli soldiers. Throughout the winter months and into the spring of 1948 they heard of more terror, villages blown up by barrel-bombs. Many Palestinians had fled across the Lebanese and Jordanian borders. The worst incident had happened in the village, Deir Yassin. The Palestinian village had been *cleaned up* with machine guns, hand grenades, and knives. Two hundred and fifty men, women, and children had been massacred. Jacques de Reynier, a Frenchman who was head of the International Red Cross pushed his way through the soldiers' lines and entered the village of Deir Yassin. He saw bodies everywhere and was about to leave when he heard a sigh. He turned and saw a ten-year old girl, mutilated by a hand grenade, but still alive.

The chief Rabbi in Jerusalem was furious, and the local Jewish people were shocked and disgusted, but the military machine was not about to be under any religious authority.

Surrounding Arab countries tried to stop the takeover of Palestinian lands but the British had pulled out and the Zionists had confiscated all the store houses of military supplies. Palestinian families were separated and many elderly died. Their Jewish neighbors and friends ached for them, and no way condoned such violence, but there was nothing they could do. The nations of the world were silent.

Palestinians came to fear one name, the Zionist organization of *Irgun*. One of their leaders was Menachin Begin, who was on the top ten terrorist list most wanted by the British. May 14th of 1948, Ben Gurion proclaimed the state of Israel, and the United States immediately recognized the new nation of Israel under Zionist rule.

The people of Elias's village, living in the abandoned homes of Gish, were left alone for almost two years. Elias's father prayed:

Forgive them, oh God. Heal their pain. Remove their bitterness. Let us show them your peace.

Then one day army trucks drove up to Gish and with a loudspeaker announced all men, young and old must come out with their hands on their heads. The soldiers kept the men of Biram in the sun all day, calling them terrorists and demanding to know where they kept their weapons. Elias was shocked, his peaceful father, brothers, and uncles terrorists? Elias could not believe such a nightmare was happening to them. Elias could see his father was praying the whole time for the soldiers. The Israeli soldiers took all the men away in the back of a big truck. The women of the village screamed and wailed for days but soon became busy with the daily struggle of survival for their younger children's sake. His mother, sister, and one brother were left alone with no food, no income, and no men. After three months of grief and fear, Elias's father and older brothers returned in the middle of the night. The soldiers had dumped them all off at the Lebanese border and shot machine gun fire over their heads and they all scattered. Elias's father and brothers had walked home, starving and traveling only at night as not to be seen by any soldiers. Many of the men of Biram never made it back; they either died or ended up in refugee camps.

After that the Palestinian men were left alone and they found out why. The Jewish settlers moved into all their villages and took over their olive and fig groves, so they needed cheap labor. Elias's father and brothers became laborers in their own fig groves. Why did they do

It? Elias's father said, "I'm afraid someone else won't know what they are doing. They'll break the branches and spoil the new growth." But this was a very big disappointment to him. This is what he told his children:

Children, he said softly, turning those sad eyes upon us, if someone hurts you, you can curse him. But this would be useless. Instead, you have to ask the Lord to bless the man who makes himself your enemy. And do you know what will happen? The Lord will bless you with inner peace—and perhaps your enemy will turn from his wickedness. If not, the Lord will deal with him.

A local Bishop would travel around to the Palestinian villages and bring some food and clothing for the people. Through this Bishop, Elias went on to school, Seminary in Paris and Jerusalem, and became a pastor of a Melkite church in Ibillin. Ibillin is a village northeast of Nazareth. He speaks eleven languages, including Hebrew. Elias Chacour has a message:

I want to disarm my Jewish brother so he can read in my eyes the words, "I love you." I have beautiful dreams for Palestinian and Jewish children together. [5]

This is the story of Palestinians the world has not wanted to hear. We have been so focused on the Jews and their suffering that we have not noticed that innocent Palestinians have paid the price for the Nazi holocaust. The Palestinians are suffering in Israel and the occupied territories. Jewish-American writer Alfred Lilienthal has put it this way, "One man's dream has become another man's nightmare."

In 1917, the population of Palestine was around 700,000. There were around 570,000 Muslim Palestinians, 100,000 Palestinian Christians, and about 50,000 Jews. The Jews were about seven percent of the population. Former Prime Minister Menachin Begin boasted of his daring deeds and the Irgun victory of Deir Yassin; that of the original 800,000 Palestinians (1948) who lived in present day Israel, only 165,000 are still there. [6]

When Israel was declared a state in 1948, the Jewish Irgun and Stern gangs massacred 254 women, children, and old men in Deir Yassin and threw their bodies down a well. Then they dynamited their homes and bulldozed the city flat. This attack on Deir Yassin was condemned by the Jewish Agency for Palestine and the Haganah organization but later leaflets were posted and loudspeaker vans toured Arab areas broadcasting, "If you don't leave your homes the fate of Deir Yassin will be your fate." Hundreds of thousands of Palestinians fled in fear with just the shirts on their back, thinking this was a war situation and they would return. But they were never allowed to return. From 475 villages in Palestine, 385 were destroyed and bulldozed away. [7] Those Palestinians that have managed to stay in their homeland are treated like second-class citizens.

They are not only treated badly but there is one horror story after another about the punishments they receive if they protest that treatment. Israel subjects Palestinians to 1200 military laws. Palestinians must carry identification cards specifying their race and religion. It is written on their ID card that if they leave Israel they may not be remitted. Arab taxis must be painted in a certain manner. Arab's phone numbers are all given the initial digit of 8. Palestinians cars must have a blue license plate while Israelis have yellow. They are systematically stopped and harassed by Israeli police. Until the 1991 Gulf War, more than 100,000 Palestinians commuted from the occupied West Bank to Israel every day to work but received only half the wages an Israeli Jew received. They were not allowed to spend the night in Israel and failure to return home was punishable by arrest. They passed check points and the border quards have a reputation for being the most abusive of all Israeli police. During Operation Desert Storm Palestinians were placed under curfew and not allowed in Israel at all. Since that war many Palestinians were never given their jobs back because the Israeli government wants to replace all Palestinian workers with Russian immigrants.

Palestinians only receive half the irrigation allotment of Jews. Palestinians provide $80 million a year in social security payment that they receive no benefits for. Israelis are allowed to carry guns but Palestinians face imprisonment for possession of a weapon. Peaceful protests, strikes, failure to carry an identification card, distribution of leaflets, displaying any Palestinian national symbol, or having a business that competes with a Jew are all considered crimes punishable by law. There are 15,190 Palestinians held in Israeli prisons. Detainees may be held without charges or a trial date for years. All charges and confessions are printed in Hebrew which they cannot read. The Israeli policy of deportation without trial has often been brutally carried out. Men are arrested in the middle of the night, taken to the desert and dropped off. They have been threatened, "If you ever come back you will be a dead man."

Since the beginning of the Intifada (unarmed struggle), December 8, 1987, 1,119 Palestinians have died, 120,847 have been hospitalized for injuries, and 483 deported. [8] Israel also practices collective punishment on Palestinians. There have been 11,255 days that 10,000 or more people have lived under curfew. 2,094 Palestinian homes have been demolished or sealed. 88,226 acres of land have been confiscated. 130,331 trees have been bulldozed, including fruit trees. [9] Israeli settlers with poison tanks on their backs and machine guns in their hands come in the middle of the night and spray vineyards which have taken at least ten years to cultivate. On April 28, 1973, an Israeli Piper plane sprayed poison over 494 acres of wheat fields on the occupied West Bank near Akraba. [10] Medical facilities, Muslim courts, and educational facilities are closed down. These collective punishments are often exercised on relatives or villages of suspected collaborators of Palestinian nationalism. Villages have been punished for protesting Jewish settlements on Arab lands. The Palestinians consider these illegal settlements in Israeli occupied territories.

There are literally thousands of written testimonies by Palestinians, Americans, and Israeli citizens to all of these charges against the Israeli government. Modern day Israel is not without their Jeremiahs and Ezekials. Dr. Israel Shahak, retired professor at the Hebrew University in Jerusalem and Holocaust survivor, is chairman of the Israeli League for Human and Civil Rights. He traveled to the United States and testified of abuse of Palestinian rights in 1975 before the House Subcommittee on International Organizations and Movements of the Foreign Affairs Committee. These and other reports received were locked up and any efforts to see them were met with refusal by Edward Kennedy, Chairman of the Senate Judiciary Subcommittee on Refugees. All information on Palestinian abuse has been treated like national security secrets. The Media have been very careful to give the American people the Israeli side of the story. But the media around the world have given Palestinian suffering fair coverage. The first such coverage was on June 19, 1977, in the London Sunday Times. A four-page article was written about testimonies of Palestinians tortured in Israeli prisons. The research for the article was done by two British reporters. [11]

Arab peoples see Israel as a part of collective power by the Western countries to further dominate the Middle East and the valuable resource, oil. It is a new frontier to conquer.

The Old Testament verses we reviewed in this chapter reveal the standard God expected the Israelis to live by. Present day Israel is hardly near that standard. Israel's first President to be, Dr. Weizmann, said, "I am certain that the world will judge the Jewish state by what it shall do with the Arabs." [12] That prophetic statement is already starting to come true.

Felicia Langer is an Israeli lawyer who single-handedly defended Palestinians in court for 22 years. After the 1967 war, Felicia saw what was happening in the occupied territories and decided to move her law practice there and defend Palestinian people against unfair treatment from the Israeli military. She is vice president of the Israeli League for Human and Civil Rights. She has written three books about her experiences: *With My own Eyes, These Are My Brothers,* and *An Age of Stone.* She has recently retired from being an active defense lawyer in the occupied territories, and is working on an autobiography and going on speaking tours in Europe and America.

Felicia Langer's efforts have not been in vain, she is presently seeing a new generation of Israeli lawyers defending Arab prisoners. Felicia says, "Only because of my strong feelings for my country am I doing what I can to save its soul. Because we (Jews) know what it is to suffer, we must not oppress others." [13]

It is obvious the Zionist government of modern day Israel needs help in solving its boundary disputes with its neighbors. America should no longer sit quiet in the face of such human rights abuses. The Peace Conferences which started in 1991 in Madrid are a step in the right direction. No matter what obstacles are encountered, these peaceful meetings between the Israeli Jews and the Palestinians should continue with the support of all Americans. The majority of both Christian and Muslim Palestinians, and Jews do want to live side by side in peace.

December 4, 1991, in Washington D.C., the Palestinian delegation celebrated the fourth night of Chanukah with the Jewish Committee for Israeli-Peace in the lobby of the Grand Hotel. Palestinian spokesman Mayor Freij lit the fourth candle on the Channukah menorah. Palestinian delegation spokeswoman Dr. Hanan Mikhail-Ashrawi is capturing the hearts of Americans. Dr Ashrawi said, "I have intense faith in American fair play. Once Americans begin to know the Palestinians, they will care and they will do something to effect a concrete change in the region." The Clinton administration inviting Prime Minister Yitshak Rabin and Chairman Yasser Arafat to Washington, D.C. to sign the 1993 Peace Agreement was just such an action. [14]

Notes:

1. George M. Lamsa, *Old Testament Light, The Indispensable Guide to the Customs, Manners, & Idioms of Biblical Times* (San Francisco: Harper & Row, Publishers, 1964), p. 267.

2. Grace Halsell, reviewed, "The Thirteenth Tribe," *The Washington Report on Middle East Affairs*, May/June 1991, p. 71.

3. James A. Michener, *The Source* (Greenwich, Conn: Fawcett Publications, Inc., 1965) p. 227.

4. Nelson Beecher Keyes, *Story of the Bible World* (Pleasantville, NY: The Reader's Digest Association, 1962) p. 57.

5. Elias Chacour with David Hazard, *Bloodbrothers* (Grand Rapids, Mich: Chosen Books, 1984) pp. ix,21,38, and 62.

6. Alfred M. Lilienthal, *The Zionist Connection, What Price Peace* (New York: Dodd, Mead & Company, 1978) p. 29.

7. Ibid, pp. 159,160.

8. Robert B. Ashmore, "Palestinian Suffering and the Nuremberg Defense," *The Washington Report on Middle East Affairs*, April 1990, p. 8.

9. These statistics are from the Palestinian Human Rights Center. Jerusalem/Chicago (312) 271-4492. Figures through Jan 31, 1992.

10. Lilienthal, p. 169.

11. Lilienthal, p. 178.

12. Lilienthal, p. 187.

13. Laura Cooley, Israeli Human Rights Attorney Felicia Langer Receives 1990 Award," *The Washington Report on Middle East Affairs,* Dec. 1990, p. 25.

14. Jack Shaheen, The Face of the Palestinian, *St. Louis Post-Dispatch*, Nov 7, 1991.

PART IV

CHOOSING TO BE CLOSE TO MUSLIMS

JESUS AND 24 OTHER JUDEO-CHRISTIAN PROPHETS IN THE QURAN

Praise me not as Jesus is praised. I am liable to err as other men. I too need forgiveness. --The Prophet Muhammad

The world does not consist of 100 percent Christians and 100 percent non-Christians. There are people (a great many of them) who are slowly ceasing to be Christians but who still call themselves by that name: some of them are clergymen. There are other people who are slowly becoming Christians though they do not yet call themselves so. There are people who do not accept the full Christian doctrine about Christ but who are so strongly attracted by Him that they are His in a much deeper sense than they themselves understand. There are people in other religions who are being led by God's secret influence to concentrate on those parts of their religion which are in agreement with Christianity, and who thus belong to Christ without knowing it. And always, of course, there are a great many people who are just confused in mind and have a lot of inconsistent beliefs all jumbled up together...But when we are comparing Christians in general with non-Christians in general, we are usually not thinking about real people whom we know at all, but only about two vague ideas which we have got from novels and newspapers. --C. S. Lewis

Living in the Middle East was very exciting for me. One of my favorite errands was buying bread. Every one or two blocks they had what the Iranians called a *noon-var.* It was a large room, flush with the rest of the buildings, and was open in the front. At night they pulled down a large metal door and put a gigantic lock on it. It reminded me of a large side-ways sardine can.

But what went on inside was the most interesting. There was an oven that looked like a big cement ball. On the side it had a hole with a light shining out of it. Then the baker took a dough ball and flung it around in his arms until it was stretched flat, very much like the way the pizza parlors make their crust in America. Then the baker would slap it onto the inside of that cement ball. I always held my breath; I thought sure the man would burn his arm, and how did he know the dough was going to stick? The cement was very hot and that was why he never had to turn the flat bread. It cooked on one side from the hot cement and it cooked on the other side from the center flame in the oven. When it was done, which only took about five minutes, the baker would stick a long poker with a hook on the end, and retrieve the big flat piece of bread.

He would then throw it on the table in front of us so the smell could drive us mad. Javad was only three, and he would bring his little hand up and rip off a piece. Then we would count: one, two, three, four, five breads, and give him a very little amount of money. Thank you, Agha Reza! That was the name of our baker.

We would rush home the half a block with the hot bread in my arms. Javad would cry, "Give me another piece, Mommy." When we got close to the house we saw an orange BMW coming down the narrow side street we lived on. "Emeh (aunt) Shahla's car," Javad declared excitedly! My sister-in-law stopped by almost every day on her way home from the University of Isfahan, where she taught Biology. On Thursdays the work day ended at noon, so we would go out with her. We would go down by the Zayandeh-rud River and there were shops and street vendors selling things. Many merchants would put a blanket on the sidewalk and spread out their things, like they do in New York City.

One shop had lamb liver kabobs, and that was the children's favorite. They would always argue, "You got seven kabobs, and I only got six." The liver kabobs came on long wooden sticks. That particular day Emeh Shahla said, "Let's walk over to Chahr-Bagh Street, I want to visit that new gold jewelry store." Chahr-Bagh meant *four gardens.*

As we were passing the narrow streets we held arms like Iranian women always do. I had three very beautiful and affectionate sisters-in-law, and I enjoyed being with them very much. All at once I looked up and saw two men with strings of lights going all around the wall of one home and they had put up a big sign. I asked, "Shahla Khanum, what are those men doing to your neighbor's house?"

She said, "They are getting ready for a Roseh."

"What is a Roseh?"

"A Roseh is a prayer meeting. They put lights all over their house and put up a big sign that says Roseh, and everyone knows they are welcome to come. A Mullah comes and reads from the Quran, and gives a sermon. The men sit in the courtyard where the Mullah is preaching and the women sit inside the house. The hostess also serves cookies and tea for everyone. Would you like to go?"

"Yes, I would like that very much," I answered. I wasn't so much interested in the prayer meeting as much as just seeing what was going on.

That night we all dressed up in nice dresses and then we wore chadors. These chadors looked like dark flowered sheets. A woman would put the center of one edge of the material on the top of her head and the material draped down around her body. Isfahanian chadors were really very beautiful because they were voile materials with floral designs.

We arrived at the Roseh and the men went to the courtyard and sat on Persian Carpets. The Mullah sat on a platform and read from the Quran. We women all went inside the house where there was a lot more visiting going on. The hot cardamom tea tasted good.

It was a good opportunity to see neighbors, and eventually the women settled down and listened to the sermon. We were inside the house but with the glass sliding doors we could see the men in the courtyard down below us. One thing I will always remember was how the men were weeping openly. I assumed they were just touched by the words the religious man was speaking, about how God loves us, and how unworthy we really are. I remember thinking how good it was that the men in the Middle East had one place where it was acceptable to sit and cry openly like that. Sometimes I wish we had a place of worship like that in America. It was very friendly.

Those days I did not understand enough Arabic or Farsi to know what they were reading in the Quran, or what the Mullah discussed at the Rosehs. I know sometimes they talked about the early history of the Arab Muslims, but the Quran has stories of Jesus and 24 other Judeo-Christian prophets. First of all, let us examine the information about Jesus in the Quran, and compare it with what is in the Bible.

In order to understand the Quran, there are a few things we must keep in mind. The Arabic name for God is Allah. But for practical purposes, I will use the English word, God, in this study. In the Quran,

God is always referred to as We or Us, which is the honorific form of the pronoun. God the most high is always referred to with reference by Muslims. Always keep in mind when reading the Quran that the angel Gabriel is speaking to Muhammad. God is speaking to Muhammad through the angel Gabriel, with the purpose of Muhammad revealing it to his people. In order to understand the Quran we must look at its literary form, which is very different from the Bible. Christians believe the Bible was written by the prophets and by men inspired by the Holy Spirit. Muslims believe the words of God dropped right out of heaven and Muhammad just opened his mouth and said them. Therefore the Bible is written in story form by second and third person story-tellers; but the verses of the Quran are often written as a direct quote from God, or from one of his prophets.

JESUS THE WORD

Quran

Surah III:45,46,48: (And remember) when the angels said: O Mary! Lo! God giveth thee glad tidings of a word from Him, whose name is the Messiah, Jesus son of Mary, illustrious in this world and the Hereafter, and one of those brought near (unto God). He will speak unto mankind in his cradle and in his manhood, and he is of the righteous. And He will teach him the Scripture and wisdom, and the Torah and the Gospel.

Bible

John 1:1-3,9,14: In the beginning was the Word: the Word was with God and the Word was God. He was with God in the beginning. Through him all things came to be, not one thing had its being but through him... The Word was the true light that enlightens all men; and he was coming into the world... The Word was made flesh, he lived among us, and we saw his glory...full of grace and truth.

JESUS PERFORMS MIRACLES

Quran

Surah III:49: And will make him a messenger unto the children of Israel, (saying): Lo! I come unto you with a sign from your Lord. Lo! I fashion for you out of clay the likeness of a bird, and I breathe into it and it is a bird, by God's leave. I heal him who was born blind, and the leper, and I raise the dead, by God's leave.

Bible

Luke 4:16,17,18: He came to Nazareth where he had been brought up, and went into the synagogue on the sabbath day as he usually did. He stood up to read, and they handed him the scroll of the prophet Isaiah. Unrolling the scroll he found the place where it is written:

The spirit of the Lord has been given to me, for He has anointed me. He has sent me to bring the good news to the poor, to proclaim liberty to captives and to the blind new sight, to set the downtrodden free, to proclaim the Lord's year of favor.

Matthew 4:23, 24: He went around the whole of Galilee teaching in their synagogues, proclaiming the Good News of the kingdom and curing all kinds of diseases and sickness among the people. His fame spread throughout Syria, and those who were suffering from diseases and painful complaints of one kind or another, the possessed, epileptics, the paralyzed, were all brought to him, and he cured them.

JESUS FULFILLING THE LAW

Quran

Surah III:50: And (I come) confirming that which was before me of the Torah, and to make lawful some of that which was forbidden unto you. I come unto you with a sign from your Lord, so keep your duty to God and obey me.

Bible

Matthew 5:17, 18, 19, 20: Think not that I am come to destroy the law, or the prophets: I am not come to destroy, but to fulfill. For verily I say unto you, Till heaven and earth pass, one jot or one tittle shall in no wise pass from the law, till all be fulfilled. Whosoever therefore shall break one of these least commandments, and shall teach men so, he shall be called the least in the kingdom of heaven: but whosoever shall do and teach them, the same shall be called great in the kingdom of heaven. For I say unto you, That except your righteousness shall exceed the righteousness of the scribes and Pharisees, ye shall in no case enter into the kingdom of heaven.

THE ASCENSION OF JESUS CHRIST

Quran

Surah III:55, 56: (And remember) when God said: O Jesus! Lo! I am gathering thee and causing thee to ascend unto Me, and am cleansing thee of those who disbelieve and am setting those who follow thee above those who disbelieve until the Day of Resurrection. Then unto Me ye will (all) return, and I shall judge between you as to that wherein ye used to differ. As for those who disbelieve I shall chastise them with a heavy chastisement in the world and the Hereafter; and they will have no helpers.

Bible

Acts 7:8,9,10,11: And he said unto them.."But you will receive power when the Holy Spirit comes on you, and then you will be my witnesses not only in Jerusalem but throughout Judea and Samaria, and indeed to the ends of the earth." As he said this he was lifted up while they looked on, and a cloud took him from their sight. They were still staring into the sky when suddenly two men in white were standing near them and they said, "Why are you men from Galilee standing here looking into the sky? Jesus who has been taken up from you into heaven, this same Jesus will come back in the same way as you have seen him go there."

JESUS THE SECOND ADAM

Quran

Surah III:59,60: Lo! the likeness of Jesus with God is as the likeness of Adam. He created him of dust, then He said unto him: Be! and he is. (This is) the truth from thy Lord (O Muhammad), so be not thou of those who waver.

Bible

I Corinthians 15:21,22: Death came through one man and in the same way the resurrection of the dead has come through one man. Just as all men die in Adam., so all men will be brought to life in Christ.

JESUS FILLED WITH THE HOLY SPIRIT

Quran

Surah II:253: Of those messengers, some of whom We have cause to excel others, and of whom there are some unto whom God spake, while some of them He exalted (above others) in degree; and We gave Jesus, son of Mary, clear proofs (of God's sovereignty) and We supported him with the Holy Spirit.

Bible

Matthew 3:16: As soon as Jesus was baptized he came up from the water, and suddenly the heavens opened and he saw the Spirit of God descending like a dove and coming down on him. And a voice spoke from heaven, "This is my..Beloved; my favor rests on him."

Philippians 2:9-11: wherefore God also hath highly exalted him, and given him a name which is above every name: That at the name of Jesus every knee should bow...And that every tongue should confess that Jesus Christ is Lord, to the glory of God.

JESUS THE MESSIAH, THE WORD, AND THE SPIRIT

Quran

Surah IV:171,172: O People of the Scripture! Do not exaggerate in your religion nor utter aught concerning God save the truth. The Messiah, Jesus son of Mary, was only a messenger of God, and His word which He conveyed unto Mary, and a Spirit from Him. The Messiah will never scorn to be a slave unto God, nor will the favored angels.

Bible

John 4:25,26: The woman of Samaria said to him, "I know that Messiah—that is, Christ--is coming; and when he comes he will tell us everything." "I who am speaking to you," said Jesus, "I am he."

Revelation 19:11-16: And now I saw heaven open, and a white horse appears; its rider was called Faithful and True; he is a judge with integrity, a warrior for justice. His eyes are flames of fire, and his head was crowned with many coronets [NJB]; the name written on him was known only to himself, His cloak was soaked in blood. He is known by the name, The Word of God. Behind him, dressed in linen of dazzling white, rode the armies of heaven on white horses. From his mouth came a sharp sword to strike the pagans with; he is the one who will rule them with an iron scepter, and tread out the wine of Almighty God's fierce anger. On his cloak and on his thigh there was a name written: The King of kings and the Lord of lords.

JESUS THE LIGHT

Quran

Surah V:46,47: And We caused Jesus, son of Mary, to follow in their footsteps, confirming that which was (revealed) before him, and

We bestowed on him the Gospel wherein is guidance and light, confirming that which was (revealed) before it in the Torah--a guidance and an admonition unto those who ward off (evil). Let the People of the Gospel judge by that which God hath revealed therein. Whoso judgeth not by that which God hath revealed; such are the evil livers.

Bible

John 8:12: When Jesus spoke to the people again, he said: "I am the light of the world; anyone who follows me will not be walking in the dark; he will have the light of life."

**JESUS, THE BREAD OF LIFE,
THE LIVING WATER, AT HIS TABLE**

Quran

Surah V:109-115: In the day when God gathereth together the messengers, and saith: What was your response (from mankind)? they say: We have no knowledge Lo! Thou, only Thou art the Knower of Things Hidden. When God saith: O Jesus, son of Mary! Remember My favor unto thee and unto they mother; how I strengthened thee with the Holy Spirit, so that thou speakest unto mankind in the cradle as in maturity; and how I taught thee the Scripture and Wisdom and the Torah and the Gospel; and how thou didst shape of clay as it were the likeness of a bird by My permission, and didst blow upon it and it was a bird by My permission, and thou didst heal him who was born blind and the leper by My permission and how thou didst raise the dead, by My permission, and how I restrained the Children of Israel from (harming) thee when thou camest unto them with clear proofs, and those of them who disbelieved exclaimed: This is naught else than mere magic; And when I inspired the disciples, (saying): Believe in Me and in My messenger, they said: We believe. Bear witness that we have surrendered (unto thee). When the disciples said: O Jesus, son of Mary! Is thy Lord able to send down for us a table spread with food from heaven? He said: Observe your duty to God, if ye are true believers. (They said): We wish to eat thereof, that we may satisfy our hearts and know that thou hast spoken truth to us, and that thereof we may be witnesses. Jesus, son of Mary, said: O God, Lord of us! Send down for us a table spread with food from heaven, that it may be a feast for us, for the first of us and for the last of us, and a sign from Thee. Give us sustenance, for Thou art the Best of Sustainers. God said: Lo! I send it down for you. And whosoever disbelieveth of you afterward, him surely will I punish with a punishment wherewith I have not punished any of (My) creatures.

Bible

John 4:13 Jesus replied: "Whoever drinks this water will get thirsty again; but anyone who drinks the water that I shall give will never be thirsty again: the water that I shall give will turn into a spring inside him, welling up to eternal life."

John 6:33-35: "...for the bread of God is that which comes down from heaven and gives life to the world." "Sir," they said, "give us that bread always." "I am the bread of life. He who comes to me will never be hungry; he who believes in me will never thirst."

John 4:34: Jesus said: My food is to do the will of the one who sent me, and to complete his work.

Revelations 19:5-9: Then a voice came from the throne; it said, "Praise our God, you servants of his and all who, great or small, revere him." And I seemed to hear the voices answering, "Alleluia! The reign of the Lord our God Almighty has begun; Let us be glad and joyful and give praise to God, because this is the time for the marriage of the Lamb. His bride is ready, and she has been able to dress herself in dazzling white linen, because her linen is made of the good deeds of the saints." The angel said, "Write this: Happy are those who are invited to the wedding feast of the Lamb."

MARY, MOTHER OF JESUS

Quran

Surah III:42-46: And when the angels said: O Mary! Lo! God hath chosen thee and made thee pure, and hath preferred thee above (all) the women of creation. O Mary! Be obedient to thy Lord, prostrate thyself and bow with those who bow (in worship). This is of the tidings of things hidden. We reveal it unto thee (Muhammad). Thou wast not present with them when they threw their pens (to know) which of them should be the guardian of Mary, nor wast thou present with them when they quarrelled (thereupon). (And remember) when the angels said: O Mary! Lo! God giveth thee glad tidings of a word from Him, whose name is the Messiah, Jesus, son of Mary, illustrious in the world and the Hereafter, and one of those brought near (unto God). He will speak unto mankind in his cradle and in his manhood, and he is of the righteous.

Surah XIX:16-35: And make mention of Mary in the Scripture, when she had withdrawn from her people to a chamber looking East, And had chosen seclusion from them. Then We sent unto her Our Spirit and it assumed for her the likeness of a perfect man. She said: Lo! I seek refuge in the Beneficent One from thee, if thou art God-fearing. He said: I am only a messenger of thy Lord, that I may bestow on thee a faultless son. She said: How can I have a son when no mortal hath touched me, neither have I been unchaste? He said: So (It will be). Thy Lord saith: It is easy for Me. And (it will be) that We may make of him a revelation for mankind and a mercy from Us, and it is a thing ordained. And she conceived him, and she withdrew with him to a far place. And the pangs of childbirth drove her unto the trunk of the palm tree. She said: Oh, would that I had died ere this and had become a thing of naught, forgotten! Then (one) cried unto her from below her, saying: Grieve not! Thy Lord hath placed a small stream beneath thee, And shake the trunk of the palm tree toward thee; thou wilt cause ripe dates to fall upon thee. So eat and drink and be consoled. And if thou meetest any mortal, say: Lo! I have vowed a fast unto the Beneficent, and may not speak this day to any mortal. Then she brought him to her own folk, carrying him. They said: O Mary! Thou hast come with an amazing thing. O sister of Aaron! Thy father was not a wicked man nor was thy mother a harlot. Then she pointed to him. They said: How can we talk to one who is in the cradle, a young boy? He spake: Lo! I am the slave of God. He hath given me the Scripture and hath appointed me a Prophet, And hath made me blessed wheresoever I may be, and hath enjoined upon me prayer and almsgiving so long as I remain alive, And (hath made me) dutiful toward her who bore me, and hath not made me arrogant, unblest. Peace on me the day I was born, and the day I die, and the day I shall be raised alive! Such was Jesus, son of Mary, (this is) a statement of the truth concerning which they doubt. It befitteth not (the Majesty of) God that He should take unto Himself a son. Glory be to Him! When He decreeth a thing, He saith unto it only: Be! and it is.

*Islam rejects putting human relationships on God. Only believers may be called brothers and sisters. The Quran's explanation for the

*virgin birth was that it was a miracle of God: He just gave the word ,
and Jesus came into being.*

Bible

Matthew 1:18-25: This is how Jesus Christ came to be born. His
mother Mary was betrothed to Joseph; but before they came to live
together she was found to be with child through the Holy Spirit. Her
husband Joseph, being a man of honor and wanting to spare her
publicity, decided to divorce her informally. He had made up his mind
to do this when the angel of the Lord appeared to him in a dream and
said, "Joseph son of David, do not be afraid to take Mary home as your
wife, because she has conceived what is in her by the holy Spirit. She
will give birth to a son and you must name him Jesus, because he is the
one who is to save his people from their sins." Now all this took place
to fulfill the words spoken by the Lord through the prophet: The virgin
will conceive and give birth to a son and they will call him Immanuel,
a name which means *God-is-with-us*. When Joseph woke up he did
what the angel of the Lord had told him to do: he took his wife to his
home, and though he had not had intercourse with her, she gave birth
to a son; and he named him Jesus.

The account of Mary and Jesus can also be found in Matthew 2,
and Luke 2.

JOHN THE BAPTIST

*The Arabic name for John is Yahya.

Quran

Surah III:38-41: Then Zachariah prayed unto his Lord and said:
My Lord! Bestow upon me of Thy bounty goodly offspring. Lo! Thou
art the Hearer of Prayer. And the angels called to him as he stood
praying in the sanctuary: God giveth thee glad tidings of (a son whose
name is) John, (who Cometh) to confirm a word from God, lordly,
chaste, a Prophet of the righteous. He said: My Lord! How can I have
a son when age hath overtaken me already and my wife is barren?
(The angel) answered: So (it will be). God doth what He will. He said:
My Lord! Appoint a token for me. (The angel) said: The token unto
thee (shall be) that thou shalt not speak unto mankind three days
except by signs. Remember thy Lord much, and praise (Him) in the
early hours of night and morning. Surah XIX:6-15:...Who shall inherit

of me and inherit (also) of the house of Jacob. And make him, my Lord, acceptable (unto thee). (It was said unto him): O Zachariah! Lo! We bring thee tidings of a son whose name is John; We have given the same name to none before (him). He said: My Lord! How can I have a son when my wife is barren and I have reached infirm old age? He said: So (it will be). Thy Lord saith: It is easy for Me, even as I created thee before, when thou wast naught. He said: My Lord! Appoint for me some token. He said: Thy token is that thou, with no bodily defect, shalt not speak unto mankind three nights. Then he came forth unto his people from the sanctuary, and signified to them: Glorify your Lord at break of day and fall of night. (And it was said unto his son): O John! Hold fast the Scripture. And We gave him wisdom when a child, And compassion from Our presence, and purity; and he was devout, And dutiful toward his parents. And he was not arrogant, rebellious. Peace on him the day he was born, and the day he dieth and the day he shall be raised alive!

Bible

Luke 3:2-6,15,16,18:...during the pontificate of Annas and Caiaphas, the word of God came to John son of Zechariah, in the wilderness. He went through the whole Jordan district proclaiming a baptism of repentance for the forgiveness of sins, as it is written in the book of the sayings of the prophet Isaiah: A voice cries in the wilderness: Prepare a way for the Lord, make his paths straight. Every valley will be filled in, every mountain and hill be laid low, winding ways will be straightened and rough roads made smooth. And all mankind shall see the salvation of God. ... A feeling of expectancy had grown among the people, who were beginning to think that John might be the Christ, so John declared before them all, "I baptize you with water, but someone is coming, someone who is more powerful than I am, and I am not fit to undo the strap of his sandals; he will baptize you with the Holy Spirit and fire.... "As will as this, there were many other things he said to exhort the people and to announce the Good News to them.

*The rest of the passages of John the Baptist can be found in Matthew 3, 11:2-19, 14:1-12; Luke 1:5-24, 3:2-20; and John 1:6-9, 15, 19-34.

OTHER JUDEO-CHRISTIAN PROPHETS

Surah IV:163-166: Lo! We inspire thee as We inspired Noah and the prophets after him, as We inspired Abraham and Ishmael and Isaac and Jacob and the tribes, and Jesus and Job and Jonah and Aaron and Solomon, and as we imparted unto David the Psalms; And messengers We have mentioned unto thee before and messengers We have not mentioned unto thee; and God spake directly unto Moses; Messengers of good cheer and of warning, in order that mankind might have no argument against God after the messengers. God was ever Mighty, Wise. 166 But God (Himself) testifieth concerning that which He hath revealed unto thee; in His knowledge hath He revealed it; and the Angels also testify. And God is sufficient Witness.

THE FALL OF LUCIFER AND
THE FALL OF ADAM AND EVE

Quran

Surah VII:10-13,16-25,27: And We have given you (mankind) power in the earth, and appointed for you therein a livelihood. Little give ye thanks! And We created you, then fashioned you, then told the angels: Fall ye prostrate before Adam! And they fell prostrate, all save Iblis, who was not of those who make prostration. He said: What hindered thee that thou didst not fall prostrate when I bade thee? (Iblis) said: I am better than him Thou created me of fire while him Thou didst create of mud. He said: Then go down hence! It is not for thee to show pride here, so go forth! Lo! thou art of those reprieved. He said: Now, because Thou hast sent me astray, verily I shall lurk in ambush for them on Thy Right Path. Then I shall come upon them from before them and from behind them and from their right hands and from their left hand, and Thou wilt not find most of them beholden (unto Thee). He said: Go forth from hence, degraded, banished. As for such of them as follow thee, surely I will fill hell with all of you. And (unto man): O Adam! Dwell thou and they wife in the Garden and eat from whence ye will, but come not nigh this tree lest ye become wrong-doers. Then Satan whispered to them that he might manifest unto them that which was hidden from them of their shame, and he said: Your Lord forbade you from this tree only lest ye would become angels or become of the immortals. And he swore unto them (saying): Lo! I am a sincere adviser unto you. Thus did he lead them on with guile. And when they tasted of the tree their shame was manifest to them and they began to hide (by heaping) on themselves some of the leaves of the Garden. And their Lord called them (saying): Did I not forbid you from that tree and tell you: Lo! Satan is an open enemy to you? They said: Our Lord! We have wronged ourselves. If Thou forgive us not and have not mercy on us, surely we are of the lost! He said: Go down (from hence), one of you a foe unto the other. There will be for you on earth a habitation and provision for a while. He said: There shall ye live, and there shall ye die, and thence shall ye be brought forth...O Children of Adam! Let not Satan seduce you as he caused your (first) parents to go forth from the Garden and tore off from them their robe (of innocence) that he might manifest their shame to them. Lo! he seeth you, he and his tribe, from whence ye see him not. Lo! We have made the devils protecting friends for those who believe not.

Bible

The story of Adam and Eve is found in Genesis 1:27-3:24.

NOAH

Quran

Surah LXXI is named Noah. Surah XXIII:23-29: And We verily sent Noah unto his folk, and he said: O my people! Serve God. Ye have no other god save Him. Will ye not ward off (evil)? But the chieftains of his folk, who disbelieved, said: This is only a mortal like you who would make himself superior to you. Had God willed, He surely could have sent down angels. We heard not of this in the case of our fathers of old. He is only a man in whom is a madness, so watch him for a while. He said: My Lord! Help me because they deny me. Then We inspired in him, saying: Make the ship under Our eyes and Our inspiration. Then, when Our command cometh and the oven gusheth water, introduce therein of every (kind) two spouses, and thy household save him there of against whom the Word hath already gone forth. And plead not with me on behalf of those who have done wrong. Lo! they will be drowned. And when thou art on board the ship, thou and whoso is with thee, then say: Praise be to God Who hath saved us from the wrongdoing folk! And say: My Lord! Cause me to land at a blessed landing-place, for Thou art best of all who bring to land.

Bible

The story of Noah is in Genesis 6:1-10:32.

ABRAHAM

Quran

Abraham has the most extensive coverage of all the prophets. The story of Abraham is found in 15 different surahs. The longest is XXI:51-71. Surah III:67,68: Abraham was not a Jew, nor yet a Christian; but he was an upright man who had surrendered (to God), and he was not of the idolaters Lo! those of mankind who have the best claim to Abraham are those *who followed* him, and this Prophet and those who believe (with him); and God is the Protecting Friend of the believers.

Bible

The story of Abraham is found in Genesis. Abraham is referred to throughout the Bible. John 8:38,39: Jesus said, I speak what I have seen with my Father; and you do what you have seen with your father. They answered, saying to him, Our own father is Abraham. Jesus said to them, If you were the sons of Abraham, you would be doing the works of Abraham.

MOSES

Quran

Moses has an extensive coverage. The story of Moses and his people is found in 12 different surahs of the Quran. The longest is Surah X:75-92. Surah VII:159,160: And of Moses' folk there is a community who lead with truth and establish justice therewith. We divided them into twelve tribes, nations; and We inspired Moses, when his people asked him for water, saying: Smite with thy staff the rock! And there gushed forth therefrom twelve springs, so that each tribe knew their drinking-place. And we caused the white cloud to overshadow them and sent down for them the manna and the quails (saying): Eat of the good things wherewith We have provided you....

Bible

The story of Moses and his people is found in Exodus 1:1- 40:38; Leviticus 1:1-27:34; Numbers 1:1-36:13; Deuteronomy 1:1-34:12.

ISHMAEL AND ISAAC

Quran

Surah XIX:54,55: And make mention in the Scripture of Ishmael. Lo! he was a keeper of his promise, and he was a messenger (of God), a Prophet. He enjoined upon his people worship and almsgiving, and was acceptable in the sight of his Lord. Surah XXXVII:109-113: Peace be unto Abraham! Thus do We reward the good. Lo! he is one of Our believing slaves. And We gave him tidings of the birth of Isaac, a Prophet of the righteous. And We blessed him and Isaac. And of their seed are some who do good, and some who plainly wrong themselves. Surah XIV is named Abraham and he prays for Ishmael and Isaac. 35,39: And when Abraham said: My Lord! Make safe this territory, and preserve me and my sons from serving idols... Praise be to God Who hath given me, in my old age, Ishmael and Isaac! Lo' my Lord is indeed the Hearer of prayer.

Bible

The story of Ishmael and Isaac is in Genesis 16:7-35:29. Genesis 18:18,19: And the Lord said, Seeing that Abraham shall surely become a great and mighty nation, and all the nations of the earth shall be blessed in him? For I know him, that he will command his children and his household after him, and they shall keep the way of the Lord, to do justice and judgment; that the Lord may bring upon Abraham that which he hath spoken of him.

LOT IN SODOM AND GOMORRAH

Quran

Lot is discussed in 11 surahs. Surah XI:77-81: And when Our messengers came unto Lot, he was distressed and knew not how to protect them. He said: This is a distressful day! And his people came unto him, running towards him--and before then they, used to commit abominations--He said: O my people! Here are my daughters! They are purer for you. Beware of God, and degrade me not in (the presence of) my guests. Is there not among you any upright man? They said: Well thou knowest that we have no right to thy daughters, and well thou knowest what we want. He said: Would that I had strength to resist you or had some strong support (among you)! (The messengers) said: O Lot! Lo! we are messengers of thy Lord: they shall not reach thee. So travel with thy people in a part of the night, and let not one of you turn around—(all) save thy wife. Lo! that which smiteth them will smite her (also). Lo! their tryst is (for) the morning. Is not the morning nigh? So when Our commandment came to pass We overthrew (that township) and rained upon it stones of clay, one after another.

Bible

The story of Lot is found in Genesis 18:20-19:38.

JACOB AND JOSEPH

Quran

Surah XII is called Joseph. It has the complete story of Joseph and his father Jacob.

Bible

The story of Jacob and Joseph is in Genesis 25:21-50:26.

Surah X is named Jonah; Surah XVII is named The Children of Israel; Surah XIX is named Mary, Surah XXI is named The Prophets, and Surah XXX is named The Romans. The Quran also has digested stories of Jonah, Job, David and Goliath, Solomon, Cain and Abel, Aaron,, Ezekial, Elijah, and Elisha. The Muslims are not familiar with the Epistles of Paul. The Pauline churches were all north and west of Jerusalem, getting into Europe. There were other apostles that carried Jesus' message Southwest, Southeast, and Northeast of Jerusalem.

Notes:

All Quran passages were taken from the Muhammad Marmaduke Pickthall, trans., The Glorious Quran, (New York: Muslim World League, 1977).

Unless specified, the Bible passages are taken from the NIV translation.

COMMON GROUND OF ISLAM AND CHRISTIANITY

Jesus' Kingdom was built differently from anyone else'ss—not by weapons, but on love. --Napolean

> I went to the Garden of Love,
> And saw what I never had seen:
> A Chapel was built in the midst,
> Where I used to play on the green.
> And the gates of this Chapel were shut,
> And "Thou shalt not" writ over the door;
> So I turn'd to the Garden of Love
> That so many sweet flowers bore;
> And I saw it was filled with graves,
> And tomb-stones where flowers should be;
> And Priests in black gowns were walking their rounds,
> And binding with briars my joys & desires.
>   --William Blake (1757-1827)

Once upon a time in the land of the United States there was a man named Robb. Robb's heart was full of love for God and Jesus was the Lord of his life. One day Robb heard a voice that said, "My good and faithful servant, your cup runneth over. I send you to a far-away land as a tentmaker. Go teach Muslim people about Jesus."

Robb answered, "Here I am Lord, send me."

Robb, his wife Sharon, and their two children Melissa and John, moved to the Middle East. Robb found a job teaching English, and they found a local church.

It did not take Robb long to make friends. He brought his first two Muslim friends, Muhammad and Ali, to church with him. But the next week they did not want to come. Muhammad said, "We do not want to come to that church because they did not treat us respectfully. We don't think they like us coming there."

Robb said, "What do you mean? I want you there."

Muhammad said, "You do not understand because you are from a faraway land; but they will never accept us in that church."

Robb did not know what to do. He went home; knelt down and prayed, "O Lord, you have sent me to the Middle East. I seek you with a pure heart. Give me wisdom and understanding as to what I should do."

Robb searched the scriptures day and night and the word became a lamp unto his feet and a light unto his way. He pondered on all that he had read. He thought, "Islam meant *submission to God,* and a Muslim was *one who submits to God.*" On this premises, he himself was a Muslim; even John the Baptist was a Muslim.

Robb decided what he must do and circumstances worked in his favor. They had to move from their apartment and they found a home on the other side of town. They said good-bye to the people at their church. Robb did not look for another church but decided to have classes in his own home. Robb discussed this decision at length with his mission board. This was something new. After all, what was it Jesus told his disciples in Matthew 13:52?

And he said to them, "Well then, every scribe who becomes a disciple of the Kingdom of Heaven is like a householder who brings out from his storeroom things both new and old."

Robb invited Muhammad and Ali and many other of his English students to his home to study religion. "What religion are you?" they asked him.

"I am one who submits to God." answered Robb.

"Well then," said Muhammad, "You are a Muslim."

"Yes," said Robb, "I guess that makes me a Muslim."

After a year or so, Robb had ten young Muslim men studying in his home. Robb loved his students; they were a warm, loving group of men. Robb was very happy. He found these men fascinating to study with. More and more, he was beginning to see that the Bible really was written for the Middle Eastern mind, and how much he had missed out on in the West. He was learning so much culture from studying with his Muslim friends.

Then one day Ali came to Robb and said, "Teacher, do you believe God could give knowledge to people through their dreams?"

"Yes I do, God spoke to people in the Bible through dreams. In the book of Numbers, God told Miriam and Aaron that he would speak to a prophet in dreams. In Genesis, God spoke to Joseph through dreams; Joseph also translated dreams. In I Kings, the Lord appeared to Solomon in a dream. King Nebuchadnezzar of Babylon and Daniel the prophet had dreams from God. In Matthew, the Lord appeared unto Joseph, Mary's betrothed, in a dream. In fact, in Joel 2 and Acts 2 God promises He will pour out his spirit and old men will dream dreams and young men will see visions."

"I have had a very unusual dream," said Ali.

"What was it?" asked Robb.

"I dreamed there were two tunnels, one of them was Islam and the other was Christianity. I went down the Christian tunnel and no one was there. Then I went down the Islam tunnel and I saw the Prophet Muhammad and I kissed him, and I look around him and there was Jesus. I asked him what he was doing in the Islamic tunnel. He said, 'Well, I came to earth and finished my mission, I brought God's word to the people, some disciples followed me and some other people followed me, and a lot of people didn't.'"

"I asked again," said Ali, "But what are you doing at this tunnel?"

Jesus said, "You will find the answer to your question in your own book, chapter Al-Hadid, verse 27."

Ali awoke and looked up the verse, and he thought, "I have never seen that verse before." It said:

...and We caused Jesus, son of Mary, to follow, and gave him the Gospel, and placed compassion and mercy in the hearts of those that followed him.

Robb told him, "Ali, the Gospel means good news, and the good news is forgiveness of sin through a repentant heart."

Robb and Ali studied forgiveness and the grace of God for the next month and one day Ali came and said, "Teacher, I have had another dream." Robb asked him to tell him about it. Ali again dreamed there were two tunnels, and he was just about to go into one when he was surrounded by a great bright light, so bright that he couldn't hear a thing but he could hear voices. Then he saw a black sea all around.

He asked what the black sea was and a voice said, "This is your misunderstanding about who Jesus Christ is."

Ali thought to himself, "Yes, I do have a misunderstanding about who Jesus is."

Then two shrouded figures came into the light so he could see them, but not their faces.

A voice said, "Choose!"

Ali said, "I can't see your faces."

"Choose!"

"I can't see your faces, which of you is right?" And then the shrouded figures pointed to each other. "Teacher, what does it mean?"

"Maybe it means God wants us to study the character of Muhammad from Jesus' point of view and study Jesus from Muhammad's point of view." Robb said. They studied and then prayed for another dream.

Ali came back one day and announced he had a third dream. In this dream he entered one of the tunnels, and the tunnels came together at the end. There was Muhammad and Jesus both standing at the end of the tunnel. Ali asked Muhammad, "What are you doing here?"

Muhammad said, "I am surrender."

Ali then turned to Jesus and asked, "What are you doing here?"

Jesus answered, "I am sacrifice."

Ali said, "Now I see, what Muhammad has been telling us all along is right. We must surrender, but we must surrender to God's sacrifice."

Robb saw the lights go on for Ali. He knew this was unpredictable, Spirit-God working in a man's heart who was seeking. Robb told Ali, "Now you are a son of the Kingdom."

Robb knew there were certain terms he should not use with his Muslim friends, one was Christian. The title Christian has been discredited by the behavior of Christians in the past.

We Christians must live with that reality, just as we acknowledge the sin status we inherited from Adam and Eve. Muslims acquaint Christianity with the Crusades and the domination of the West. Were the Crusades any less of a sin than eating a forbidden fruit? Muslims were on the receiving end of death and destruction, and are not likely to forget it; if they were trying to forget it they have the Gulf war to refresh their memory. Unless we acknowledge death and destruction of innocent people as sin, and show a repentant heart, Muslims will not even believe we are candidates for God's kingdom. Robb was not in the Middle East to promote an earthly kingdom, but the heavenly kingdom.

Muslims also do not relate to putting human qualities on God, so Robb never called Jesus the son of God. The Quran calls Jesus the *Word*, the *Messiah*, the *slave of God*, and the *prophet filled with the Spirit of God*.

Some local Christians may feel not calling Jesus the son of God cuts the heart out of the gospel. Look at it this way. If you insist upon using certain terminology you may as well not even initiate what will be a short and painful encounter for both sides. This is the main bottleneck of Christian-Muslim relationships.

Paul didn't use the same terminology with the Greeks and the Jews. That is why he says in I Corinthians 9:20 "To a Jew, I am a Jew." He did not really mean he was a Jew; he meant that he understood how Jews think, what meaning they put behind words, and what their needs were. That was one of the reasons Timothy was such a valuable asset to Paul; his mother was Jewish and his father was a Gentile. He understood two cultures.

If you knew that when you said Jesus is the son of God, a person would imagine God having sex with Mary, would you still say it? No, because that is blasphemy. There! That is what the Muslim may think. Would you want a Muslim to think you actually believed that? Of course you wouldn't. There is a cultural miscommunication here that cannot always be explained. I have come across something similar in the way Americans pronounce Iranian names. We could not predict how they were going to pronounce the names. By the time we had our third child we wrote four different spellings on a piece of paper in the recovery room in the hospital, and asked the nurse to read them all. The spelling she pronounced correctly we used for the birth certificate. That child has no problem with his name being mispronounced.

There are gross cross-cultural misunderstandings. One missionary went to a native tribe and months passed by and the village people were cold and unresponsive to the missionaries. They finally asked an old man in the village, "Why don't people become friendly with us."

The old man said, "You have strange ways. When you came here you brought some tin cans with you. One can had a picture of corn on it, and then you opened it up and it had corn inside and you ate it. Another can had a picture of meat on it and you opened it up, it had meat inside, and you ate it. Then when you had your baby you brought small tin cans with pictures of babies on them you opened them up and you fed the insides to your baby." It was very logical for them to think these missionaries were cannibals. How were they to know the baby food contents were not the same as the picture like the other tins. [1] The only way misunderstandings like this can be straightened out is through communication.

Someone must take that step out in compromise to bridge the gap of misunderstanding. Christians are often taught they should not compromise the gospel. What gospel? If your friend has not even seen the gospel in what you have said or done, all you are compromising is your methodology. You don't have to worry about compromising your moral principles because most Muslims have very high morals. They honor their parents, uphold family unity, and don't drink or smoke. Most Muslims are classic teetotalers (they love to drink tea).

Paul addresses these kind of dilemmas in I Corinthians 8, 9, and 10. In chapter 10:24 Paul says, "no man should be looking for his own advantage, but everybody for the other man's." If our behavior is offensive we must do an evaluation like Robb did. The Bible does not give methodology. All the terms Robb uses are in the Bible.

If Muslims relate to Jesus' human side, that is no problem. The Nicene Creed says Jesus is very man. The Bible is full of verses pertaining to his human side. John 5:19 says "..I tell you most solemnly, the Son can do nothing by himself; he can do only what he sees the Father doing: and whatever the Father does the Son does too." In John 5:24 Jesus says "I tell you most solemnly, whoever listens to my words, and believes in the **One** who sent me, has eternal life; without being brought to judgment he has passed from death to life." In John 5:30, Jesus says, "I can do nothing by myself; I can only judge as I am told to judge, and my judging is just, because my aim is to do not my own will, but the will of him who sent me." In John 6:44 Jesus says, "No man can come to me, except the Father which hath sent me draw him: and I will raise him up the last day." In John 7:16 Jesus answers the Jews, "My teaching is not from myself: it comes from the one who sent me." In Matthew 12:32 and Luke 12:10 Jesus says, "And anyone who says a word against the Son of Man will be forgiven; but let anyone speak against the Holy Spirit and he will not be forgiven either in this world or in the next."

This is not the whole picture of who Christ is, but it is a biblical truth. Christians don't always cover the whole picture of salvation when they are speaking on eternal security; they don't bring in all of the aspects of judgement when they are concentrating on God's love. In the same way, we can look at a Muslims perspective as common ground between us. As Christians, we cannot deny while Jesus was dying on the cross, God was still on his throne in heaven, sustaining his creation. God's Word was with him in the beginning; and when His Word was made flesh and dwelt among us there was a separation. In John 4:24 Jesus said, "God is a Spirit: and they that worship him must worship him in spirit and truth."

When Muslims talk about Jesus, they are relating to the man that walked the earth for 33 years. Most Americans relate to Jesus as the living word on the right hand of God. These are the dual aspects of Christ. Maybe we can learn from each other.

Many Americans are not even relating well to the metaphor of God as the father. That is because this metaphor was very applicable in the ancient Jewish culture, but our fathers have been taken out of the home by the industrial revolution. People in the American culture no longer receive that same kind of nurturing from their fathers and that is making it hard for them to relate to God's love. These are all cultural misunderstandings.

In I Corinthians 9:9 Paul refers to an Old Testament verse which says, "It is written in the Law of Moses: you must not put a muzzle on the ox when it is treading out the corn." Here he uses this verse to express financial needs that are holding back his ministry. In I Timothy 5:18 he uses this verse in reference to the honor that elders in the church need to further their ministry. Christian layman need respect and freedom to minister to others. What many churches do to Christians is to muzzle them by forcing their methodology (which is usually cultural) on people that are sincerely trying to minister to others. It is like constraining them with a muzzle while they are trying to get their spiritual work done. Christians in return may try to force that methodology on the Muslims. That is why people like Robb may have to minister to Muslims without the involvement of the local church.

One of the greatest missionaries that ever went to Muslims was Samuel Zwemer. He felt God calling him to Arabia. He adopted the motto of Genesis 17:18: "O that Ishmael might live before Thee." No mission board would sponsor him; they called him "foolish" for wanting to go to such a fanatical people. Zwemer and a friend formed their own organization, The Arabian Mission. He went to Arabia in June of 1890. He married, and two of his young daughters died of dysentery in Bahrain. He wrote more than 50 books about Muslims, and spent much of his life traveling and educating Christians about Muslims. In China he was even invited to mosques to speak because of his knowledge of Arabic and Islam. Samuel Zwemer went alone. Was he foolish? He wasn't any more foolish than Peter was in Luke 5:5. His message still resounds powerfully today: "Master, we have toiled all the night, and have taken nothing: nevertheless at Thy word, I will let down the net." [2] You see, our responsibility is to make our lives the good news of Christ, and the rest is up to the Holy Spirit. What the Spirit chooses to do in people's hearts is up to Him.

God is working in His own way in each man's heart. We must let the Holy Spirit do His work. Many times Christians think they must argue and defend Christ. Christ doesn't need us to defend him if we are being offensive. We need the Holy Spirit to defend us, and He will most likely have to clean up the mess we have made in another person's heart.

Thank God for Christians that have a heart to reach out to Muslims in friendship; but their job will be twice as hard if they are trying to make friends with an offended Muslim. With the methodology that has been put to practice in America, most Muslims you meet will be somewhat offended.

Another very important aspect of Middle Eastern culture is that things move very slowly. God's timing for a Muslim will be much slower than with a Westerner. Middle Easterners take a very long time to make their point. Americans are used to life in the fast lane, and seem very impatient to Middle Easterners. We had one American neighbor in Iran that every time you talked to him he would say, "I've got to get going."

Iranians would ask, "Why is he always in such a big hurry, what is it he has to go to?" They couldn't figure out what could be so important that you would make people feel like you couldn't talk to them for a few minutes. I tell Americans that if you are visiting with a Middle Easterner in person, or on the telephone, there are many polite ways to end the conversation graciously: "It was nice seeing you," "I will let you go," "Please say hello to your family, we will talk again real soon," etc., etc.

Before a Muslim will be interested in your philosophy of life he must see some strength in you he doesn't have. According to the Bible, patience is a strength and impatience is a weakness. God's timing is not necessarily our timing. How have you proved yourself to be a friend, that a Muslim should respect your spiritual advice? Have you helped weather any crisis in your Muslim friend's life? Did you comfort him when you saw he was broken-hearted over the Gulf war? Did you sympathize with him when he felt he was at the end of prejudice attitudes? Have you helped answer his questions about the American lifestyle? Are you concentrating on the things you have in common, rather than your differences? Are you moving more slowly in activities so he can keep up? Are you finding his new perspectives interesting and sincerely trying to understand where he is coming from? Ask questions: Why do you find it offensive when it is said that Jesus is the son of God? What do you think about this verse?

One day I asked a Muslim friend, "If you don't believe Jesus died on the cross, what do you make of this verse in the Quran that says Jesus said, 'Blessed am I the day I will be raised from the dead?'"

She said, "I think that Jesus is telling us that if we live for God our spirits will come alive, and we will live forever with God in eternity."

I responded, "I certainly have to admit that you have taken the spiritual meaning well." We need to concentrate on those things we agree on. What do my Muslim friends need from me? They need love and acceptance; only then will they see Christ and his kingdom.

Jesus proclaimed the kingdom of God. Robb decided to study the kingdom of God with his students. Let's look at some of the information Rob and Ali may have studied. What other doctrines do Christians and Muslims have in common? What forms of worship do Christians and Muslims share?

When Jesus began to preach, in Matthew 4:17, he said "Repent: for the kingdom of heaven is at hand." A very clear theme in the Quran is the glorious throne of God, a dominion, and an eternal kingdom over which God reigns in sovereignty. Jesus' main message was about the kingdom of God. I have heard some Christians say the kingdom of God will not come into being until the Messiah comes, but the Bible is very clear about the kingdom starting here and now. In Luke 11:20 Jesus said, "...the kingdom of God has come to you." Luke 17:20 tells us, "Once, having been asked by the Pharisees when the kingdom of God would come, Jesus replied, 'The kingdom of God does not come with your careful observation, nor will people say, 'Here it is,' or 'There it is,' because the kingdom of God is within you.'"

God meant for his kingdom to start back with his people when He led them out of Egypt. He went before them in a pillar of fire. But the people demanded a kingdom patterned after the ungodly nations around them. In I Samuel 8:5 The Israelites came to Samuel and said, "...give us a king to rule over us, like the other nations." Samuel felt very rejected and went to God about it. In verse 7 God told Samuel, "..Obey the voice of the people in all that they say to you, for it is not you they have rejected; they have rejected me from ruling over them." So God let them have an earthly king, of which Saul was the first. King David was the divinely anointed king. Through David God hoped to bring people back to his heavenly kingdom; He told David his kingdom would last forever. Matthew lists the genealogy of David until to Jesus.

Then Jesus tries to explain to the Pharisees that God has this special kingdom that He wants them to participate in, but again they fail to find the kingdom of God. After that, Paul admits the religious leadership was taken from the Jews, and gives a very stiff warning to Christians in Romans 11:20,21: "..they were cut off, but through their unbelief; if you still hold firm, it is only thanks to your faith. Rather than making you proud, that should make you afraid. God did not spare the natural branches, and he is not likely to spare you."

Here we see God working with the local culture, even though it was not to his perfection. God then turns to a new group of people, giving them a chance to participate in his kingdom. It is a rare privilege to be a part of the kingdom of God.

God has always worked with people, creating them with a free will, coordinating events around their behavior, and using whoever has a tender heart toward Him. Whenever America gets involved in another war in the Middle east, the people at my church can see my grief and they say, "God is in control." I tell them I choose to see God as the great coordinator; He has to work around men's mistakes. St. Augustine puts it well:

> *Since God foresaw all things and, hence, that man would sin, our conception of the supernatural City of God must be based on what God foreknew and forewilled, and not on human fancies that could never come true, because it was not in God's plan that they should. Not even by his sin could man change the counsels of God, in the sense of compelling Him to alter what He had once decided. The truth is that, by His omniscience, God could foresee two future realities: how bad man whom God had created good was to become, and how much good God was to make out of this very evil. [3]*

Robb and Ali discussed the kingdom of God. Ali admitted he knew Muslims that made commitments and went to Mecca but their behavior had not really changed. Robb had to admit that he also knew Christians that had dedicated their lives to follow Christ and obey God, but they did not act like sons of the kingdom either. Of course, we will not see the kingdom in all its fullness until the Messiah comes but wherever the people of God dwell we should see signs of the kingdom of God. Both the Quran and the Bible have much to say about God's kingdom.

Quran

Surah LVII:4,5:...who created the heavens and the earth in six days; then He mounted the Throne. He knoweth all that entereth the earth and all that emergeth therefrom and all that cometh down from the sky and all that ascendeth therein, and He is with you wheresoever ye may be. And God is Seer of what ye do. His is the Sovereignty of the heavens and the earth, and unto God (all) things are brought back.

Surah IX:129: ...He is Lord of the Tremendous Throne.

Surah XXIII:86: Say: Who is Lord of the seven heavens, and Lord of the Tremendous Throne?

Surah XXXI:26: ...He is the Absolute, the Owner of Praise.

Surah LXX:3,4:...God, Lord of the Ascending Stairways (Whereby) the angels and the Spirit ascend unto Him in a Day where of the span is fifty thousand years.

Surah XL:15: The Exalter of Ranks, the Lord of the Throne. He casteth the Spirit of his command upon whom He will...

Surah LXXXV:14,15: And He is the Forgiving, the Loving Lord of the Throne of Glory.

Surah VII:54: ...mounted He the Throne...and hath made the sun and the moon and the stars subservient by His command.

Bible

Psalm 45:6: Your throne, God, shall last for ever and ever, your royal scepter is a scepter of integrity.

Psalm 47:7-9(NJB): God is king of the whole world: play your best in his honor! God is king of the nations, he reigns on his holy throne...He reigns supreme.

Psalm 93:2: Thy throne is established of old: thou art from everlasting.

Psalm 145:10-13: All thy works shall praise thee, O LORD; and thy saints shall bless thee. They shall speak of the glory of thy kingdom, and talk of thy power; To make known to the sons of men his mighty acts, and the glorious majesty of his kingdom. Thy kingdom is an everlasting kingdom, and thy dominion endureth throughout all generations.

Hebrews 12:28,29: We have been given possession of an unshakable kingdom. Let us therefore hold on to the grace that we have been given and use it to worship God in the way that he finds acceptable, in reverence and fear. For our God is a consuming fire.

After those beautiful descriptions the Quran and Bible give us of the kingdom, we may pay more attention when Jesus says in Matthew 6:33..."Seek ye first the kingdom of God, and his righteousness; and all these things shall be added unto you." Being a part of the kingdom of God is much more than just being good; it is being part of something exciting with a wonderful purpose.

Adam and Eve were once in God's eternal kingdom in the Garden of Eden, what the Quran calls Paradise. But men lost their knowledge of the worship of God until there was only one godly man left, Noah. Men had willingly left, or become lost from God's kingdom. King David saw it in Psalm 14:2,3(NJB) "Yahweh is looking down from heaven at the sons of men, to see if a single one is wise, if a single one is seeking God. All have turned aside, all alike are tainted; there is not one good man left, not a single one." Isaiah seemed to understand that the Messiah was going to have to come and take the burden on himself; in chapter 53:6 he says, "All we like sheep have gone astray; we have turned every one to his own way; and the Lord hath laid on him the iniquity of us all." Later, Paul the apostle, a citizen of the Roman Empire repeats the Psalms of David, and in Romans 10:23 says, "all have sinned and come short of the glory of God."

This paints a pretty bleak picture of mankind. What can we do? When we know God has this wonderful kingdom, how can we find our way back to it? We know God loves us and wants us to be a part of his kingdom. He is calling us, but we must find our way. Jesus is called the Word in the Quran, and in Surah X:94 it says, "And if thou (Muhammad) art in doubt concerning that which We reveal unto thee, then question those who read the Scripture (that was) before thee."

In Matthew 13 Jesus tells us in parables of two ways that men find the kingdom. One man is walking in a field and stumbles over a treasure. He hides it, and overjoyed, goes to sell everything he owns just to buy the field so the treasure will be his. The second man is a merchant who knows there is a precious pearl, and he is looking for it. When he finds it, he sells everything he has and buys that one pearl.

I have an American friend who was not taught about living for God in her childhood. When she grew up her social life consisted of nightclubs and parties. At one party, over a bottle of wine and a package of cigarettes, someone shared the *good news* with her and invited her to church the next day. As they were standing for Bible reading in church she looked down, and in Matt 22:14 the words "..for many are called but few are chosen," jumped off the page at her. She felt God saying, "I want you." She went home, got on her knees and said, "I don't know what that girl has Lord, but I want it." She then surrendered her life to God. Debra stumbled on a treasure. The kingdom took her by surprise. On the other hand, I have shared with you in this book about my life-long search for something I knew I didn't have, a relationship with a personal God. But I was raised in church. Why didn't I enter the kingdom of God in church.

Jesus says there are two things which keep people from entering the kingdom of God. These are the same things which I saw in other people that prevented me from finding the kingdom of God in my church. In Mark 7:7-9,13, Jesus refers to God's words in Isaiah:

"This people honors me only with lip-service, while their hearts are far from me. The worship they offer me is worthless, the doctrines they teach are only human regulations." Jesus said, "You put aside the commandment of God to cling to human traditions. How ingeniously you get around the commandment of God in order to preserve your own tradition!"

The second thing that prevents men from entering the kingdom of God is in John 12:42,43:

And yet there were many who did believe in him, even among the leading men, but they did not admit it, through fear of the Pharisees and fear of being expelled from the synagogue: they put honor fro m men before the honor that comes from God.

I guess the best way to say this is that men often worry more about what the people around them think than what God thinks of them. It is a sad commentary, because most Christians covet the love and respect of the Christian community. It is difficult for people to do what is right when they know that action will alienate them from the group of people they care so much about. Some people may have to step out alone, even from the church, like Robb had to do in our story. There is a beautiful Iranian writing I saw in a friend's home. It is God speaking and He says,

If you have everyone, but you don't have Me, you have no one.

If you have no one, but you have Me, you have everyone.

If our motives are to please men instead of pleasing God, that will keep us from entering the kingdom. In Matthew 7:21,24 Jesus says, "It is not those who say to me, Lord, Lord, who will enter the kingdom of heaven, but the person who does the will of my Father in heaven... Therefore, everyone who listens to these words of mine and acts on them..." If Jesus says we must do God's will to enter His kingdom, we must know more of what God's will really is.

The Middle Easterners are more familiar with the monarchy system. Every kingdom has a theme, a constitution, subjects, and a king. The British system is the Monarchy that Americans are the most familiar with. Of course today the Queen of England does not have absolute power as the kings once did. Henry the VIII with all his wives is a classic example. If you look back at the British history, their main theme was world domination through power. In the early 20th Century, England ruled a good percentage of the world, but by mid-century most of the leadership had slipped from their hands. The British people had a set of rules (and some rights) to live by. They had their Queen.

A friend of mine compared the kingdom of heaven to Norway during World War II. The Nazis had taken over Norway and the Norwegian king fled the country. He set up his government in exile and carried on business as normally as possible. The Norwegian population in Norway cooperated with the ruling Nazi government but the first allegiance of their hearts was to the exiled Norwegian Monarchy.

The difference between the earthly kingdoms we have seen, and the kingdom of God is that God is absolute ruler; His loyal subjects are to be absolutely submitted to his will. The perfect monarchy is designed to have a completely loving king whose subjects carry out His plan and desires to perfection. In Matthew 22:37-40 Jesus said, "You must love the Lord your God with all your Heart, with all your soul, and with all your mind. This is the greatest and the first commandment. The second resembles it: You must love your neighbor as yourself. On these two commandments hang the whole Law, and the Prophets also." Why should we give allegiance to this heavenly kingdom? Because no one cares about us as much as our King does, and it is the only way we will know complete joy and peace.

The theme of the kingdom is domination of the world through *love*: God's love for us, our love for God, God's love for others, and our love for others. It is not a domination of man over man, but rather God dominating men's hearts within the context of their own cultures. I have a little exercise I have used over the years when I do not feel I like someone. I imagine a little beam of light from heaven shining down on that person, and how much God loves him or her. It really does give me a better attitude. If God loves someone that much, they have worth and I must treat them as though they are worthy. Love gives worth. If I say I love God, I must love what He loves and who he loves, just because His love has given it worth. That includes the whole of creation.

Some other characteristics of the kingdom of God are: I Corinthians 4:20...the kingdom of God is not just word, it is *power*.

Hebrews 13:28..We have been given possession of an *unshakable* kingdom.

II Peter 1:11...the *eternal* kingdom of our Lord and Savior.

I Corinthians 15:50..flesh and blood cannot enter the Kingdom of God. I John 3:2..*now* we are the sons of God. John 3:5...unless a man be born from above (*Spiritual*), he cannot see the kingdom of God.

Romans 14:17 ..the kingdom of God does not mean eating or drinking this or that, it means *righteousness* and *peace* and *joy* brought by the Holy Spirit.

Luke 4:18...*good news* to the poor,...*liberty* to the captives, ..to the blind *new sight*,..to the downtrodden *freedom*, ..Lord's year of *favor*!

Notice there is no mention of certain groups being more special than any other. Not nationality, wealth, beauty, nor color makes any difference in the kingdom of God. God is a spirit and He is concerned with the spiritual awakening of the whole world, and every segment of society.

The kingdom is	*The kingdom is not*
love	fear
power	weak
unshakable	destructible
eternal	of this world
now	only later
spiritual	physical
righteousness	sin
peace	war
joy	anger
good news	bad news
liberty	controlling
new sight	blind
freedom	bondage
favor	rejection

When we make judgements as to what are a part of the kingdom of God, this list can help us discern.

The kingdom of God has a constitution.

1. Subjects must not feel anger in their hearts toward fellow men. (Matt 5:21-26)

2. Subjects must not have impure thoughts in their hearts. (Matt 5:27-32).

3. Subjects must be honest and keep their word. (Matt 5:33- 37)

4. Subjects must not retaliate. (Matt 5:38-42).

5. Subjects must love and pray for their enemies. (Matt 5:43-48).

6. Subjects must tithe, fast, and pray to God, not to impress other people; pray after this pattern: (Matt 6:1- 18)

    > Our Father in heaven,
    > Hallowed be thy name.
    > Thy kingdom come, Thy will be done,
    > as in heaven so on earth.
    > Give us bread for our needs from day to day.
    > And forgive us our offenses,
    > as we have forgiven our offenders.
    > And do not let us enter into temptation,
    > but deliver us from evil,
    > for Thine is the kingdom, and the power,
    > and the glory, forever. Amen. [4]

7. Subjects must invest time and effort in eternal purposes rather than earthly. (Matt 6:19-24).

8. Subjects must not be judgemental toward fellow man, but rather judge themselves first. (Matt 7:1-5).

9. Subjects must go to God with all their needs. (Matt 7:1- 7).

10. Subjects must obey the *Golden Rule*: do unto others as you would have them do unto you. (Matt 7:12).

One day my Christian friend Debra called me and was so discouraged because she had failed to obey the constitution of God's kingdom. I sympathized with her and said, "You are just too hard on yourself, you can't be perfect all the time."

Debra answered, "Don't ever tell me that again, in Matthew 5:48 Jesus said, 'You must be perfect just as your heavenly Father is perfect.'" She felt God expected obedience from her and she wanted to be obedient. She was obeying Matt 7:1-5 by judging her own behavior.

Matthew 5 gives a description of the subjects who live in complete obedience to the constitution of the kingdom of God:

Blessed are the poor in spirit: for theirs is the kingdom of heaven.

Blessed are they that mourn; for they shall be comforted.

Blessed are the meek: for they shall inherit the earth.

Blessed are they which do hunger and thirst after righteousness: for they shall be filled.

Blessed are the merciful: for they shall obtain mercy.

Blessed are the pure in heart: for they shall see God.

Blessed are the peacemakers: for they shall be called the children of God.

Blessed are they which are persecuted for righteousness' sake: for theirs is the kingdom of heaven.

Let us now look at the character of the king:

Matthew 21:5 "..Look, your king comes to you; he is *humble*, he rides on a donkey and on a colt.."

Revelation 17:14..he is *Lord* of lords, and King of kings: and they that are with him are called, and chosen, and faithful. I Timothy 1:17 Now unto the King *eternal, immortal, invisible*, the only *wise* God, be honor and glory for ever and ever.

Luke 1:34...his reign will have no end.

John 18:36,37 Jesus answers Pilate, the Roman governor..My kingdom is not of this world: if my kingdom were of this world, then would my servants fight,..Thou sayest I am a king. To this end was I born, and for this cause came I into the world, that I should bear *witness unto the truth*. Every one that is of the truth heareth my voice.

Revelation 19:11-16 The first battle of the End...And now I saw heaven open, and a white horse appear; its rider was called *Faithful* and *True*; he is a judge with *integrity*, a warrior for *justice*...He is known by the name, The *Word of God*. Behind him, dressed in linen of dazzling white, rode the armies of heaven on white horses. From his mouth came a sharp sword to strike the pagans with; he is the one who will rule them with an iron scepter, an tread out the wine of Almighty God's fierce anger. On his cloak and on his thigh there was a name written: The King of kings and the Lord of lords.

In the Bible the complete plan of the kingdom is revealed. At the creation, Jesus as the Word was present. Then, born of a virgin, the word became flesh and dwelt among men. Christ was crucified, and raised again the third day. Mark 16:19 tells: "after the Lord had spoken unto them, he was received up into heaven, and sat on the right hand of God." At the end of God's plan for man's redemption, Jesus will give his kingdom to God like a gift and God will become all in all. The separation of God and his Word will no longer be necessary. The subjects will be dwelling in the eternal heavenly kingdom.

In John 6:39, Jesus said, "And this is the Father's will which hath sent me, that of all which he hath given me I should lose nothing, but should raise it up again at the last day." I Corinthians 15:24-28 Paul tells, "After that will come the end, when he hands over the kingdom to God the Father, having done away with every sovereignty, authority and power. For he must be king until he has put all his enemies under his feet and the last of the enemies to be destroyed is death, for everything is to be put under his feet.--Though when it is said that everything is subjected, this clearly cannot include the One who subjected everything to him. And when everything is subjected to him, then the Son himself will be *subject* in his turn to the One who subjected all things to him, so that God may be *all in all*."

The Zwemer Institute conducts Muslim Awareness seminars in churches in America. They point out the Muslims are more resistant to Western forms of worship than the actual message of the gospel. What do we think about when we say *forms of worship*? Zwemer categorizes Muslim behaviors into three categories: differing religious practices, neutral worship forms, and neutral cultural behaviors. Examples of differing religious practices would be: confessing Muhammad, pilgrimage to Mecca, or polygamy. Examples of neutral worship practices are prayer posture and times, washing before prayer, reverence for the word of God, caring for the poor, and fasting. Muslims pray morning, noon, and night. Christians respect that discipline. Muslims have a ritual of standing and leaning over and touching their forehead to the ground in prostration to God. This is the way many prophets in the Old Testament prayed, and it is very good exercise. My husband's grandmother was in her eighties and very limber yet. I'm sure that ritual standing, kneeling, and prostrating before God three times a day, at least 15 minutes a time, was a contributing factor.

One day my children had gone to the rest room in the Minnesota Zoo and when they came out my son said there was a man in there washing his arms up to his elbows and washing the top of his feet. Javad recognized this action but he said the Americans in there were taking a second look. About five minutes later we saw the fellow come out, go up on top of the hill and do his ritual prayers to God.

The only other place you will see anyone wash that way is in an operating room. Doctors scrub up to their elbows before surgery. I never really thought about it when we lived in Iran. I just accepted this ritual washing as one of their customs, but never thought of doing it myself. We all laughed at my mother-in-law when she would buy a long sleeved blouse without a button at the cuff, and then would have to rip the seams on the sleeves so she could wash her arms before she prayed.

But after our return to America in 1981, our children picked up scabies from a petting zoo. We had never heard of scabies, and the doctors were not much better. They knew it was called the *seven-year itch*. It didn't take me long to figure out why they called it that; scabies were microscopic bugs. We changed doctors three times, and covered our bodies with poison creme. Finally. I went to the University of Minnesota medical library and got two books on scabies. I learned something very interesting; 60 percent of the scabies stayed between your elbow and your wrist. The first thought that crossed my mind was, "No wonder Muhammad incorporated this washing into the prayer ritual." Middle Easterners have never heard of scabies, because if you wash your arms to the elbow three times a day no scabies would have a chance to burrow under your skin.

Many of the old testament religious traditions were also preventative medicine. Actually, this was quite related to my own prayer life because when we got scabies I was a new Christian, attending Bible Study Fellowship. I had asked other people to pray for us, but had little knowledge about how to pray and had not prayed myself. After nine months of fighting scabies I was an experienced prayer warrior. Romans 8:28 became a reality in my life, "And we know that all things work together for good to them that love God, to them who are the called according to his purpose." Scabies helped me to learn to pray.

Christians could learn from the Muslims reverence for the word of God. They keep their holy book wrapped in a nice cloth, and keep it high, and kiss it when they take it in their hands. Try kissing the Bible once and see how tender it makes you feel toward God and his word. Caring for the poor is something Muslims and Christians have in common. Fasting is a spiritual discipline Muslims take very seriously. Fasting is one of the more difficult disciplines. Fasting can be a very rewarding experience, even as much as giving up certain foods for lent. In the Christian community, thanks to Richard Foster, fasting is back in the books as a spiritual discipline. Foster recommends fasting from anything that distracts from your walk with God, all the way from advertisements to the telephone. The purpose is to simplify your life, clear your mind and listen to that still small voice.

Examples of neutral cultural behaviors would be dress styles, eating habits, social behaviors, design of houses, educational system, style of gardening, child rearing and art forms. Muslim women in Iran either wore veils, or modest dresses. Many are reluctant to wear swimming suits, even in America. I found their dress code stylish, but conservative. After living in the Middle East, I myself have developed an awareness of what impression my clothing would give to others. Modesty is a virtue very much valued in women.

Middle Eastern food is among the most delicious, and nutritious in the world. The people eat bread and rice with mildly-spiced stews, and lots of fresh fruit and vegetables. Middle Eastern restaurants in America are attracting many Americans. American and Middle Eastern social behaviors are different in many ways. Middle Easterners move more slowly, and they love to be together without necessarily accomplishing anything obvious. They are very successful in their careers but their friendships are purely for enjoyment. They enjoy being together and just visiting. They are very personal, and share their feelings for each other. They notice little things about each other and comment on them; they encourage each other often. They go to extremes to make sure their guest is comfortable and feels appreciated.

I loved the predictability of the Middle Eastern social system. They have all these little unwritten social rules that were almost like a direction book. There is structure to their social system. If you are a kind person and practice all the little social niceties, you are accepted and liked. Children are given a lot of attention.

Middle Easterners have a great zeal for education. In the Middle East there are very few extracurricular activities in the schools but the students receive more honor for their scholastic achievements. Every class honors a first student, much like we have a first chair in the violin section of an orchestra. If parents want to impress others, they say their child is the first student in the class. Parents tell their children, "The only job you have to do is to study very hard." Middle Eastern parents do not believe teenagers should go out with their friends or even get a driver's license until they are college age. They say this is the time of your life to be with your family and get good grades in school.

Middle Easterners love flowers, and plant elaborate flower gardens. In fact, the word *paradise* is an old Persian word which meant garden. We have all seen the Middle Eastern arts lately in America. The paisley is the most classic Persian design, although many Middle Eastern countries may claim it for their own. The paisley design is a stylized fern tree (commonly called the Cyprus tree). Shiraz, Iran is famous for its tall narrow fern trees that curve at the top. Middle Eastern design will be with us for awhile because the interior decorators are using it. We have seen jewelry with Arabic writings on them in local shops. Middle Eastern art is in fashion.

Our favorite is Persian carpets. Once you have Persian carpets in your home, it is very difficult to live without them. The rich color and design bring so much warmth to a room. They are a very good investments because they become more valuable with age. In the Middle East people buy carpets as they can afford them and then give their children each a carpet when they get married.

With the slower life-style in the Middle East, artists and weavers may spend days or weeks, or months on their art. A hand woven carpet may take months or years to weave. Other Iranian art includes pictures, or miniature frames with wood, copper, and ivory (imitation) inlays, calligraphy writings, miniature paintings on ivory, carved pewter and copper plates, paintings on leather, painted and baked ceramic tiles, porcelain painted copper pots, clay pottery, and wax statues.

Europeans have long appreciated Middle Eastern art and now we are seeing more of it in America.

To summarize, Muslims believe God is one, the creator of heaven and earth. They believe in five holy books, three of which are in the Bible. Muslims believe in the Judeo-Christian prophets in the Bible, concluding that Muhammad was the last prophet. They believe in angelic beings. The Quran has extensive coverage on the day of judgement with elaborate descriptions of the suffering in hell. Muslims believe in the sovereignty of God; Surah II:138 says (We take our) colour from God, and who is better than God at colouring? We are His worshippers. This is a reference to the same practice that the Christian baptism was derived from, the dying of materials in the ancient world. They would submerge the material into the dye and when they brought it out it would be a different color. That is symbolic of the old man who becomes the new man through his relationship with God. Muslims believe God is in control of everything that happens in the world.

We have our faith in God in common, we both relate to Christ even though a bit differently, we have most of the essential beliefs about God in common. Some of our worship forms are cultural and we can learn from each other. The ancient culture has much to teach Westerners about friendship and family relationships. George Gilder in his book *Men and Marriage* tells how the American culture is constantly being replenished by the influx of foreigners with their strong family relationships and their willingness to sacrifice for their children's educations. We American Christians have much in common with Middle Eastern Muslims.

Notes:

1. Ralph D. Winter and Stephen C. Hawthorne, ed., *Perspectives on the World Christian Movement, A Reader* (Pasadena, California: William Carey Library, 1981) p. 373.

2. J. Christy Wilson, A Life Worth Emulating, The Legacy of Samuel Zwemer. *Sharing God's Love with Muslims, A Zwemer Institute Newsletter.* Winter, 1987, p. 1.

3. St Augustine, *City of God* (New York: An Image Book, Double-day, 1958.) p. 304.

4. George M. Lamsa's translation from the Aramaic of the Peshitta, *HOLY BIBLE from the ancient Eastern text,* (Harper San Francisco).

SOLVING MYSTERIES

That Jesus' message is so great and so powerful lies in the fact that it is so simple and on the other hand so rich, so simple as to be exhausted in each of the leading thoughts which he uttered; so rich that every one of these thoughts seems to be inexhaustible and the full meaning of the sayings and parables beyond our reach. --Adolf von Harnack (1851-1930)

In the formation of early church doctrines there was dissension, personal jealousy, intolerance, persecution, bigotry. That out of this welter should have arisen the Bible, with its fine inspiration, would seem to present a plausible basis for belief in its Divine origin. --The Lost Books of the Bible

I grew up in a small church that was mainly concerned with evangelism. The problem was that we spent all our social time with the people in that church, and there was very seldom anyone new to evangelize. I'm afraid to say I became tired of hearing the gospel story. The members of our congregation never discussed religion outside of church. The conversation went directly to clothes, recipes, or their children. After all, we all knew the gospel story so well; it was simple.

The sad part was that I really loved to read. If someone had just told me about C. S. Lewis and the *Chronicles of Narnia* or Martin Luther and the Reformation, it would have been wonderful. If I could have learned more about the women of the Bible, it would have helped. As a young girl, it was difficult to relate to Paul. He didn't seem to be very fond of women after all. But I guess the people of our church didn't know about those things themselves. I entertained myself with secular books like *King of the Wind*, and *The Call of the Wild*. They were good stories about relationships and commitment.

In my teens I decided that I had had enough of church and was going out to learn about the world. It didn't take me long to find out the world wasn't much more stimulating; people were mostly concerned with making money and having fun. I wasn't really that interested in either, so again I buried myself in my books. I moved on to books like the *Scarlet Letter*, Thomas Hardy stories, Khalil Gibran, and historical accounts of Europe and the founding of Israel.

Then when I was 18 I met a very interesting boy. He was from Iran. He said, "Persia, you know, like Persian carpets." I had heard of Persian carpets. His name was Bahram. Bahram was a Muslim and he knew all the Bible stories; even better than I did. And he really enjoyed talking about them. He had majored in literature in high school and had read all kinds of wonderful books. Bahram had memorized 500 line poems and he translated them from his language for me. For Christmas he bought me the whole series of Khalil Gibran books. I was in love. It looked like Christians and Muslims believed the same things.

It was not until 13 years later when I was touched by the Holy Spirit that I realized the difference is that Muslims see only the mystery of the gospel.

I returned to church with my children. I met a dear Christian friend named Debra. She taught me about all the famous Christian authors and I had a pile of books I thought I would never get through. But again the church was telling us the gospel is simple. Was it really simple or was it too mysterious like the Muslims said? I thought I would find out for myself. Let's see what the Bible has to say about it.

The King James version uses the word *simple* 16 times. In most of these verses *simple* means shallow, or ignorant. In the NIV Bible, Proverbs 9:13 changes *simple* to undisciplined and Psalm 116:6 changes it to simple-hearted. In Psalm 116:6, purely-motivated would probably be a clearer description of the meaning. The word simplicity is used once in II Corinthians 1:12:

> *For our rejoicing is this, the testimony of our conscience, that in simplicity and godly sincerity, not with fleshly wisdom, but by the grace of God, we have had our conversation in the world, and more abundant to you...*

The NIV changes this to *the holiness and sincerity that are fro m God.* So it is actually referring more to the Christian community's behavior. Not one of these is calling the gospel a simple concept.

In contrast, the word *mystery* is used 21 times. The word *mystery* is directly referred to in the gospel 16 of those times. The NIV changes the word *mystery* to *secrets* in I Corinthians 2:7, 4:1, and Mark 4:11. *Mystery* is changed to *deep truths* in I Timothy 3:9. Romans 11:25 says:

> *For I would not, brethren, that ye should be ignorant of this mystery, lest ye should be wise in your own conceits; that blindness in part is happened to Israel, until the fulness of the Gentiles be come in.*

What did Paul mean by this verse? Could it be that the Jewish religious leaders thought they had God all figured out with their endless books of law. And when they dedicated their lives to obeying those laws, they felt like they had done quite a good job and in their minds became a part of an exclusive pious community.

In Mark 7:9, Jesus tells the Pharisees they reject the commandments of God to keep their traditions. That blindness in part can also happen to Christians if we are not humble before the mystery of God.

There is one part of the mystery that Paul reveals to us in Ephesians 3:3-6(NIV):

> *The mystery made known to me by revelation...then you will be able to understand my insight into the mystery of Christ, which was not made known to men in other generations as it has now been revealed by the Spirit to God's holy apostles and prophets. This mystery is that through the gospel the Gentiles are heirs together in the promise in Christ Jesus.*

It further explains in Galatians 3:28,29, that there is neither Jew nor Greek, there is neither bond nor free, there is neither male nor female: for ye are all one in Christ Jesus...If ye be Christ's, then ye are Abraham's seed, and heirs according to the promise.

As for the rest of the mystery of God Paul says in I Corinthians 13:12 that we now see as a poor reflection in a mirror but there will be a time when we shall see Him face to face. I Timothy 3:16(NJB) says: Without any doubt, the mystery of our religion is very deep indeed:

> *He was made visible in the flesh, attested by the Spirit, seen by angels, proclaimed to the pagans, believed in by the world, taken up in glory.*

If Paul thought the mystery was important enough to bring it to our attention 16 times, how is it that the church has ended up with what A.Z. Tozer calls *Instant Christianity:*

The American genius for getting things done quickly and easily with little concern for quality or permanence has bred a virus that has infected the whole evangelical church in the United States and, through our literature, our evangelists and our missionaries, has spread all over the world... By "Instant Christianity", I mean the kind found almost everywhere in gospel circles and which is born of the notion that we may discharge our total obligation to our own souls in one act of faith, or at most by two, and be relieved thereafter of all anxiety about our spiritual condition. [1]

Muslims see many Christians as people who claim to have made a commitment to Christ but do not see the honest, peaceful, spiritually disciplined person they should expect. They look at Islam which means *surrender to God* and have been raised with the pillars of practice. What these pillars are, are spiritual discipline; fasting, prayer, worship, and tithing. Children are taught in school to practice these disciplines. Most Muslims will be quick to tell you that Islam is a way of life. Once they hit Western secular society they lose the support of the corporate disciplines. But they still have themselves to compare with the average Christian. One Muslim man said, "Should I exchange my way of life for one hour Sunday morning? I look at some of these people claiming to be Christians and wonder if I would like to change from what I am to what they are. I'm afraid I just can't justify the action. On the other hand, I have seen a few Christians I would want to be like!"

Christians have a challenge. The Bible gives a standard of life that is a mystery until it is practiced. Traditional marriage, Christian ethics, and monism sound like nonsense to the world because people are not seeing the practical outworking of it.

Frank Tillapaugh, a Baptist minister from Denver, has a series of tapes called *The Church Unleashed*. He says American Evangelical Christians have center stage in the world today, but it is only temporary. He challenges the church to act now in rising to the occasion of a changing world. It has been through the efforts of Christian para-church organizations, publishing houses, and colleges that center stage has been achieved. The churches are still weak. He says if you put a new Christian in an average church for two years, that Christian will be crippled in his or her ability to think *ministry*; the average church is a commentary to the white middle class American.

Our mind-set must change and many churches are rising to the challenge of revival. Tillapaugh says we have a message of absolutes, set and revealed in scripture but the Bible does not give us methodology. Many churches are making a renewed effort of restructuring their methodology to meet the needs of their own people and potential people that may come in. Facilitating special groups within larger churches is becoming a popular method of drawing senior citizens, singles, and teens. Why not Muslims?

In Minneapolis, we attended Quran-Bible studies and the Iranians loved them. People would take turns having the studies in their homes. Each family would bring an ethnic dish and we would have a social time. After dinner all the children would go play; the older children watching out for the younger ones. Then the adults would have a study time. Verses from the Quran were read and then the equivalent spiritual concept was addressed from the Bible. After the reading, there was open discussion with the group.

First we had one Iranian-Christian couple, and they taught in Farsi. They even taught us some praise songs written by Iranians. The Iranians seemed to really enjoy singing those songs in their own language. That couple moved away and another young Iranian couple took their place. They were also very effective, but were later tragically killed in a car accident along with their infant daughter. An American couple that had been former missionaries to Iran took over the sessions, and even in English the attendance grew. Finally, there was such a big group that no home could handle it. What these former missionaries needed to do was rent a hall and spend all their time preparing for these sessions. We heard they had traveled to churches trying to get financial support, but were unable to get support for that particular ministry. Later we learned they moved to California and started a church with Iranians. The Iranians kept asking me, "What happened to our religious socials?"

Teenagers are often eager to participate in special outreach activities but it is often overprotective parents that are the problem. I have heard more than one parent repent of the sin of not entrusting their teenager to God, and refusing the church to allow special interest ministries for their youth. One young man asked, "When are they going to let us do something useful for the Lord?" Classes on church history and other religions are very helpful to the Christian youth going off to college where they will be exposed to a plurality of beliefs. Teenagers are at their peak of energy and desire. They must be allowed to burn off that energy for the Lord. Let their walk with God be the most stimulating force in their lives. I Corinthians 16:1 said: "they addicted themselves to the ministry of saints." This is not referring to spiritual highs but to the joy of ministering to others. This would be the ideal group to start a *Make a Muslim Friend* ministry. Another group in the church rising to the challenge is women's ministry. A group of women from Hope Presbyterian Church in Minneapolis invited a group of foreign women on a weekend retreat. It was at a hotel. The church women had a fund raiser and earned enough money so that they could invite the foreign women free of charge. One woman from the church was a beauty consultant and she donated her time. The foreign women were lined up bright and early Saturday morning to have their makeup done and their fashion colors evaluated. When they finished with the outer beauty they had a Bible study about inner beauty. Some of the foreign women had to be home Saturday evening and couldn't sleep over. One Christian woman's dear husband picked up the foreign women in his van. He sat in a hotel room for ten hours with two young children so he could be there to give them rides home that evening. His wife stayed at the hotel to help entertain their guests the entire weekend. That retreat became a family project for them. Many of those foreign women are now attending church, along with some of their husbands. The very aware and educated women of the twentieth century are challenging the methodology of the church.

Frank Tillapaugh says his church has bases all over the city in any building that can facilitate a Bible study or sharing time. The church must not ask, *if*, but they must ask, *how* can it be done. It is God who works through the church; not as a building or institution, but as people sharing love with others. This is part of the great mystery Paul tells us not to be ignorant of.

There is another mystery. A number of years ago I had done a thorough study of the Quran and I had many questions. I went to the Muslims. "Why is it," I asked, "that in the Quran, it says if you have any doubt about these words, go to the Scriptures before you and confirm them, but Muslims do not read the Bible?"

"Because," they answered, "the Bible has been changed." They said Muslim scholars had assumed the Bible and the Quran were the same until 90 years after the books of the Quran had been compiled and published. Then they went back to the Bible and saw there were differences in the accounts of Jesus, the trinity, and even heaven. The conclusion they came to was that Christians must have changed the Bible.

Of course I could not accept that explanation, but I felt in my heart that there must be some other explanation. What was it?

Some of the questions that come up in Christian-Muslim dialogue are: Does the Quran talk about a triune God? Is it permissible for a Muslim to read the Bible? Did Jesus talk from the cradle? Did Jesus, as a young boy, make a clay bird come alive? Would an honorable prophet of God like Jesus ever be allowed to die a shameful death such as crucifixion? Was Jesus raised from the dead, or was it a substitute on the cross? Will Huris serve men in heaven? Are Huris physically sexual beings? Many people take these issues very seriously.

The Quran seemed to be in line with the theology of Christ when I read it. I felt as though I was getting a digested coverage and was constantly being referred back to the Bible. Was it possible in Muhammad's day that Christian writings were common knowledge and the Muslims considered the Quran *God's last revelation to mankind*, as they still do today? Was it Muhammad's desire that his people be a *people of the Book* also? It would have made sense considering it took the Christians almost 700 years to come up with an Arabic Bible. The Bible was not translated into Arabic, which was the closest language to Hebrew, until after Islam was well established. With the creative style of writing in the Middle East I knew the differing details of the Bible stories would not concern Easterners as it would Westerners. Even with all this I had a feeling there was something we didn't know. What was it the Quran was referring to when it said, "That which the People of the Book differ among themselves."

I started to read everything I could get my hands on about church history and the theology of Christ. People around me didn't understand why I was searching like that. My Christian friend Debra said, "What is it with you, can't you just believe it?"

I answered, "This does not have to do with believing, there is something more that I don't know."

She sighed, "Maybe it's your Muslim background."

My brother John, who is a missionary in Irian Jaya was home on furlough and I questioned him. "Wasn't Jesus a man while he was on earth?"

"Yes of course; he was very, very human."

"Then why is it that Christians seem to get nervous when you mention that?"

John turned and gave me a long look and then said, "I guess it's because most Christians knowledge on the theology of Christ is quite limited."

I continued to search. I found a few good books like *The Everlasting Man* by G.K. Chesterton, and read the book of Hebrews in the Bible over and over.

One day a friend of mine gave me a bag of old books. She said, "Here, why don't you see if these would be of any interest to you, you are into this stuff." I opened the bag and took the books out one by one. I read the titles: *The Book Nobody Knows, When God was Man,* and *The Meaning of Christ*. These books were published in the 1920's and 40's. "Maybe these will give me the answers I've been looking for," I thought. I read them eagerly, and *The Meaning of Christ* seemed like the perfect book to base my theology of Christ on. It even had a chapter called: the ragged edge of blasphemy. That thought assured me I wouldn't miss a bit of the theology of Christ.

I thought maybe I should show it to my Bible study lecturer and see what she thought about it. I waited for her evaluation; if she didn't affirm it, I could be back to start again.

She brought the book and said, "This is a wonderful book; too bad it's out of print."

The author of *The Meaning of Christ,* Doctor Robert Johnson said:

> *The church has always been squeamish about attempts to psychoanalyze Jesus, or to simplify him by an identification of what in him was divine and what was human. The framers of the early creeds pointedly refused to be lured into this temptation, and in grateful awe they affirmed the mystery that he is very God and very Man.*

Dr. Johnson gave a beautiful analogy about Jesus. He suggested that seeing God in Jesus is like looking through a window seeing a garden. If we focus too much on the window, the garden will be a confused mass of color. In the same way we must look through Jesus to see God. There is only one God; that is the hypothesis of Christianity. We must not make Christ another God besides God and we should in no way substitute him for God. This is the way Muslims often feel when they go to some churches. They feel the church is so into Jesus that it has forgotten about God. In the evangelical community today it is popular to say, "I believe Jesus is God." That shows you have the right theology. But that is a gross oversimplification of who Jesus is and it is very misunderstood by Muslims.

In an attempt to balance these spiritual concepts about Jesus, the early churches made statements of faith, called creeds. They all said, "Jesus was very God and very man." The creeds were not so much a statement about what they did believe but rather boundaries to what they didn't believe. Why did they find it necessary to say *Jesus was very God and very man*, and what laid beyond the boundaries of what the church didn't believe? These were questions that were still unanswered for me.

I was at a writer's colony, Hedgebrook Cottages, on Whidbey Island, Washington. In the evening I would have supper at the farmhouse with four other writers. We would discuss our writings and our spiritual experiences. There was quite a nice library in the sitting room and one of the other writers said, "Judith, here's a book you might enjoy reading." It was called *The Gnostic Gospels,* by Elaine Pagels. I took it to my cottage and read it and immediately knew this is what I had been looking for. This book told what had been outside the boundaries of the early creeds. I went back to the writers and told them what a valuable resource they had shown me. They asked, "Haven't you read the Dead Sea Scrolls and the book called *The Lost Books of the Bible*?" I was very embarrassed to admit that our church had not ever mentioned these writings, but assured them I would read them all.

The Gnostic Gospels told a story about an Arab peasant that had found a large earthenware jar buried outside the town of Naj Hammadi, near the Nile River in Egypt. Inside the jar were 13 papyrus books, bound in leather. The peasant was quite disappointed, expecting something more valuable, like gold. He took them home and his wife used some of them to start the fires in the hearth. Thirteen of the books eventually ended up at an antique dealer. Some of the books were sold on the black market, but most of them were placed in the Coptic Museum in Cairo, Egypt. The books were found in 1946 but never really entered the public domain until 1972 and 1977.

The Coptics were the Egyptian Christians and the books had to be translated from their unique language. In an effort to free themselves from the cumbersome hieroglyphic writing, the Coptic Christians wrote their spoken Arab language in Greek letters. They added seven letters to accommodate for the extra sounds not present in Greek. This combination of two languages was mainly used by the Christian Arabs and whomever they shared with.

Scholars of religious history were very excited about this find. Historical writings of the early church had mentioned the heresy of the gnostics, but these 13 books were like the last pieces of the puzzle. These texts were outlawed as heresy by the church in the late second century, but many copies were secretly kept in monasteries for study until at least the fourth century, and who knows, maybe longer. One such monastery was St. Pachomius, near the cliff where these papyrus texts may have been secretly buried by the monks when Athanasius, powerful Archbishop of Alexandria, ordered a purge on all *apocryphal books* of heresy. Scholars feel these texts were preserved in this earthen jar for up to 1600 years. [2]

What is in these texts that was so threatening to the orthodox church? Are these books the answer to what was and is beyond the boundaries of the Christian creeds? Yes, they are.

The gnostic gospels, it seems were written by followers of the disciples and other early church scholars. The sect developed out of a desire to *know oneself* in a more mystical way. They believed *self knowledge* was knowledge of God. They wanted to discover the divine from within. They felt ignorance, rather than sin was the cause of suffering. They understood the gospel not as a set of answers, but the beginning of a search. To know oneself at the deepest level was called *gnosis*. They expressed their gnosis through poems, new myths, conversations with Christ, and accounts of visions. It was a form of creative writing. Some of these writings were beautiful elaborations of spiritual concepts. One text called *The Authoritative Teaching* describes the soul seeking God:

...the rational soul who wearied herself in seeking—she learned about God. She labored with inquiring, enduring distress in body, wearing out her feet after the evangelist, learning about the Inscrutable One...She came to rest in him who is at rest. She reclined in her bedchamber. She ate of the banquet for which she had hungered...She found what she had sought. [3]

I actually identified a bit with that poor soul.

Unfortunately, many of the writings did pass over the boundaries of the church creeds and into heresy, even though the names of many of the books were very credible. The Gospel of Thomas is probably the most famous one, and there was the Gospel of Mary Magdalene, The Gospel of Phillip, The Letter of Phillip to Peter, The Gospel of Truth, and more. Religious scholars feel the books show influence of Egyptian, Babylonian, Jewish, Persian, and Greek mythology or mysticism. Edward Cronze, a British scholar of Buddhism said that there was evidence of Buddhist contact with Thomas Christians in India. The Gospel of Thomas indicates the believer and Christ receiving their being from the same source:

Jesus said, "I am not your master. Because you have drunk, you have become drunk from the bubbling stream which I have measured out.... He who will drink from my mouth will become as I am: I myself shall become he, and the things that are hidden will be revealed to him." [4]

There were also other elaborations such as describing Jesus as the reader's spiritual *twin brother*. Women were given mystical characteristics or scorned. Sexual metaphors were used to describe spiritual experiences. The only examples we would have anywhere near that kind of literature is Ezekial 16 and the book of Hosea, in the Bible. We must try to understand that the world was in a state of enormous transition from paganism to Christianity. Even the Israelites, who introduced monotheism to the world, had been infiltrated by pagan gods and mythology. In I Kings, chapter 11 it tells how Solomon married women who worshiped other gods and at their request, he built high places for Chemosh and Molech; detestable gods of Moab and the Ammonites. In verse 5 it says he followed Ashtoreth, the goddess of the Sidonians. Because of these pagan influences, the Christian Gnostic sect was a great threat to the early church.

Irenaeus, the orthodox Bishop of Lyons was not as worried about what they had already written as he was about what they were going to come up with next, and who was to be the authority. In the year a.d. 180 Irenaeus said, "Heretics boast they possess more gospels than there really are." Irenaeus complained that in his time such writings had already won wide circulation—from Gual to Rome, Greece, and Asia Minor. [5] This may be the explanation for the church's authoritarian attitude that developed into repression in later years.

Let us look at a number of controversies between the Gnostics and the Orthodox Church. Some scholars feel the Christian creed: "I believe in one God, Father Almighty, maker of heaven and earth" was made to exclude a heretic Marcion (a.d. 140) and his followers. Marcion saw a contrast between the war-faring God of the Old Testament and the loving God of the New Testament and concluded there must be two gods. [6] This certainly did explain the *differences between the people of the book* the Quran referred to.

This could explain the Muslim's objection to the trinity. In Surah 4:171, the three natures of the trinity are described:

> *The Messiah, Jesus son of Mary, was only a messenger of God, and His word which he conveyed unto Mary, and a spirit from Him.*

The nature of the trinity is peppered throughout this objective statement about Jesus. He is called God's word, the Messiah, Jesus son of Mary, and the Spirit.

If the Arabs of the day had heard gospels from the gnostics passed down from generation to generation, they would have gotten a different version of the trinity. One controversy during early Christianity was God the father, God the mother, or both. The monotheistic religions of today; Judaism, Christianity, and Islam are quick to point out that God is not of any gender. But many people feel God is portrayed as masculine. Although Mary is called mother of God by Catholics she is never called God, the mother. The gnostic's Apocryphon of John has a mystical vision of the trinity:

> *The (heavens were opened and the whole) creation (which is) under heaven shone and (the world) trembled. (And I was afraid, and I) saw in the light....a likeness with multiple forms...and the likeness had three forms.*

To John's question the vision answers:
"He said to me John, John why do you doubt, and why are you afraid?....I am the one who (is with you) always. I (am the Father); I am the Mother; I am the Son." [7]

They had another version of the trinity. The secret book of John:

....he said... "I am a jealous God and there is no other God beside me." But by announcing this he indicated to the angels...that another God does exist; for if there were no other one, of whom would he be jealous?....Then the mother began to be distressed. [8]

The superior female God often humiliated the male God; like in the Hypostasis of the Archons:

...he became arrogant, saying, "It is I who am God, and there is no other apart from me."...and a voice came forth from above the realm of absolute power, saying, "you are wrong Samael" (which means God of the blind). And he said, "If any other thing exists before me, let it appear to me!" And immediately, Sophia ("Wisdom") stretched forth her finger, and introduced light into matter, and she followed it down into the region of Chaos.. ...And he again said to his offspring, "It is I who am the God of all." And Life, the daughter of Wisdom, cried out; she said to him, "you are wrong, Saklas." [9]

This would explain why Muhammad may have had the impression that some Christians believed the trinity was God, Jesus, and Mary. The author of *Islam Revealed*, Dr. Anis Shorrosh also speaks of the heretic Mariamites, who had made Jesus the son and God the husband. [10]

Was it possible that Christian writings outside the canon of the Bible could have been passed along the trade routes by the Arabs? The Egyptians were fellow Arabs. Even if the books had been banned, the Arabs were great story tellers; as they are today. The Quran would have been right to condemn this heresy. In Surah V:116 Allah asks,

O Jesus, son of Mary! Didst thou say unto mankind: Take me and my mother for two gods beside Allah?

The orthodox church reacted violently to the gnostic writings. Bishop Irenaeus admitted many women were attracted to the gnostic congregations. The orthodox church had even lost the wife of a deacon to a gnostic church. This clarifies some of Paul's seemingly contradictory statements about women. The first years after Christ's life on earth women were active in leadership positions in the church but this may be about the time Paul writes his prickly passages about women in the Bible. It was a time of great social change and the coming together of many diverse cultures.

Jesus speaking from the cradle is another phenomenon in the Quran that has puzzled Christians. There are two sources of early Christian writings that give an account of Jesus speaking from the cradle, *The Gnostic Gospels* and *The Lost Books of the Bible.*

The Egyptian gnostic teacher Valentinus said he first experienced Paul's teaching through a vision, and Jesus the infant talks to him:

He saw a new born infant and when he asks who he might be, the child answered, "I am the Logos." [11]

The story of Jesus speaking from the cradle is also found in The first Gospel of the INFANCY of JESUS CHRIST, chapter 1:1-3:

The following accounts we found in the book of Joseph the high-priest, called by some Caiaphas: He relates, that Jesus spake even when he was in the cradle, and said to his mother: Mary, I am Jesus the Son of God, that word which thou didst bring forth according to the declaration of the angel Gabriel to thee, and my father hath sent me for the salvation of the world. [12]

The Quran gives similar accounts of Jesus speaking from the cradle, first in Surah III:46:

He will speak unto mankind in his cradle and in his manhood, and he is of the righteous.

Secondly, in Surah XIX:29-33:

Then she pointed to him. They said How can we talk to one who is in the cradle, a young boy? He spake: Lo! I am the slave of Allah. He hath given me the Scripture and hath appointed me a Prophet, And hath made me blessed wheresoever I may be, and hath enjoined upon me prayer and almsgiving so long as I remain alive, And (hath made me) dutiful toward her who bore me, and hath not made me arrogant, unblest. Peace on me the day I was born, and the day I die, and the day I shall be raised alive!

Another story about Jesus' childhood in the Quran talks about Jesus making a clay bird come alive. Ancient Christian writings also had that story. The first Gospel of the INFANCY of JESUS CHRIST, chapter XV:1,2,6 says:

And when the Lord Jesus was seven years of age, he was on a certain day with other boys his companions about the same age. Who when they were at play, made clay into several shapes...He had also made the figures of birds and sparrows, which, when he commanded to fly, did fly, and when he commanded to stand still, did stand still; and if he gave them meat and drink, they did eat and drink. [13]

The Quran, Surah V:110 has God reminding Jesus of this incident:

....how thou didst shape of clay as it were the likeness of a bird by My permission, and dids't blow upon it and it was a bird by My permission....

The orthodox church reacted violently to the teaching that Jesus was half human and half divine; therefore he did not really suffer on the cross. The gnostic's *Second Treatise of the Great Seth* says:

It was another...who drank the gall and the vinegar; it was not I. They struck me with the reed; it was another, Simon, who bore the cross of his shoulder. It was another upon whom they placed the crown of thorns. But I was rejoicing in the height over....their error...And I was laughing at their ignorance. [14]

The *Apocalypse of Peter* was a similar interpretation of the living Jesus laughing above the cross with a substitute dying. With this in mind let us look at Surah IV:157 in the Quran:

And because of their saying: We slew the Messiah Jesus son of Mary, Allah's messenger—they slew him not nor crucified, but it appeared so unto them; and lo! those who disagree concerning it are in doubt thereof; they have no knowledge thereof save pursuit of a conjecture; they slew him not for certain.

Muslim theologians differ in their interpretation of this verse. Was it possible Muhammad had heard gnostic Christians give this account of how Christ's spirit separated from his body, or that another took his place, and he himself did not suffer? On the other hand, this verse could also agree with the Christian interpretation that the Jews were bragging that they had gotten rid of Jesus, but they were only used to carry out a divine plan. God was in control of Jesus' mission to die as the perfect sacrifice for forgiveness of man's sin. Christians believe Jesus went to the cross himself, died, and suffered as a man. This is a great inspiration to Christians in that he completely identified with men and their suffering. If we really want to get technical, the Romans crucified him, not the Jews. Again, in the Quran, Surah XIX:34 Jesus confirms his own death and resurrection:

> *Peace on me the day I was born, and the day I die, and the day I shall be raised alive!*

The orthodox church reacted to the heresy that Christ did not suffer on the cross. One church patriarch, Tertullian, traces this heresy to the time of Roman persecution of Christians. Christians were being put in the arena to be eaten alive by wild beasts, tortured, crucified, or beheaded. The church felt the Christians endured suffering through identifying with Christ's suffering on the cross and claimed the blood of martyrs as the seed of the church. Rightfully so, the people watching the Christians die brave deaths were so impressed that they also wanted to join their faith. It was also understandable that some Christians were so afraid that they developed a theology to excuse themselves.

Some gnostics actually did not think things should be settled in such a violent way. At this time, many Christians fled to Persia and started what became a large group of Christians called Nestorians. It stands to reason that the outside persecution from the government would add to the internal organizational problems of the early church.

Probably the most difficult issue that has surfaced when Christians read the Quran is the reference to Huris in heaven. Huris are Eastern mythical characters. They are beautiful wide-eyed females that carry a flask and serve a drink. In Persian poetry the Sufis refer to the Saqis, which are also beautiful ladies serving a drink. The terms Huri and Saqi are often used interchangeably with angels, or the spirit of God who communicates a message. The drink is wine; it is symbolic of the Spirit of God which produces a feeling of being filled with the Spirit. The Sufis were Muslims and alcohol is absolutely forbidden in Islam.

One day we received a card from Iran with a photo of a beautiful painting. It was a miniature painting and quite difficult to see. Miniature artists paint with a magnifying glass and many of them go blind after years of this profession. I saw the picture had a mud man and seven beautiful black haired women with wings standing around him. They were trying to stick a red heart on this mud man's chest. One of the black haired, winged beauties had run to an ornately decorated building with a cup in her hand.

I got out my magnifying glass and took a closer look. I saw that the beautiful woman knocking on the door was weeping! I said, "Bahram, look at this painting, it looks like a story. Do you know what it is?" He thought for a couple of days and finally remembered the poetry of Hafez, an Iranian poet who rewrote the Quran in poetry. He found the story of this painting and here is the translation:

Last night I dreamed that angels stood outside the tavern door, and knocked in vain, and wept; They took the clay of Adam, and, it looked like, moulded a clay cup while all heavenly beings slept.

Oh dwellers of the Hall of Chastity!

Bring love's passionate red wine to me, because Adam is dust, and only your spirit is life.

For God's love was too much for heaven to bear, so he looked for a messenger elsewhere.

and because of Adam, my name is written in the book of Life.

Between my Lord and me such intimacy lies, that it makes the Huris glad in Paradise.

They flit through green grass with songs of praise.

But a hundred fantasies of things and desire overwhelm me, and Father Adam goes astray, tempted by one poor grain of corn.

But through his search and God's grace, the soft breath of truth reaches his ears.

For there are seventy-two differing doctrines he hears, and tempting untruths call him endlessly.

But that is not the fame of Love's true fire which makes the candlelight shadows dance in rings.

But to the warmth a moth is drawn in desire, and he is sent forth with scorched and drooped wings.

This poem talks of Huris trying to help God create Adam. They realize that they don't have the necessary ingredient, which is God's spirit. One of the Huris has gone to the building where God dwells (called the halls of chastity) with her cup to get it filled. She is knocking on the door and weeping because no one has answered the door and she knows without God's spirit the mud man can never live. [15]

This wonderfully creative poem has altered details but the spiritual concept is there: only through receiving God's spirit can humans, made of dust, have life. The Psalmist in Chapter 116, verse 13 says:

I will lift up the cup of salvation and call on the name of the Lord.

I have heard Christians say that Muhammad and the Quran promised sex in heaven. That is not true. The Quran does not say anywhere that anyone will have sex with Huris. Surah XLIII:70 says believers will enter the garden with their wives and that they will be glad. Surah XLIV:54 says believers will be wed to Huris. Huris are described as chaste companions in some places, and in other places called the fair ones with wide lovely eyes. Now some people may immediately think of sex because humans relate in a very physical realm, but that is not what the Quran says.

No one really knows what the activities will be with husband and wife in heaven. Some people believe relationships will have spiritual significance, rather than physical significance. The joy of the sexual relationship here on earth may be only a taste of the ecstasy of the spiritual relationship we will have with God in heaven. To others, that may be disappointing. The Bible says believers will be like angels. One Arab friend read the verses about Huris, and said, "To me, this means if someone doesn't have anyone in heaven, there will be spares." Most Muslims do not believe it has any sexual implication, rather it is symbolic of an emotional benefit in heaven; there will be no loneliness in heaven, for women as well as men.

Like one Arab Christian said to me, "No one really knows exactly what is going to be in heaven; we just know God will be there and we want to be there too." Surah XLIV:57 in the Quran does say the supreme triumph of heaven is the bounty from thy Lord.

We know it is possible to misinterpret scriptures because we have seen it done with the "health and wealth" theory in Christianity. It is very effective persuasion to promise people all the physical benefits they ever dreamed about if they just live for God, but it is not spiritual truth. The Quranic verses about Huris have no doubt been conveniently used for persuading men to do monumental feats of bravery, but extra meaning has certainly been read into the passages.

In the church of the first century there were writings about virgins in heaven. Hermes, brother of Pius, bishop of Rome, wrote the book of *Hermes*. It was read publicly in the churches as an extra writing, not included in the canon of the Bible. Hermes had a vision of heaven, and in the third part, *Similitude IX*, he is taken by the Angel of Repentance and introduced to 12 virgins whose names are Faith, Continence, Power, Patience, Simplicity, Innocence, Chastity, Cheerfulness, Truth, Understanding, Concord, and Charity. The angel leaves Hermes alone with the virgins while he goes to take care of other business:

So I remained with those virgins: now they were cheerful and courteous unto me; especially the four, which seemed to be the chiefest among them...Thou shalt sleep with us as a brother, not as a husband: for thou art our brother, and we are ready from henceforth to dwell with thee; for thou art very dear to us. 100. Howbeit I was ashamed to continue with them. But she that seemed to be the chiefest amongst them, embraced me, and began to kiss me. And the rest when they saw that I was kissed by her, began also to kiss me as a brother; and led me about the tower, and played with me. 101 Some of them also sung psalms, others made up the chorus with them. But I walked about the tower with them, rejoicing silently, and seeming to myself to be grown young again. 102. When the evening came on, I would forthwith have gone home, but they withheld me, and suffered me not to depart. Wherefore I continued with them that night near the same tower. 103 So they spread their linen garments upon the ground; and placed me in the middle, nor did they anything else, only they prayed. 104 I also prayed with them without ceasing, nor less than they. Who when they saw me pray in that manner, rejoiced greatly; and I continued there with them till the next day. 105 And when we had worshipped God, then the shepherd came and said unto them: You have done no injury to this man. They answered, Ask him. I said unto him, Sir, I have received a great deal of satisfaction in that I have remained with them. 106 And he said unto me, How didst thou sup? I answered, Sir, I feasted the whole night upon the words of the Lord. They received thee well then, said he; I said, Sir very well.

Later, *The Lost Books of the Bible* says these books were hidden away for 1500 years, and only translated and made available in this century. [16]

The institution of the church with her Bishops, creeds, and canons, was not able to bring the gnostics under her authority but she successfully forced them underground by the fourth century. It is possible that gnostic texts were successfully hidden in Eastern churches and monasteries after the year a.d. 400. The Naj Hammadi find is evidence of that.

The Eastern church broke from the Western church in the late fourth century. The Council of Chalcedon alienated Monophysite believers in Syria and Egypt. The Monophysite doctrine originated in Constantinople (Turkey). They claimed Jesus the man was independent of Jesus the eternal Word, therefore Mary could not be called the Mother of God. Of course, the Pope in Rome's reaction to that led to the break of the Eastern church. For 250 years the Byzantine patriarchs tried to reconcile the Eastern Monophysites but were unable to do so. [9] By a.d. 570 when Muhammad was born, the church was already split into the Western church and the Eastern church. Muhammad had established contact with Christians and the Quran mentions the differences among the *People of the Book* repeatedly. With Egypt and Arabia being neighbors, and having such similar cultures, chances are Muhammad heard more of the Eastern Church's side of the story. *The Gnostic Gospels*, also called the *Naj Hammadi library,* and the writings of early Christian authorities found in the *Lost Books of the Bible* have helped us understand what some of those differences were.

Looking back at ancient Christian writings from the first century church gives us insights into the writing styles of the day. Many of the themes in the Quran that seem so foreign to us were present in earlier religious writings.

Notes:

1. A. W. Tozer, *That Incredible Christian*, (Harrisburg, Pennsylvania: Christian Publications, Inc., 1964), p. 23.

2. Elaine Pagels, *The Gnostic Gospels*, (New York: Vintage Books, 1981) pp. xi-xiii.

3. Ibid., p. 135.

4. Ibid., p. xx.

5. Ibid., p. xv.

6. Ibid., p. 33.

7. Ibid., p. 18 or 61.

8. Ibid., p. 69.

9. Ibid., p. 70.

10. Dr. Anis A. Shorrosh, *Islam Revealed, A Christian Arab's View of Islam* (Nashville: Thomas Nelson's Publishers, 1988), p. 114.

11. Pagels, p. 23.

12. *The Lost Books of The Bible* (New York: Bell Publishing Co, 1979), p. 38.

13. Ibid., p. 52.

14. Pagels, p.

15. G. M. L. Bell, trans., *Selected Sonnets from Divan of Hofez.* (Tehran, Iran: Eghbal Publications, 1986) p. 23, my changes from old English to more familiar vocabulary.

16. *The Lost Books of the Bible*, p. 254.

AMERICAN CHRISTIANS IN THE MIDDLE EAST PROCESS

When the church aligns itself politically, it gives priority to the compromises and temporal successes of the political world rather than its Christian confession of eternal truth.   --Charles Colson

Pain and suffering will come to every human being who employs himself in evil—Jews first, but Gentiles as well; renown, honor and peace will come to everyone who does good—Jews first, but Gentiles as well. God has no favorites.   --Romans 2: 9-11

My brother was in town visiting and he mentioned there was a church in our city that he had heard was very dynamic. "Could we visit it this Sunday?" he asked. We all agreed and attended that very next Sunday.

It was promotional Sunday and all of the teachers were sitting at tables signing people up for their classes. We were invited to a Wednesday evening class called *The Middle East in the End Times.*

We called our Arab friend Saed, and invited him to come with us. Saed asked, "They won't mind if I'm Muslim will they?"

"Of course not," I said, "we all worship the same God."

This class was to have a number of guest speakers and the first speaker started out by saying, "We are living in the end times. That is evident by the fact that the Jews are all returning to the new state of Israel. The Arabs will never live in peace with Israel. In Ezekial 38 it says Gog, of the land of Magog, is the enemy of God and its people will come from the north. This is the communist Soviet Regime. With the help of Iran, the Arab countries, Libya, and Ethiopia, this nation will attack Israel. This dispute will ultimately precipitate the battle of Armageddon. This last battle will be a nuclear holocaust, and will take place in the valley of Megiddo in Israel. There will be a remnant of Jews who will survive because they are God's chosen people."

Our friend Saed turned to us with a very alarmed look on his face. He raised his hand and asked, "Why do you think the Arabs will never live in peace with Israel? The Palestinians have already recognized Israel."

"No, the Arabs will never recognize Israel!"

Saed said, "That is not true, the Palestine Liberation Organization has put their past behind them. They first made a statement supporting United Nations resolution 242, and 338, recognizing Israel and denouncing terrorism on Nov. 15, 1988 at the Algiers declaration, and again on Dec. 13 and 14, 1988, at U.N. speeches in Geneva. In Stockholm, Dec. 7, 1988, the Palestinian National Council said it was ready to sit down at the table with whatever representatives Israel chooses to discuss their differences."

Then Saed asked, "You say the Jews are God's chosen people but what about the thousands of Christian and Muslim Palestinians who have been run out of their homes and killed? They are all worshipping God too."

All at once a man sitting in the row in front of us turned around and said, "Ishmael has been thrown out!"

After class, Saed was very distraught. "What do they mean Ishmael was thrown out; do they think God does not love Arabs anymore?"

"Saed," I said, "these people obviously do not understand that passage in the Bible. The only reason Abraham put Ishmael out was because God promised He would take care of Ishmael. Isaac was to carry the bloodline to the Messiah. But God loved Ishmael and all men equally. He promised to make him a great nation, and He did. Look at all of the poetry, the music, and the mathematics we have learned from the Arabs. They are a great people. Saed, the book of Romans, in the New testament says "...they are not all Israel, which are of Israel." Galations 3:9,28,29 says that those who believe are blessed with Abraham...There is neither Jew nor Greek (the Lamza Bible says *Aramaean*), there is neither bond nor free, there is neither male nor female: for ye are all one in Christ Jesus. And if ye be Christ's, then are ye Abraham's seed, and heirs according to the promise."

The speaker approached us and asked, "Are you people from the Middle East?"

"Some of us are," I answered, "and my friend here feels you are prejudicing people against Arabs."

"Well, I realize this is not very good news for the Arabs," He answered. "But we take God's word literally here."

"But sir, the Bible literally says in Isaiah 54:7 and Romans 10:15 that the gospel is supposed to be good news for all people. God so loved the world, and what you told us tonight is a modern day interpretation of prophesy."

"Sir," broke in Saed, "this kind of teaching just encourages the kind of massacre of Palestinians that happened last month in Jerusalem."

The speaker said, "That happened because Palestinian terrorists attacked the Jewish worshippers at the Wailing Wall."

"Where did you receive that information?" asked Saed.

"From Christian radio."

"Then your Christian radio is wrong, I will tell you the truth about what happened." And this is the side of the story Saed told us.

The evening of October 8, 1990, three Jewish political groups met in the northern outskirts of Jerusalem to organize a march for the following day. Many religious pilgrims were in town because of a major Jewish holiday, the Feast of the Tabernacles. Many secular Jewish groups take advantage of these religious holidays to hold anti-Arab demonstrations. The next day, the march started about five o'clock in the morning and proceeded to all parts of the city, including the Arab sections in East Jerusalem. The police stopped all Arab traffic to let the Jewish marchers, who were screaming anti-Arab slogans pass. Even some of the Soviet immigrants were getting right into the swing of things.

Twice a year, during the Tabernacles and the Passover holidays, these marches pass through all the streets of Jerusalem. This one was as violent as usual. Groups of settlers, religious youth organizations and various right wing groups attacked the Arab section of the Old City, breaking windows and cursing Islam and Christianity. One particular group called the *Temple Mount Faithful* was on its usual procession to enter the grounds of the two Muslim Mosques and set the corner stone for the Jewish temple. This activity has been banned by the Israeli government because members of this group have repeatedly tried to destroy the Al Aqsa Mosque and the Dome of the Rock, sacred to one billion Muslims in the world.

That same morning, about 8 a.m., a group of 20,000 Jewish

worshippers were gathered at the Wailing Wall (believed to be the ruins of the second temple that was destroyed by the Romans in a.d. 70) for a religious ceremony. This ceremony was watched by Palestinians above the Wailing Wall, but proceeded in an orderly fashion and was dismissed at 9:30 a.m. The crowd dispersed. At 10:15 the area before the Wailing Wall was largely deserted. About this same time the marchers reached the area and marched to the Spring of Shiliah, located near Silwan, an Arab neighborhood. The Jewish marchers and the Silwan Arabs started screaming abuses at each other and a Muezzin from the Silwan mosque started calling "Allah Akbar" (God is Great) from the loudspeaker to distract the angry people.

All week Palestinian Muslims had been persuading people to come and defend the Dome of the Rock and Al Aqsa Mosque from the *Temple Mount Faithful*, so there were 3000 Palestinians inside the walls of the Haram Al-Sharif (Noble Sanctuary) compound. When they heard the Silwan Muezzin give the call, the Muslims thought the attack on their mosques had begun. Also hearing the call, Israeli police started shooting tear gas into the Haram Al-Sharif compound; and it landed next to some Palestinian women. One hundred to two hundred Palestinians then rushed toward the Police, picked up stones from a near by construction site and threw them at their attackers. To try and stop the violence the larger group of Palestinians made a human chain between the police and the stone-throwing Palestinians. At this point the police shot three Palestinian youth, one of which was holding tight in the human chain. The police were outnumbered so they retreated from the compound.

At 11:00, the Imam on the loud-speaker called, "Move inside the mosques...Al Haram is a place for worship, not for fighting...there are dead and wounded." [1] The Palestinians ran into the Haram Al-Sharif compound and locked the gates. Military reinforcements soon arrived, border guards, police and secret police in civilian clothing broke the gates down and proceeded to shoot Palestinians for almost two hours. The Imam continued begging for the Palestinian lives on his loudspeaker, "Captain of police, stop the shooting and come to talk with us. We don't want bloodshed. We need medical assistance. The responsibility for the shooting is on the shoulders of the police."

Within 15 minutes, ambulances started coming to take the wounded to the hospital. The ambulance crew said there was tear gas everywhere and there was shooting coming from every direction. A nurse was told only to treat the seriously wounded, although she said they themselves needed treatment for the tear gas. Groups of terrified Palestinian volunteers came to help the ambulance crew. The Israeli police started shooting the volunteers and ambulance crew. Fatmah, a nurse, gives this account from her hospital bed:

The first was a young man shot in the face. Then they brought us a man who had been shot in the chin. The third was hit in the shoulder. The fourth man was very serious. He had been shot in the back and the bullet came out of his stomach. The last one had been hit in the head. He was bleeding profusely from his right eyeball. I put my hand over his eye socket and blood began pouring out of his mouth. I put my other hand over his mouth and blood started coming out of his ear. After several minutes, I discovered he had no pulse...I went to give oxygen to the man shot in the back and then something happened to my arm. I fell to the floor of the ambulance. I didn't realize what had happened at first but when I looked down, I noticed that my right arm was dangling and there was blood everywhere. I screamed to Eissa, the other staff nurse, for help. I thought we were going to die so I began praying. [2]

The Ambulance doctor, Dr. Tareq Abu Al-Hawa, realized Fatmah had been injured so decided to start back for the hospital immediately. As they started out, Israeli police riddled their ambulance with machine gun fire. Fatmah was then hit three more times in the chest; Eissa received wounds in the throat and abdomen. The wounded passengers were hit again and Dr. Tareq Abu Al-Hawa was shot in the ankle. Another staff worker at the hospital said he made a second trip with this same ambulance, even though it was already full of blood and the windshield was shattered. He also was hit with two plastic bullets which shattered in his leg. He said they were all dressed in clearly marked white medical uniforms, so there was no doubt that the Israeli police knew they were medical staff. While this was all going on, the Imam kept calling from the mosque, "Don't you know the meaning of mercy? Stop shooting! Stop killing! Stop the massacre!"

Back at the hospital, Palestinians gathered and every time a death was announced, they chanted, "God is Great, with spirit and blood we redeem you, oh martyr." In response to these outbursts of grief, Israeli soldiers shot tear gas through the maternity ward windows. Hospital staff rushed in to evacuate newborn babies. [3]

In America, news agencies reported that Israeli police shot at Palestinian terrorists because they were throwing rocks on the worshippers at the Wailing Wall. This was the official report from the Israeli government. Reports from four Palestinian and Jewish human rights groups, many eyewitnesses, and three video tapes revealed the Israeli version was wrong. The Palestinians charged that the Israeli police initiated and killed Arabs in cold blood.

Three amateur cameramen had filmed the entire sequence of events, and the UN Security Council representatives viewed one of the videotapes. The Security council passed a resolution calling for a UN investigation of the massacre; Prime Minister Yitzhak Shamir refused them permission and said the Israeli government was doing its own investigation. Of course, the result of the investigation came out the same except they admitted that the police had used excessive force. One of the police charged with the killings, Aryeh Bibi, was promoted to full commander of the Israeli Police Manpower Division.

An American reporter and journalist instructor, Michael Emery of Los Angeles, flew to Jerusalem and viewed the three video tapes personally and made these statements:

Palestinians did not hurl stones on Jewish worshippers; Israeli police initiated the conflict with Palestinians; Palestinians, fleeing from Israeli police bullets, picked stones from a construction site and tossed them in the direction of their attackers. Many of these fell in the vicinity of the Western Wall, but there were few, if any Jewish worshippers still there when the first stones fell. [4]

Dr. Israel Shahak, chairman of the Israel League for Human and Civil Rights in Jerusalem, said the Israeli government was expecting trouble on this Jewish holiday, but was short of police because of all the protest demonstrations and other forms of civil disobedience by Palestinians. Israeli Prime Minister Yitzhak Shamir ordered the police to render rapid suppression of any riots in the city. To make up for the shortage, they assigned the *Special Police Unit* trained in karate and Israeli methods of breaking bones and in hitting the sensitive parts of the body. Their purpose is to cause maximum pain without killing. This group is called out to deal with the worst Jewish criminals, and Palestinian Arabs. Dr. Shahak says this mass murder on Temple Mount can only be understood in terms of the racism and oppression experienced by Palestinians in the occupied territories. Palestinian casualties were 18 dead and 350 to 400 injured. He said by the small number of injuries on the Israeli side, it was obvious there were no stones thrown on Jewish worshippers. [5]

The remaining Palestinians in the compound were handcuffed and set in the hot sun for hours. Some Palestinians had remained in the mosques. Many of them were also taken into custody by the police for God knows what punishment.

Faisal Husseini is chairman of the Arab Studies Institute in Jerusalem and very influential among Palestinians in the occupied territories. He is one of the Palestinian representatives for the Israeli-Palestinian Peace talks. Husseini is said to be at the top of an assassination hit list among Israeli extremists and is, with a few other Palestinians, living under heavy guard. Husseini was there the day of the Temple Mount (Haram Al-Sharif) massacre and was miraculously spared. He said as the bullets passed by his head, he said this prayer:

Lord, my breast is heavy with bitterness, let me not hate.

Lord, my heart is filled with pain, let me not avenge myself.

Lord, my soul is fearful, let not that fear turn into hatred.

Lord, my body is weak, let me not despair.

Lord, I am one of your worshippers standing at a crossroads. Sustain my strength.

Lord, to believe is to love, to forgive and never to doubt. Faith is a light that guides the way, do not extinguish that light.

Lord, protect our unarmed uprising and grant us the strength to resist striking back at those who hurt us.

Lord, we want only to be free and not to enslave others.

Lord, we seek a state to provide a home to which our dispersed people can return. We do not seek to destroy the states or homes of others.

Lord, we have nothing, except our faith in you.

Grant us the feeling of certainty. Grant us the will to stay.

Lord, let forgiveness and mercy suffuse us.

Let the blood spilled from our bodies strengthen us and fortify us against hatred and revenge.

Lord, hear my prayers.

Show my people and me the true path. [6]

We have heard it said that a Christian should be someone with a Bible in one hand and a news periodical in the other. Trying to make friends with a Middle Eastern Muslim and not understanding his grief about the Palestinian situation is impossible. It is being politically unaware. We can have all the knowledge about Islam but when they see we have no knowledge about the world around us, they doubt our simple solutions to all problems in general.

Muslims are confounded by the American Christian's silence at the persecution of the Jerusalem church in Israel. In April of 1990, 150 Jewish settlers moved into St. John's Hospice, a Greek-Orthodox group home. The hospice was located in the Christian section of East Jerusalem. It was half a block from the Church of the Holy Sepulchre and all three religious groups: Christians, Muslims and Jews, were outraged. One hundred fifty clergymen from nine major sects gathered to officially close the doors of the Church of the Holy Sepulchre, as well as the church of the Nativity and other religious sights, in a day long protest. The Nusseibeh family, the keepers of the keys of the church, said the church doors had not been closed for 800 years, since the Crusades. In an act of support for the protest, Muslim leaders closed the Al Aqsa Mosque and the Dome of the Rock to visitors. The takeover was even denounced by American government officials and American Jewish lobby groups.

This incident occurred during the height of tourist season, and the Greek Orthodox Church staged a protest in front of the hospice. A Greek Orthodox priest reached up to remove the star of David from above the door of the Christian hospice; Israeli police shot tear gas into the crowd. The elderly Greek Orthodox Patriarch, Diodoros I, fell down and the cross on his scepter was broken. The Israeli Supreme Court made a decision to evict the Jewish settlers but some remained, and are guarded by Israeli police.

An investigation showed that the Shamir government had put up $1.8 million in Israeli government money to help with the purchase, which was made from a drug dealer. It was supposedly purchased from a Panamanian man. [7] It would make sense that a building owned by the Greek Orthodox church would have been purchased from the church itself. It is this kind of underhanded dealing that has characterized much of the buying of Palestinian lands, because Palestinians do not want to sell their land.

Pastors in clerical garb from the Roman Catholic church and the Greek Orthodox church have been dragged through the streets and beaten by Israeli soldiers. Then when their congregations wanted to protest, the soldiers entered their mass and fired machine guns under the pews. Many Palestinians feel this persecution was related to the ordination in 1988 by the Pope John Paul II of Rev. Michael Sabbah as Roman Catholic patriarch of Jerusalem. Sabbah was the first Palestinian to be appointed to this post, and his ordination in Rome was the same day that one of the priests had been beaten.

After the shooting, the church leaders gathered and issued a statement of support for the Palestinian uprising. They called for Christians to hold a week of fasting and prayer for the grievous suffering of their people on the West Bank and Gaza, and for them to achieve their legal rights. Up until this time the church leaders had tried to stay out of this kind of controversy. Roman Catholic, Greek Orthodox, Armenian patriarches, Anglican, Lutheran, Greek and Syrian Catholic bishops, the leaders of the majority of the 200,000 Christians on the occupied territories, Israel, and Jordan were represented in this effort. The church was under attack. [8] Jerusalem Christians are being driven out by higher taxes, confiscation of property, closing of Palestinian Universities and discrimination in employment. In 1967 there were 14,000 Christians in Jerusalem, today there are only 10,000, and it is estimated that if their persecution continues there will only be 7000 left in five years. Christianity is being threatened with extinction in the Holy Land. [9]

American Churches give little notice of the suffering of 100,000 Christian Palestinians in Israel and the occupied territories. I grieved that Sunday in April of 1990 for the Jerusalem church. It was one week after Easter, when we had celebrated Christ rising from the tomb. There had been a very small article in the newspaper about the churches and mosques (in sympathy with the churches) being closed in Jerusalem after the hospice takeover. But American churches did not mention it. How is it we can pray for the peace of Jerusalem but not even acknowledge the Church of the Holy Sepulchre, site of the empty tomb of Jesus, is having a crisis? Are we so out of touch with the Eastern Christians who have kept the faith alive in that part of the world where Jesus walked and ministered to all people, that we don't even have one little prayer for them? This is why Muslims feel they are seeing a second crusades. During the Crusades, Christian Arabs claim they were treated just as badly as Muslims, just because they were Arabs.

Not all churches have ignored the Palestinian plight. Since Iraq's invasion of Kuwait, Pope John Paul II has taken a tough and realistic line on the 1991 Gulf conflict. Because of the Roman Catholic church in Jerusalem, the Pope has been more aware of Christian Palestinian's problems. The Vatican states the present conflict began with the settlement of European Jews in Palestine, the creation of the Israeli state after the European Holocaust and World War II, and with the mass expulsions of Palestinians. The Vatican refuses to recognize Israel until it redefines its own boundaries and addresses Palestinian rights. The Vatican's representative, Archbishop Renato Martino stated:

> *The Arab-Israeli conflict is the root issue underlying all Middle East strife. The Holy See insists on the urgency of finding a solution to the questions of Lebanon and Palestine while resolving the Persian Gulf Conflict. [10]*

Upon Golda Meir's visit to the Vatican in 1973, Pope Paul told her he found it hard to understand why the Jewish people, who are supposed to act mercifully, respond so fiercely in their own country. The Vatican persists in its policy of Palestinian rights, and international control- trusteeship of Jerusalem to be administered by the three monotheistic faiths. [11]

In 1989, the Executive Council of the Episcopal Diocese of Michigan submitted to Moshe Aumann, the Israeli Embassy's minister-counselor, a protest of human rights abuses in Israel. [12] Both the British and Netherlands council of Churches visited Israel to show solidarity with their Palestinian brothers and sisters. Anglican Bishop Samual spoke warmly of the Arabs and Jews who are coura-geously coming together and trying to build bridges of reconciliation despite the cost, noting that, "It is such people who hold the key to the future; for them we must pray." [13]

In June of 1990, the 202nd General Assembly of American Presbyterians reaffirmed the self-determination of Palestinians with full civil liberties for both Arabs and Jews. [14] Sam Bandela, regional director for Asia Habitat for Humanity is involved in a project for Palestinians and later for invaded, occupied, and war-torn Lebanon. [15]

New Zealand's Althea Campbell, Secretary of Christian World Service Information, visited the Holy Lands and then went on to visit the Middle East Council of Churches in Cyprus. Gabriel Habib, Secretary of MECC, said this to her:

The Jews believe they have a divine right to the land, and the Palestinians believe they have a human right, not only from possession of the land for thousands of years, but also given to them by modern international law. The Jews believe divine right is superior to human right. But as Christians, we believe God and the human being have been reconciled in Jesus Christ incarnate. Therefore the divine right and the human right have been reconciled.

Mr. Habib believes the Jews and Palestinians are both the children of Abraham. Now, that concept must be applied to the Israeli-Palestinian situation. [16]

The American Christian Fundamentalists and many Evangelicals have wholeheartedly and unconditionally supported the Zionist state of Israel. People have become confused about Zionism. I myself grew up in a Fundamentalist church and I know there are many sincere Christians who want to do their best for the Lord. I wondered how it was possible that people who were so kind hearted that they couldn't declaw a cat, could be so cold-hearted toward the Palestinian people.

As children, we were taught Biblical Zionism. It was a time when the Bible was interpreted more allegorically than literally. There was a time Zion and Jerusalem had more heavenly meanings and were for Christians to take for their own. We used to sing the old song, "We are marching to Zion, beautiful Zion, the beautiful city of God." This meant our life was a pilgrimage on earth and our real destination was heaven. Augustine's book, the *City of God* (a.d. 413-426), was allegorical. The aim of this book was to restore confidence in the Christian church which would take the place of the earthly power, Rome.

Augustine believed the role of government faded in the face of the importance of the salvation of the soul. Government is part of an earthly city, but our first allegiance was to the city of God. He believed the church was the historical representative of the Kingdom of God on earth. Augustine believed the first resurrection occurred with baptism, where the faithful are introduced into the Kingdom of God. In other words, the Kingdom has come, God's will should be done on earth as it is in heaven, through the church. He believed justice would be served with the witness of history. [17]

But many present day Fundamentalists have called themselves dispensationalists and they say we are living in the last dispensation. Because the Jews are returning to Israel they say Jesus is coming soon. They preach Armageddon Theology. Dispensationalists do not get upset about the world being destroyed because they are also premillennialists. They say, "When the bombs fall, we're going up." Dispensationalists believe they are going to be raptured before the tribulation, so they will not have to share in any of the suffering. Dispensationalists believe the biblical land of Zion and the modern day Zionist Israel are one and the same. They teach that whoever controls the area around the land of Palestine, the Sinai, and the Suez canal holds the balance of power in Europe, Asia, and Africa. Hal Linsey's book, *The Late Great Planet Earth,* describing premillenial dispensationalism has sold millions of copies. The Reagan Administration was seeped in Armageddon Theology and its foreign policy was reflective of those beliefs. Many dispensationalist premillennialists believe the Jewish Temple must be rebuilt so Jesus can reign over the earth from that building.

But there is one thing dispensationalists do not always tell their congregations. On the location where most Jewish priests say the Temple should be built, now stands one of the Muslims most sacred worshipping sites, Haram Al-Sharif. These grounds, housing the two mosques, Al Aqsa and the Dome of the Rock, have been under Muslim rule since a.d. 637. It remained in Muslim hands except for the 88 years the crusaders of Europe held it (1099-1087).

The Haram Al-Sharif was built by the Mamluk Turk, Sultan Solyman the Magnificent, in the 16th century. The Muslims believe the rock inside the Dome of the Rock is where Muhammad prayed and experienced a trip to the seventh heaven with the angel Gabriel. The

Jews believe that rock is where the Old Testament sacrifices were made. There have been hundreds of attempts to destroy the mosques by extremist groups in Israel, the most famous being the Gush Settlers.

Sheikh Muhammad Shakra, director of Al-Aqsa Mosque said Israelis have done extensive excavations under the Muslim worship sites and they have not found any clues that the temple ever stood there. According to Adnon Husseini, who was in charge of Muslim properties, there are now five buildings with structural problems because of all the digging the Israelis have done.

The Muslim Arabs are in constant fear that their two holy worship sites will be destroyed, and the 1990 massacre in Jerusalem was a direct result of this fear. Modern day Zionists believe the Mosque must be destroyed and the Temple erected in its place.

In 1980, Israel illegally annexed Arab East Jerusalem and the nations of the world protested by moving their embassies from West Jerusalem to Tel Aviv. With the encouragement of the Israeli government, a group of Fundamentalist Christians opened the International Christian Embassy in fashionable West Jerusalem. Israeli officials attended the grand opening, and 1000 Christians from 23 nations pledged their support. The embassy has a number of functions, mainly to foster support for Israel in other nations. It also put together, in cooperation with the Israeli tourist department, a ten day tourist promotional package. All accommodations exclusively made by El Al.

The International Christian Embassy sponsors the Christian Zionist Congress in Basel, Switzerland. In 1985, a series of resolutions were written by Jan Willem van der Hoevan of Holland, spokesman for the International Christian Embassy. The resolutions urged all Jews in the world to return to Israel, even the American Jews. He believes every Christian should facilitate their doing so. Israel was also urged to annex the West Bank, even though it has one million Palestinian inhabitants. Michael Anderson of Cornerstone spoke with van der Hoevan and was concerned by what he called his fiercely one-sided stand. He also met with Pastor Habi, even though the young pastor risked being arrested because of the late hour. Pastor Habi said oppression not only degrades its victims, it also degrades the oppressor:

Every day Palestinian Christians in Israel, who have held the torc h of the faith unbroken here for the last two thousand years, think more and more about leaving. We are losing hope. We are oppressed by elements within fundamentalist Judaism, seen as traitors by Palestinian Muslims, and not seen at all by Western Christians...yet I still hope. But why is this nothing to our Western brothers and sisters? [18]

The most dangerous function of the International Christian Embassy is its support of reconstruction of a new Jewish temple on the site of Haram Al-Sharif, where the two mosques are setting. They have had a cassette tape available for five dollars about plans to build a temple on the Haram Al-Sharif grounds. The Embassy said Christians wanting to donate money to the building of the temple are referred to a man called Stanley Goldfoot. Goldfoot immigrated from South Africa in the thirties, and some people call him an Israeli terrorist. According to the Israeli newspaper *Davar*, Goldfoot placed the bomb in the King David Hotel which killed a hundred people in 1946. [19] He was also one of three-member team of the Stern Gang who assassinated Counte Bernadotte, head of the Swedish Red Cross and part of a United Nations team in Israel, in 1948. [20] Goldfoot does not claim to be a religious person but his philosophy is whoever controls the Temple will have power in Israel. Goldfoot is associated with wealthy and influential Fundamentalist Christians in America who raise money for the building of the temple. They also financially support the training of young rabbis to sacrifice animals for when the new temple is built. They work under a number of organizations, a few being The Jerusalem Temple Foundation, Jewish Christian Cooperation, and Mission to America. Reverend James E. DeLoach of Houston's Second Baptist Church said it cost them quite a bit of money to bail 29 Israeli terrorists out of jail in Israel who had been caught on the Al-Haram grounds with dynamite. [21]

Edward Saed, a Christian Palestinian who was exiled in 1948, is a University Professor at Columbia University. In 1992, he decided to travel with his family, back to his homeland. Saed went looking for his childhood home in Jerusalem with a map and a copy of the title deed. What he found was the International Christian Embassy. He expressed his frustration:

To have found my family's house now occupied not by an Israeli Jewish family but by a right-wing fundamentalist Christian and militantly pro-Zionist group, run by a South African Boer no less! Anger and melancholy overtook me, so that when an American woman came out of the house holding an armful of laundry and asked if she could help, I could not bring myself to ask to go inside. [22]

I decided to call an evangelical missionary (who wishes to be kept anonymous) who was home on furlough and ask him what he knew about the International Christian Embassy in Jerusalem. He confirmed this information about the embassy. He said the Christians in Palestine will not have anything to do with the Christian Embassy because it is strictly of a political nature and supports the secular Zionist government of Israel. This of course contributes to the suffering of the local Christians, as well as the Muslims. This kind of political climate often puts missionaries in a dangerous position.

The Messianic Jews in Israel resent the embassy the most, because their interests and feelings are not represented at all. The International Christian Embassy makes it sound like they are speaking for all Christians, but in reality they do not speak for any of the local Christians. Messianic Jews in Israel are considered traitors and many of them do not dare write on their identification cards that they are followers of Christ. The Israeli government says there is no such thing as a Messianic or Completed Jew. If they specify their religious belief the government will no longer consider them Jews and they will forego the privileges that accompany that status. At that point, they are not a whole lot better off than Palestinian Arabs.

December 25, 1989, the Israeli High Court ruled that Nozrim (followers of the Nazarene) will not receive automatic citizenship like other Jews. In the first century after Christ, a council of rabbis proclaimed them heretics and made up twelve prayers for them. One of the prayers said, "May the apostates have no hope, may the dominion of wickedness be speedily uprooted in our day, may the Nozrim quickly perish and not be inscribed together with the righteous."

The Israeli Knesset passed an Anti-Missionary Law in 1977. They claimed Christians were taking advantage of unfortunate Jews and made it a criminal offense for a Christian to do anything for a Jew that would contribute to his becoming a Christian. It is punishable by five years in prison and a fine of 50,000 Israeli shekels. The Jewish convert will receive three years in prison and a 30,000 shekel fine. Author Louis Bahjat Hamada said he was very encouraged by what he saw from the Israeli Messianic Jews and Christian Palestinians:

> *I was told there were about 25 Christian congregations throughout Israel—made up of nearly 4,000 Jews and many more thousands of Arabs. Both groups of believers risk family persecution and government harassment. However, Jewish and Christian Arabs love one another in Christ, and their bold witness in the midst of strong opposition was very inspiring to me. [23]*

Author and former speech writer for Lyndon Johnson, Grace Halsell, traveled to the Holy Lands with a Jerry Falwell tour and was very disappointed that she did not meet any Palestinian Christians. She sought out Palestinian Christians on her own. She spoke with Brother Joseph Loewenstein, President Emeritus of Bethlehem University. Grace asked him how the Israelis benefited by having Falwell's followers not to see Palestinian Christians. He said the militant Zionists want to control the minds of American Christians so that they will go along with government policy, no matter what it is. He said he was not at all pleased with the American policy, it is genocide of the Palestinian people.

Grace talked with Jonathan Kuttab, Palestinian Christian Human Rights Lawyer. His feelings were:

> *For the evangelical-fundamentalists such as Falwell, the cult of Israel is higher than the teachings of Christ. Falwell's Zionism is about politics. The Average American finds this mythology very appealing. It is not demanding, nor is it a moral or highly ethical religion. It is a macho religion of the small, ultrapowerful Israel, which is not a sissy. Their God is a cross between Superman and Star Wars, a God who zaps here and there with a fiery, swift sword and destroys all enemies. He is proof for those of weak faith that the Bible is still true and alive. For them, it's almost as if Joshua were in the daily newspaper.*

Kuttab said he did not understand Christians who just came to see dead stone monuments but do not desire to see the *living stones*. He said Falwell prefers not to see Palestinians because their very existence interferes with his mythology. Jonathan Kuttab said, "I, and countless other Palestinian Christians would welcome the opportunity to visit and talk with all Christians who visit here." [24]

Although the Vatican has taken a stand against Palestinian suffering in Israel, American Catholics have had to live with the strong Israeli lobby in America. Anyone who dared to criticize the Israeli government policies was publicly accused of being anti-semitic or spreading Arab propaganda. One man, Rabbi Marc Tanenbaum, was put in charge of monitoring activity within the American Christian community. On August 10, 1960, Rabbi Tanenbaum, Executive Director of the *Synagogue Council of America*, in a confidential memo to directors and officers of the organization, claimed successes in pressuring the World Council of Churches to unconditionally support the state of Israel and to stop all efforts on behalf of Palestinian refugees. Public criticism of Israeli government policy has not been tolerated in America. The Israeli lobby with all its numerous organizations has called "anti-Semitism" for every little criticism of the Israeli government.

The Anti-Defamation League has a list of names of their enemies who can expect harsh attacks on their professional and personal lives. This organization, which was created to combat discrimination, has been under investigation in California for allegedly giving sensitive police information (from their hate crime unit) about Arab Americans and others, to Israel and the Aparteid government of South Africa. The Arab-American community in Santa Clara County filed a lawsuit against ADL. [25] Tom Gerard, a former San Francisco police officer is suspected of accepting thousands of dollars in exchange for sensitive files on Arab-Americans. Some of Gerard's files were found in the San Francisco offices of the Anti-Defamation League. Gerard's files contained more than 1,000 names of Americans involved in fundraising activities for Middle Eastern organizations. The problem with this is that some action which may be a part of our American freedom could be a crime in Israel or South Africa. Then when an Arab-American who has expressed his opinion goes to visit family in Israel, the minute he steps off the plane he may be arrested. Many Arab-Americans fear for their lives. San Francisco police have agreed to meet regularly with members of the Arab community in order to become more sensitive to their culture and concerns, and to overcome negative images. [26]

Jewish Americans have been made to feel guilty that they are having a nice comfortable life in the West while the Israeli Jews are making all the sacrifices for the state of Israel. Jewish Americans who had misgivings about the kind of state Israel had become faced dire consequences. Richard Cohen said his telephone was an instrument of torture. Alfred Lilienthal had been formally excommunicated by some rabbis in New York because of his crusade for a peaceful reconciliation of Jew and Arab. Grace Halsell interviewed Mark Bruzonsky, a Washington, D.C. writer. Mark called political Zionism a tarnished dream. He had worked for Jewish Zionist organizations. He was enthusiastic about Zionism and considered it the self-determination of all Jews. But, he said he learned too much. He learned that Western Christians have been instrumental in the development of Israel, and the persecution of Arabs. A Jew is supposed to blindly support Zionism. Bruzonsky defines modern day Zionism:

Some define Zionism as the end of exile and the ingathering of all Jews. Most Arabs define Zionism as a form of racist colonization. And delegates to the United Nations at one point voted to condemn Zionism as a form of racism. George Orwell said Zionism had the usual characteristics of a nationalist movement, but the American version of it seems to be more violent and malignant that the British. And the British historian Toynbee defined Zionism as the worship of a false god—an idolatrous religion...I term Zionism a political, expansionist, colonial-type movement that led to the creation of Israel, and I term the Zionist as one who accepts the rationale of Israel's actions, regardless of how dangerous or wrong they may be. [27]

With the 1993 signing of the Peace Agreement by Israeli Prime Minister Yitzhak Rabin, it will take much of the pressure off the American Jews. It will now be more socially acceptable to want peace with Palestinians.

Dispensationalist teaching has crept into modern day Bible commentaries. Traditional commentaries have always said they were not certain who Gog and Magog were. But many modern day commentaries have labeled the Soviet Union as the evil empire who is going to attack Israel, with the help of Iran, Iraq, Syria, and Ethiopia. All these countries are called the enemies of God and people have developed irrational fears about these countries. These modern day prophesies are usually found in the commentary of Ezekial 38 or 39. When we look at the former Soviet Union with its diversity of nationalities, religions, and languages, this modern day commentary is too general to be of any relevance. Now with the breakup of the Soviet Union, this interpretation of prophesy is obsolete.

Another contemporary commentary has made the Persians fair game. The commentary on Esther 1:7 says the Persians never made any important decisions except when they were drunk. The commentary on Esther 6:1 calls King Xerxes a wild man. Westerners have a limited understanding of Eastern culture. Middle Easterners have never been big drinkers of alcoholic beverages. But, before Islam, at Middle Eastern weddings it was social compulsory to drink, and better to get drunk. In Esther 1:8 King Xerxes changes this social obligation to drink:

> *By royal command, however, drinking was not obligatory, the king having instructed the officials of his household to treat each guest according to his own wishes. [28]*

Secondly, whoever did this research used Herodotus, a Greek historian, as their source; the Greeks and the Persians were in competition for the world power at that time. That would be like going to the Soviet Union for American history during the Cold War. In fact, history tells us that Alexander the Macedonian (the Persians do not call him Great) burned Persepolis, the summer palace of Persia, in April, 330 B.C. The Persian side of the story was that Alexander was having a drunken victory party and burned Persepolis on the dare of a young maiden. Supposedly, he faced a grievous hangover the next day for burning such a magnificent architectural structure with the royal archives containing the chronicles of the Persian kings. This was a historical loss for the whole world.

The commentary saying Xerxes was a wild man was referring to the Battle of Salimas, off the island of Cyprus. In that battle, King Xerxes lost his entire fleet of ships because of a storm. Kings used to go with their armies, and the devastation of losing all those men and resources drove him to whip the sea. The Persian version of that story is that the sea calmed. Of course, they admit it could have been a coincidence.

Herodotus has a reputation for being a very creative historian. Encyclopedia Britannica admits that Greek sources are often prejudiced against the Persians and tend to view events from their own point of view. Brian M. Fagan in the *Rape of the Nile,* says this about Herodotus:

...the many inaccuracies, stemming in large part from Herodotus' liking for the fanciful and marvelous and his gullible acceptance of tall stories told by temple caretakers, were perpetuated for centuries. Yet British Egyptologist Sir Alan Gardiner's assessment of Herodotus as the "Father of History" and a "great genius" is probably fairer, for he was experimenting with what at the time was a totally new literary art form. [29]

The Bible should not have unnecessary character assassination in its commentary. Especially when the Bible and historians have given the Persians such a wonderful coverage. King Cyrus is called God's anointed in Isaiah 45. King Xerxes married a Jewish maiden and was so in love with her that he saved the Jewish race from an evil prime minister. Queen Esther's uncle Mordeci became honored above all men in the kingdom. This is very precious information to the Persians who had most of their history burned by foreign invaders.

When Bible commentaries are written, or classes are taught, we should ask ourselves, "If a person I cared about from that ethnic group was sitting here or reading this, would I still say this?" The spreading of the gospel should not have cultural biases in it. When Middle Easterners come into a church and hear this teaching which they feel is prejudiced toward them, they are very offended and never want to come back. They say, "The Westerners have put their political repression in their Holy Book now and are feeling self-righteous about how their governments have persecuted us. The gospel is supposed to be good news (Isaiah 52:7) for all men. It would be wise to check the commentaries of a study Bible before giving it to a Middle Easterner."

After the bombing of Libya, the persecution of Palestinians, and lastly, the bombing of Iraq, I have asked Christians how they can justify this kind of killing of innocent people. Some of them have actually given me this answer, "That's what God's people did in the Old Testament." Ralph Winter, professor of missions at Fuller Seminary explains why it is unacceptable for Christians to imitate all behaviors from the Old Testament. The *Books of the Law,* or the *Torah,* not only explain the strange source of evil but also describe a counter-campaign and follow that campaign through many centuries.

The first eleven chapters of Genesis give an introduction to the whole problem. Three things are described: 1) a glorious and "good" original creation; 2)the entrance of a rebellious, evil, superhuman power who is more than a force, actually a personality and the result; 3)a humanity caught up in that rebellion and brought under the power of that evil. [30] So the Old Testament not only describes the relationship of God to his chosen people but presents a strange source of evil that has temporary success much of the time. The rest of the Bible tells how the Kingdom, the Power, and the Glory of God penetrates that occupied territory, how God sent Jesus Christ to reconquer evil and redeem his fallen creatures. That is what the cross is all about. Are we going to go back and pick behaviors out of rebellious, evil, superhuman power and use it as an excuse to do the same thing? Not me! I want to pick my behaviors from Jesus Christ's victory over evil with good, and be redeemed by the blood of the lamb, because there are dire consequences. God's Kingdom strikes back.

These negative nuclear Armageddon interpretations of the Bible are not right for Christians. The time of the Gentiles will be full when Christians are being witnesses of Christ unto the ends of the earth. Matthew 24:14 says "..this Gospel of the Kingdom will be preached in the whole world as a testimony to all nations, and then the end will come." If we men blow each other up in greed, hatred, and prejudice, God will let us live with our mess. Jesus said, "Blessed are the peacemakers, they will be called the children of God."

I myself received quite a different message from Ezekial than the dispensationalists. The judgements Ezekial makes on the nations were made to prove something to the Israelites who were living in captivity in Babylon. The Jews wanted to know why they should have to live for God in this strange land when all the heathen were living a worldly and ungodly existence but appeared to be more blessed than they themselves had ever been.

We hear that today from people. Why should I have to be good when everyone else is doing it? Look at so-and-so; he's not a Christian but he's wealthier and appears to be having a much better time than we are. That's what Ezekial was trying to tell his Jewish brothers and sisters. "You live for God, and God will see to it that the heathen get their due. This is what's going to happen to the Babylonians, the Edomites, etc, etc. You don't see it now, but it will be so." It was not that God thought those people were any less than the Israelites; God loves all people equally. In Amos 9:7 (TJB) He says:

Are not you and the Cushites (Ethiopians) all the same to me, sons of Israel? It is Yahweh who speaks. Did not I, who brought Israel out of the land of Egypt, bring the Philistines from Caphtor, and the Aramaeans (Syrians) from Kir?

So as Christians, how are we supposed to relate to Israel? First of all, are we asking the same question the disciples asked Jesus on the Mount of Olives? (What a Christian friend of mine refers to as *Peter's dumb question*.) Jesus answers the question by rebuking the disciples, and then giving them the Great Commission. Acts 1:6-9:

Now having met together, they asked him, "Lord, has the time come? Are you going to restore the kingdom to Israel?" He replied, "It is not for you to know times or dates that the Father has decided by his own authority, but you will receive power when the Holy Spirit comes on you, and then you will be my witnesses not only in Jerusalem but throughout Judea and Samaria, and indeed to the ends of the earth." As he said this he was lifted up while they looked on, and a cloud took him from their sight.

In other words, Jesus is telling them, "That is none of your business, God will take care of that end of it. Your business is to be spreading my good news that the kingdom of God has come; the king is Jesus; the good news is repentance of sin; and the end result is eternity with God." Can we as Christians wholeheartedly support policies of the state of Israel if we know Palestinian Christians and Muslims are suffering as a result of those policies. The apostle Paul struggled with some of these same issues: In Romans 3:8 he says some have accused Christians of saying that they can do evil if good may come of it. Paul says, "God forbid." In other words, an unjust process cannot bring justice. Cruelty to one group does not bring good for the other. This is not the way God fulfills prophesy. Christians are to carry out the great commission and God will see to the rise and fall of great nations according to their righteous behavior. As Christians, we can wholeheartedly support the peace between Israel and the Palestinian people. The whole world will benefit from peace in this area of the world.

How exactly are we, as Christians, supposed to bless the modern state of Israel? We must want the same things for Israel that God wants for Israel. In order to know God's will we must always go to the Bible. Israel was given their own commission to contribute to the salvation of the world in Genesis 12:2, Acts 3:25, and Galations 3:8...and in thee all the families of the earth be blessed. Pumping Israel full of weapons to kill their neighbors is not blessing Israel. In Isaiah 6-12 (TJB) God tells Judah, "Is not this the sort of fast that pleases me—to break unjust fetters and undo the thongs of the yoke, to let the oppressed go free, and break every yoke, to share your bread with the hungry, and shelter the homeless poor, to clothe the man you see to be naked and not turn from your own kin? Then...You will rebuild the ancient ruins, build up on the old foundations. You will be called "Breach-mender, restorer of ruined houses."

In Isaiah 59:8,9 he says, "You don't know what true peace is, nor what it means to be just and good; you continually do wrong and those who follow you won't experience any peace, either. It is because of all this evil that you aren't finding God's blessings..." According to Galations 3, the only way to get out of under the curse is through the redemption of Christ. Verse 9 says "If you belong to Christ, then you are Abraham's seed, and heirs according to the promise." There is no Biblical justification for Christians to excuse Israel's persecution of Palestinians. It is only through righteous witness that others will know of God's love.

It is not a matter of whether Israel should be a state; the world has shown a supportive posture toward Israel, including Palestinians. They have the most to gain. The issue is what kind of a state Israel is going to be. With the signing of the 1993 Israeli, Palestinian Peace Agreement in Washington, a seed has been planted. But it must grow. Attitudes of all parties must change in order to secure a lasting peace in this area. It is time for Israel to set their fears aside and trust God, and then start trusting the people around them. In Matthew 23:23 Jesus reprimanded the spiritual and political leaders of the day: "...you have neglected the more important matters of the law—justice, mercy and faithfulness." The best way Christians can bless Jews is to help them make true peace with their neighbors, the Arabs. Our generation of Americans has had to live with the quilt of the Jewish Holocaust. Are our children going to have to live with the guilt of what is being done to Palestinians? We will never convince Muslims we care about them when we do not stand for justice on their behalf. How will we answer to God? In Genesis 9:5,6 after the great flood God blessed Noah and said:

I will demand an account of your lifeblood. I will demand an account from every beast and from man. I will demand an account of every man's life from his fellow men...for in the image of God man was made.

Notes:

1. Grace Halsell, "The Hidden Hand of the Temple Mount Faithful," *The Washington Report on Middle East Affairs*, Jan 1991, p.8.

2. Ibrahim Dawad, "The Jerusalem Massacre As Seen By Medical Rescue Personnel," *The Washington Report on Middle East Affairs,* Dec 1990, p. 46.

3. Ibid., p. 46.

4. Halsell, p. 8.

5. Dr. Israel Shahak, "What Really Happened at the Haram Al-Sharif/Temple Mount Massacre?" *The Washington Report on Middle East Affairs* Dec 1990, p. 47.

6. Faisal Husseini, "Grant Us the Strength to Resist Striking Back at Those Who Hurt Us," *The Washington Report on Middle East Affairs*, Dec 1990, p. 48.

7. Laura Cooley, "Whose Hospice? Whose Jerusalem?" *The Washington Report on Middle East Affairs*, June 1990, p. 10.

8. Ivan Kauffman, "Attack on West Bank Church Goes Unreported," *The Washington Report on Middle East Affairs.* May 1988, p. 14.

9. Dr. Judith G. Martin, professor of world religions at the Univ of Dayton, "Three Reasons Why the Vatican Can't Establish Diplomatic Ties With Israel," *America,* 106 W. 56th St., NY, reprinted by Washington Report on Middle East Affairs, Feb 1992, p. 71.

10. David Scott, Compared to Vatican, US Bishops Seem to Apply Double Standard," *The Washington Report on Middle East Affairs,* Feb 1991, p. 52.

11. Alfred M. Lilienthal, *The Zionist Connection* (New York, NY: Dodd, Mead & Company, 1978) pp. 493-505.

12. Reverend L. Humphrey Waltz, "Catholic Bishops Press on Mideast Peace," *The Washington Report on Middle East Affairs,* Dec 1989, p. 39.

13. L. Humphrey Waltz, PLO Recognition Urged by British and Dutch Church Councils," *The Washington Report on Middle East Affairs,* May 1990, p. 41.

14. Presbyterian General Assembly's Middle East Resolution, *The Washington Report on Middle East Affairs*, July/August 1990, p. 29.

15. Reverend L. Humphrey Walz, "Habitat's Hopes for Mideast Housing," *The Washington Report on Middle East Affairs*, Feb 1991, p. 53.

16. "Cry for Justice in Israel-Palestine," 2 *Crosslink*, July 1990, A New Zealand newspaper article sent to us by a friend.

17. "Christianity," *Encyclopedia Britannica Macropaedia*, Vol. 16, p. 370:1a.

18. Michael Anderson, "In the Image of God, Things are not as clear-cut as they might seem in the land of Israel," *Cornerstone Magazine*, Vol 21, Issue 100.

19. Grace Halsell, *Prophecy and Politics*, (Westport, Connecticut: Lawrence Hill & Company, 1986) p. 97.

20. Rita Fairchild, "The Assassination of Counte Folk Bernadotte," *The Washington Report on Middle East Affairs*, Sept 1990, p. 37.

21. Halsell, p. 100.

22. Edward W. Said, "Palestine, Then and Now, An exile's journey through Israel and the Occupied Territories," *Harper's,* Dec 1993, pp. 47-55.

23. Louis Bahjat Hamada, *Understanding the Arab World*, (Nashville: Thomas Nelson Publishers, 1990), p. 186.

24. Halsell, p. 27.

25. Miranda Ewell, "Spying-case questions, Deputy D.A. quits board of Anti-Defamation League." San Jose Mercury News, Friday, April 16, 1993.

26. Rachelle Marshall, "Secret Files on Arab Americans Sold by U.S. Police Officer to Israel," *Washington Report on Middle East Affairs*, March 1993. Rachelle Marshall is a member of *New Jewish Agenda*.

27. Halsell, p. 141.

28. George Lamsa, *Old Testament Light, The Indispensable Guide to the Customs, Manners, & Idioms of Biblical Times,* (San Francisco: Harper & Row, Publishers, 1964), p. 404.

29. Brian M. Fagan, *The Rape of the Nile, Tomb Robbers, Tourist, and Archaeologist in Egypt.* (New York: Charles Scribner's Sons, 1975), p. 16.

30. Ralph D. Winter, "The Kingdom Strikes Back, The Ten Epochs of Redemptive History," *Perspectives on the World Christian Movement,* A Reader (Pasadena, California: William Carey Library, 1981), p. 137.

A MORE EFFECTIVE METHOD IN REACHING OUT TO MUSLIMS

Our dogmatic proclamation, our western methodology, and our development projects must be permeated with the incarnate Christ. Let us draw near to share their grief and speak to them. We are not Christians preaching to Muslims; we are not Westerners trying to communicate with Easterners; we are not the developed seeking to lift the undeveloped. We are fallen men embracing fallen men. We share their grief so they will share the joy of His presence.   --H.M. Dard
"Reflections at a Muslim Grave"
Ishmael, My Brother

Years ago, my mother used to say to me, "In this world Elwood, you must be oh so smart or oh so pleasant." For years I was smart, but I recommend pleasant.   --Jimmy Stewart in *Harvey*

Hossein Ali had married an American girl. One of the things he had admired about her was her faith in God, even though she was a Christian. The Quran teaches that Muslims may marry the virtuous women of those who had received the scriptures before them. [1]

They had lived in the Middle East for a few years but decided to return to America when their children were still quite young. Hossein Ali wanted his children to learn about God and there wasn't an organized Islamic center in their area; so he allowed his wife to take the children to church. One Sunday he even decided to go himself and see what they were teaching his children.

He was greeted at the door by the senior pastor who shook hands with him and said, "Welcome brother; we worship the same God, please come and worship with us." Hossein Ali found people very warm and loving at that church, and it seemed to be a good influence on his wife and children. In fact, his wife seemed to be emotionally maturing, and he could see an inner strength developing in her.

A few years passed and life was good. One day Hossein Ali

received a promotion at work and was to be transferred to a smaller city in the heartland of America. Hossein Ali said, "We are going to see how real America lives."

They bought a lovely new home, and his wife began visiting churches in the new town. Hossein Ali started attending two different churches with the family. He was beginning to feel more at home in church, and they had some challenging classes on how to live a Godly life. All his life he had heard that Jesus was a great prophet and a supreme teacher, and it was interesting to study some of his teachings.

First, the pastor from one church came to visit them. He was friendly and even discussed Islam quite intelligently. It seemed a bit odd to Hossein Ali that the pastor would suggest he change the plaque on his wall of *Allah* to Jesus. After all, Allah meant *Almighty God*. "Well," he thought, "he probably doesn't know that."

Then one evening a group from the second church came to visit them and Hossein Ali's wife and children all gathered around. They had served their guests tea and cakes as was customary in a Middle Eastern home. The pastor of this church then asked him a very strange question. The pastor asked Hossein Ali if he died tonight did he know for sure he would go to heaven? Hossein Ali said, "I hope I would. I have a very strong faith in God, and I can look back over my life and see God's hand on me since I was a child, in fact, the way we came out of the Middle East...."

But the pastor didn't let him finish, and told Hossein Ali that is not what he meant. Hossein Ali quickly said, "But I believe in Jesus, in fact there is much in the Quran about Jesus." Hossein Ali's wife quickly went and brought the Quran, but the pastor would not even look at it.

Instead the pastor said, "That is not the same thing. In the Bible it says even the devils believe in God."

Hossein Ali felt a hot burning sensation go through him. How could this man come in his home as a guest and insult him this way in front of his wife and children. Didn't he know Middle Eastern men were the masters of their home and demanded ultimate respect from the family members? What was his wife thinking of him; she had turned an ashen color. She had not even admitted to their guests that she was a Christian herself. The pastor saw that Hossein Ali and his wife became distant and unreceptive, and the group excused themselves and left.

Hossein Ali was going on a business trip and while he was away he visited the pastor in their former church. That pastor was very sympathetic. He said, "I'm very sorry Hossein Ali, you must feel very hurt." Hossein Ali felt a little better to know all Christians did not have preconceived ideas about who he was and what he believed but somehow it wasn't enough.

In the meantime, his wife had gone to the church to talk to the pastor. The pastor that visited them was not there and she told his assistant pastor about what had happened. He told her that those people that do not submit to the authority were of a rebellious nature. This made Hossein Ali's wife very angry. She said, "Why should my husband submit to your authority. The Bible is an ancient literature written to Middle Easterners in a way they can understand. Your oversimplified Western techniques are offensive to him."

The assistant pastor turned very red and proclaimed loudly, "The New Testament was written in Greek and that is what we study in seminary. What are your credentials?"

By this time, Hossein Ali's wife was shaking all over. She said, "I have every reason to believe my cultural experience in the Middle East will be a great benefit to my overall understanding of the scriptures." With that, she excused herself and left. On her way out of the church she ran into the senior pastor and explained to him how he had upset her husband. He could see that Hossein Ali's wife was very shaken and quickly agreed to write a letter to her husband.

She realized she was out of line in losing her temper, and the next day sat down and wrote an apology letter to the assistant pastor for being disrespectful to his position as a pastor. She assumed he received the letter, although she never heard anything from him.

As the days passed, Hossein Ali became more and more depressed; his wife tried to comfort him. This was the one nightmare she had never imagined would happen. Didn't these people understand what this man had already been through: the loss of his family, his homeland, his culture, and his language? The letter arrived from the pastor but at the end of it he said, "We can't both be right. Either you are right and I am wrong, or I am right and you are wrong. I believe I am right." It was insult upon insult.

The second month she joined her husband in depression. Even the children didn't want to go back to that church anymore because their father had changed; he no longer laughed and played with them like he had before.

Hossein Ali's wife tried to write a few letters to the head pastor but would end up throwing them away because she could see her own anger in them; she knew that was wrong. At the end of the third month she finally had a four page letter that she felt good about. She tried to explain the cultural and political implications of sharing the gospel with a Middle Easterner. She gave the letter time to reach its destination and then she called to make an appointment to speak to him. His secretary said it would be two weeks before she could get in to see him; he only took appointments in the late afternoon. She could feel the old resentment rising in her again. "Not a very convenient time for women; the time they must prepare supper. He turned my household upside down in one evening and now I have to wait two weeks to get in to speak to him," she thought. She calmly told the secretary to make the appointment the soonest possible time.

The day she was to visit the pastor she prayed, asking the Lord to make her heart right. She opened her Bible and it fell to the passage of Philippians 1:27 "...let your conversation be as it becometh the gospel of Christ: that whether I come and see you, or else be absent, I may hear of your affairs, that ye stand fast in one spirit, with one mind striving together for the faith of the gospel."

When the pastor heard how upset Hossein Ali had become he said, "I am not in the habit of apologizing for the gospel." She said it had nothing to do with being ashamed of the gospel. That night Hossein Ali did not even get a chance to hear the gospel from the pastor. She explained that in reality what he had done was reject Hossein Ali as a person, he had rejected his faith in God the Father, and had rejected his effort to understand who Christ was. Hossein Ali felt rejected as a whole by the Christians anyway, and this confirmed his belief that trying to be a part of the Christian community was a useless effort in the first place.

The pastor explained that this evangelical approach was very successful in reaching out to the average American. However... he did admit he had not met a Muslim previous to his encounter with Hossein Ali; and that he would be happy to come and apologize to Hossein Ali if it would make him feel better and come back to church.

The Pastor did return one evening with a group of friends, graciously apologized, and invited Hossein Ali back to church. The apology did help even though Hossein Ali never went back to that particular church; he attended other churches. Hossein Ali said, "With this church the water of my soul has left and I have no dignity left to face these people with." He was not quite sure he would ever feel a welcome part of any church ever again.

How can we more effectively share God's love with Muslims. The outreach just described was not only ineffective but served to alienate the Muslim from the church.

Sharing God's love can only be done by establishing communications, by conversation, and by becoming familiar with their culture. When Muslims visit our churches or even move in next door, they surely should be visited. But the assumptions we make about the average American can not be applied to their situation. We need to look at a relationship with Muslims as a longer-term project. We must become familiar with them. Once we get acquainted with them and their culture, we must become their friends and establish trust. What we must do is earn the right to share God's love with Muslims. Close friends share everything in their hearts; that is the natural outworking of a close friendship.

The purpose of the first visit to a Middle Easterner's home should be to get to know them. Show some genuine interest in who they are and what their culture is like. Ask them lots of questions, and be a good listener. It is important to let *them* define who they are. We often have misconceptions about Muslims and may be surprised to find out who they really are. One offense to Muslims is that Islam is always grouped with Hinduism and Buddhism. Islam is a monotheistic faith and is technically grouped with Christianity and Judaism. Ask them questions about their faith, about their food habits, or about what activities they enjoy the most. Ask them how they feel about different experiences they are having in America. It may be helpful to record new information in a personal journal, and review it from time to time.

How about the statement Hossein Ali made, "I believe in Jesus?" Why was that statement ignored by the pastor? Often we have defined for ourselves what certain things mean coming from a Muslim. Rather, the pastor could have asked Hossein Ali what he meant by that statement and taken a look at his Holy Book. We must never assume we know what their beliefs are. In the Bible the disciples asked Jesus:

.... "Teacher," said John, "we saw a man driving out demons in your name and we told him to stop, because he was not one of us." "Do not stop him," Jesus said...."for whoever is not against us is for us. I tell you the truth, anyone who gives you a cup of water in my name because you belong to Christ will certainly not lose his reward. And if anyone causes one of these little ones who believe in me to sin, it would be better for him to be thrown into the sea with a larg e millstone tied around his neck......and be at peace with each other."
(Mark 9:38-50 NIV)

The question is whether we can know in one short evening what is in a man's heart. So often men hardly know their own hearts, but they need to be given the benefit of the doubt. It would have been better if the pastor would have said, "Well, that's wonderful; we will look forward to you worshipping with us." That way Hossein Ali would be studying the Bible and if his concept of Christ was different, he would receive his correction from God's word. Only the Spirit of God can speak to men's hearts; our job as Christians is to love. They will know we are Christians by the love they receive from us. Keep the first visit primarily social and ask them if you can come back again.

In between the first and second visit to a Muslim's home, we could take some time to study up on Islam. We must study history and be willing to face up to some of the deep historical reasons for the separation of Christians and Muslims. The Bible tells us, "For God hath not given us the spirit of fear, but of power and of love, and a sound mind." II Tim 1:7 (KJV). We must have faith that Christ will give us the light of his wisdom in our search for truth. The search for truth often involves being objective and being willing to listen to some criticism; then doing some research to decide if that criticism is justified. In reading Muslim material we must keep the words of Richard Foster, author of *Celebration of Discipline in mind*:

The first reading of a book involves understanding the book: what is the author saying? The second reading involves interpreting the book: what does the author mean? The third reading involves evaluating the book: is the author right or wrong? Most of us tend to do the third reading first and never do the first and second readings at all. We give a critical analysis of a book before we understand what it says. We judge a book to be right or wrong before we interpret its meaning...the time for critical analysis of a book comes after careful understanding and interpretation.[1]

Because we do often define for ourselves who other people are, we need objective resources. These may include encyclopedias, or books written by people who have lived in the Middle East. The newspaper is much more reliable than the television media. Television has presented the Middle Easterners in a very negative light. Their political struggles have been presented as criminal activities. The press never really addresses the source of the problem, and gives little or no history at all. It concentrates on the sensationalism. There is a reason behind everything, but the television viewer is presented with the effects rather than the cause. The short news reports most radio and television gives are so inadequate that there is no way the listener could begin to understand the true circumstances of the Middle Eastern problems.

More in depth studies are necessary for the Westerner to develop insight into the different cultural and political motivations. In order for us to receive objective opinions and viewpoints there must be a Middle Easterner there to represent his people. Programs with discussion groups, personal interviews, or tours of particular countries are valuable resources. All people have a tendency to be biased toward their own side of the story. Professors of Middle Eastern studies in American colleges may have wonderful insights into Middle Eastern people, but they are still Americans. I have developed a deep respect for Edward Said, a Palestinian American who is Parr Professor of English and Comparative Literature at Columbia University. He is an American who grew up in Palestine, studied in Egypt, England, and America; therefore he has viewed a number of cultures. He recognizes the strengths and the shortcomings of both the Eastern and Western cultures. Edward Said, or persons like him can contribute valuable insights into any discussion on the Middle East. A healthy discussion group is one in which all sides are represented, and allowed to give their opinions. As Americans, we are never going to understand Middle Eastern terrorism until we understand the problems that have forced people into such desperate acts of aggression.

The thing we need to be aware of is that there is material given only in our perspective and by our definitions. In his book *Orientalism,* Edward Said reveals how offended the Muslims are by the Westerners definition of them:

> *"Mohammedan" is the relevant (and insulting) European*
> *designation; "Islam" which happens to be the correct Muslim*

name, is relegated to another entry. The "heresy...which we call
Mohammedan" is "caught" as the imitation of a Christian imitation
of true religion.

What he is saying here is that because Christians worship Jesus
they think Muslims worship Muhammad. From our study in this book
we see that is simply not true. What has happened is that early
Christians defined Islam themselves from their own perspective of
religion. Rather, they should have found out from the Muslims what
the valid practice of their faith was.

In the same way the West has preconceived ideas about the Middle
East, the Middle East has their impressions of the West that have been
shaped by various experiences. Muslims may feel an American has a
lot of cheek presenting himself as the example of Christianity after the
things they have seen from the West.

There has been enmity between the Christians and the Muslims
since the Crusades. The harsh, exploitive treatment from first Europe,
and then America that we have discussed has built walls of misunderstanding with the Middle East. The movies from the West are full of
sex and violence. In 1981, the evening soap opera Dallas was one of
America's top exports. One Middle-Easterner had mistaken Dallas for
a documentary on American culture. Turkey had censored Dallas
because they said it was too immoral for their people to watch. In
addition, the Middle Easterners have often been offended by
irresponsible, immoral behavior of the secular American community in
their home countries. The drinking of alcoholic beverages is either
against the law or forbidden by religion in most Muslim countries.

As a Christian, you may say, "What does this have to do with me?"
You are probably just as offended by immoral soap operas and
alcoholism as the average Muslim. Unfortunately, in the same way we
in America get a bad impression from all Middle Easterners through
the image of the terrorist on the nightly news; they get a bad impression of all Americans by the bad examples they have seen. We must be
aware that we also have a stereotype to live down before we can
communicate effectively with them. Muslims will be very appreciative
of any interest shown in their culture. Your interest in them will also
encourage them to be interested in your culture. In reality, they have

more of a need to learn about American culture from you because this will help them integrate into the local social system. Social isolation can very easily turn into loneliness.

After a number of contacts, the lines of communication should be opening up. The next step would be to invite your Muslim friend to your home. Middle Easterners also enjoy picnics, the theater, or concerts. This would be a good time to take advantage of children's performances with coffee and dessert afterwards. This leads us to our second process in which communication is established and we move on to becoming good friends. Mutual trust and respect is essential for a good friendship.

A Christian must open up this relationship to mutual trust. The necessary ingredient in trusting a Muslim is the same ingredient that must be present in trusting any fellow human being: trusting God. When we can't open up our hearts to people, we are not trusting God.

Jesus said to love your enemies. He knew we couldn't trust our enemies; if they were trustworthy we wouldn't consider them our enemies. We must trust God and love others. We must face reality with the political situation; Muslims seem to have fallen into enemy territory by our political definitions.

But Christians must operate at a point above theology, above politics, and above culture. We must operate at a point of the complete love of Christ where there are no barriers. Why does Paul say a woman may win her husband over without talk, but by her behavior? (1 Peter 3:1 NIV) Sometimes love means not trying to prove your point. There are times when proving you are right serves no purpose. Rather, Paul shows us the most excellent way: "...and if I have faith that can move mountains, but have not love, I am nothing. Love is patient, love is kind. It always protects, always trusts, always hopes, always perseveres.." 1 Corinthians 13:2,4,7 (NIV).

We must allow Muslims the freedom of their own choice. God gave men the freedom to choose eternity with Him or apart from Him. We as God's people must give others that kind of freedom without withdrawing our love from them. We must ask God to fill our hearts with that kind of love and then we will trust. In trusting God we carry out His methods and wait for His results.

Hossein Ali obviously did not do well with the *let's get right down to business* approach, but it was much more than that that offended him. The pastor did not understand that in the Middle Eastern culture the father of the home is not spoken to in that manner in front of his family. The Grolier book, *Lands and People,* gives an insight into the Middle Eastern family :

> *The Iranian family is a very close-knit unit. At its center is the father or another older male, who is known as the master (agha). He is absolute ruler in his home and commands total respect and obedience.*

Hossein Ali never really heard the gospel that night because being told he might die was very humiliating to him in the presence of his family. Secondly, Middle Easterners are much more sensitive about death. Maybe the reason for that is that the father's life brings such security to the family members. People are much more interdependent in the Middle Eastern cultures.

Hossein Ali spent the next few minutes trying to redeem himself in the pastor's eyes, and when he couldn't accomplish that; he felt judged and condemned to death. We must remember, a pastor is presenting himself as a representative of God's word; his presence carries much authority. Then finally, Hossein Ali felt he was being compared to devils.

Hossein Ali later said to his wife, "How could he compare me to devils; they are God's rivals. I am doing my best to live a godly life; to be an educated, disciplined person and even attend church." Hossein Ali was a faithful husband, a good provider and a loving father. In fact, the very reason he was in this country was so his family could have a better life. He had given up his native country which he loved, to be here with them.

Interestingly enough, Hossein Ali had a good point. The whole message of the passage in James 2 that the pastor was quoting from is that actions speak louder than words. James 2:18 (NIV) says: " But someone will say, you have faith, I have deeds. Show me your faith without deeds, and I will show you my faith by what I do." The pastor was quoting the next verse, James 2:19 (NIV): "You believe there is one God. Good! Even the demons believe that—and shudder." This verse was taken out of context because there was no way anyone could judge another's character in one hour's time. Hossein Ali felt he had graciously welcomed the pastor into his home, but his hospitality had been returned with confrontation and rejection. What Hossein Ali needed was to be accepted, to be shown a hand of friendship, and to feel trusted. What he really needed was some good news; any Middle Easterner we meet has already had enough bad news to last them a lifetime. By the words of Romans 10:15 (KJV) " ...as it is written, How beautiful are the feet of them that preach the gospel of peace, and bring glad tidings of good things!" Middle Easterners, or any Third World people for that matter, need some good news; they have had enough bad news.

Hossein Ali had other experiences in church which made him suspect he was being welcomed in the door, but not accepted into the people's hearts. He felt they didn't trust him. He had often heard the men planning to play racketball or other activities together, but he was never invited. The Christian men often seemed uncomfortable with him; he often felt like he was trying to get into a private club. Finally one fellow from the church invited Hossein Ali over for dinner, but while they were gathered around the table the fellow made one of those odd statements Hossein Ali often encountered. He said, "You know, I watch those terrorists on television and they look like regular people; just like you." Hossein Ali felt he should be getting used to being compared to odd things but somehow he again felt confused. In the Middle East they have an expression: " The thief does not have horns and a tail." You cannot tell a thief by the way he looks either. Of course he knew if he responded by comparing this fellow with common criminals in America, of which there many more than Middle Eastern terrorists, it would only complicate the situation further. After all, it wouldn't be a gracious thing to say when you are a guest in a man's home. Most of all, it wouldn't do anything to develop trust between two people. In other words, a Christian is not always aware of the great effort the Muslim has made to be their friend.

Christians must trust the Muslim's motives first. The Muslim's reason for moving toward the church is for the spiritual benefit and the social integration it provides. However, at this point they may not necessarily be ready to accept all the church has to offer. For the spiritual benefit we must depend on the Holy Spirit to speak. Upon reviewing in this book the practice of Islam, accepted writings, and basic theology, we should trust and respect their worship of God, their emphasis on justice, and their reverence attached to the Quran as God's Holy word. Even though Muslim's may show a reluctance to read the Bible, they have a sense of deep respect for it as God's word also. The Quran has this to say about the Bible and God's people:

> *You will find the Christians nearest in affection to us because they have humble spiritual leaders among them. Surah 5:82*

> *Argue not with the people of the Scripture but if you get in a situation say "your God and our God are one, and unto Him we surrender." Surah 29:46*

> *And if you are in doubt concerning that which We reveal unto you, then question those who read the Scripture before you. Surah 10:94*

Muslims are deeply hurt to be rejected by the *People of the Book*, whom they have been instructed to respect by the Quran. Muslims have experienced deep depression when a Christian discontinues their relationship because their charity was not bringing expected results. There is a difference between charity and love, and no one wants to be a charity case. They need to know we respect them as much as they respect us. That will prevent us from destroying their feeling of self-worth. Muslims need to know there is something they are doing right, and indeed they are doing something right. In John 6:45, Jesus himself said: "No man can come to me except the Father which hath sent me draw him: and I will raise him up at the last day. It is written in the prophets, ...Every man therefore that hath heard and learned of the Father cometh to me."

Although the Christian may feel there are many doctrinal differences, our review of Muhammad's life shows that he was not presenting an alternative god. Through his references to Jesus and the Judeo-Christian prophets it is obvious that he believed he was worshiping the same God as the *People of the Book*. In fact, Muhammad believed the Ka'bah in Mecca was built by Abraham as a shrine to the one true God; then the idol-worshipping Arabs later erected 360 idols there. In A.D. 632, Muhammad entered the Ka'bah and smashed the idols, leaving only a wall painting of the baby Jesus resting in Mary's arms. [2] Muhammad felt at that time he was reestablishing the Abrahamic religion. Early Muslims turned toward

Jerusalem in prayer until Muhammad was rejected by the Medina Jews; he then changed the direction of prayer to Mecca. Again, Allah means *God* in Arabic, even Christian Arabs use that same word for God. This is a crucial point with the Muslims.

By saying "those who have learned of the Father come to me," Jesus is presenting the knowledge of God as a prerequisite to knowing Himself. He is saying that there is more than one way to receive him. We have the three Persons of the trinity in which to receive knowledge of who Christ is. My own experience was listening to a sermon on Ezekiel, and it was in Bible study two years later that I really realized that Jesus was my Savior. The Muslim's knowledge and worship of the first Person of the trinity, which is God, should be encouraged by Christians.

There are many things we can do to make the social integration less painful for them. We need to be interested in their land, their culture, and their language for their sake as well as our own. We need to give them a special time to present their background to a class or a group of people they are with the most. This would prevent them from constantly having to explain who they are during discussions. This would also make a world of difference in the group's understanding and trust of them. Let's put it this way; if a member of our class visited a foreign country, we would like to hear about it, especially if they visited a mission. The Muslim could be asked to give any additional information he had on local Christians or mission activity in his area. One particular church was small enough that they were able to turn over a Sunday evening service to families that had lived in other countries. One evening was presented by the African families, and one was presented by a Middle Eastern family. They didn't necessarily give their personal convictions but rather a religious overview of their particular country. The congregation found it very educational and enjoyed tasting ethnic foods and viewing their artifacts. Most of all, it helped them feel close to those families.

If there was concern over one person in the class having extra attention, a series of socials could be planned where each person in the group could share the background about his or her life. This would be a wonderful time for everyone to get to know each other.

The Middle Easterner's cultural contribution to Bible study is enormous. The Old Testament culture of the Middle East has not changed that much; tradition is very strong. Even many of the words from the Bible are similar to the present day Middle Eastern languages. The Hebrew word for God, Yahweh, is similar to the Arabic word for God, Yahhou. Also, in Genesis 33 when Jacob re-unites with his brother, he brings gifts to Esau. This is still a practiced tradition in the Middle East today. The class will benefit from this type of cultural information.

Christians believe they can't earn their way to heaven; that it is through the grace of God we are saved. But, Christians *can* earn their way into a Muslim's heart. Through established communication, mutual trust and our own witness, we earn the right to share God's love with others. Are we demonstrating service to God that anyone would want to emulate? Would a Muslim be better off if they were like us? Are we offering them anything better than what they already have?

Jesus' message will come through to them by our behavior. Are we motivated by money and pride? Are we resisting the influence of the world in our lives? Are we committed to our families? Do we live a disciplined life? Muslims have grown up with a strong teaching in the area of spiritual discipline. Our inner man must be shining through our outer exterior. That inner man can only be developed by meditation, prayer, fasting (not necessarily food), and study. This is the way we position ourselves before God so He can do that inner work. If we have not practiced these spiritual disciplines, it will show.

Is our nationalism and pride in our earthly kingdom overshadowing our submission to our Heavenly Kingdom? This would be a great stumbling block to our Muslim brothers and sisters.

When Christians have opened their minds and hearts to a Muslim Iranian and said, "I don't understand why Iran is angry with us but I ask you to forgive us for any wrong motives in our relationship with your country," this brings down great walls of resentment. Christian love can be a healing balm to all hurts. A warning is in order that with that opening, your friend may proceed to explain in detail what the wrong motives were. Your national pride at this point must be put aside because defensive answers will prove to your friend that you may not be as sorry as you said you were. It is good to just listen and go home and spend some time in prayer. Ask God to give you the patience and understanding to continue in your friendship that you may be a positive influence even in that great political process. *Long Ago and Far Away* had a story about a man who spent his life planting acorn seeds, and a great forest grew over the mountains. The narrator, Christopher Plummer, said, "How is it that one man's mission can be more powerful than the work of many nations."

Probably the most difficult area of communication is our cultural practice of Christianity. If we watched a Christian from the other side of the world worship, it would be immediately obvious to us what aspects of our practice are cultural. These cultural differences are even greater with the Middle Eastern Muslims. We can reduce offense by modifying some of our behaviors, or not expecting them to enjoy all our forms of worship. We must be aware that our message is not always presented in a way that they can understand. Muslims are not familiar with our style of music; therefore they may feel embarrassed to sing. Allow them that freedom to just listen; they may get more out of it than it appears.

Muslims have been taught that there should be no images of God or prophets. This was for the same purpose as the second commandment in the Old Testament: prevention of any idol worship. They will become accustomed to pictures of Jesus hanging everywhere but may never enjoy them as we do. Especially, many of our pictures show Jesus, who they know was a Middle Easterner himself, with blond hair.

The Muslim's traditional food habits and cleanliness habits are similar to those laid down for the Israelites in the book of Leviticus. So if there are any social functions with pork served, it would be good to have an alternative meat for the Muslim guest. Many Muslims have heard all the reasoning of why those traditions are not necessary anymore, but they have never developed a taste for pork. They would much rather not eat it; but they do not want to appear impolite.

Middle Eastern Muslims were not accustomed to worshipping in mixed company. They will accept that social standard here but will be more sensitive to women's presence and dress. Revealing sun dresses or shorts worn in a worshipping place will seem disrespectful and distracting to their discipline of worship. If this situation arises it may be better to have the men sit beside each other and the women sit together.

Upon our return from Iran one summer our six year old son said, "Mommy, everyone here is naked." The contrast was obvious even to such a little one. Revealing bathing suits are really quite shocking after living in the Middle East where women either wear the veil or are dressed very modestly. If Middle Easterners have lived in America for a number of years they may not be as sensitive to this issue.

We brought one Muslim fellow that couldn't speak any English to a Sunday School swimming party. He said, "This group of women must be religious."

I said, "Yes, why do you say so?" He had noticed that they were all wearing modest, one piece swim suits. What we wear really does give a message to others.

The last thing Muslims often comment on is our treatment of our Holy book. They may notice that we handle it in a more casual way than they are used to. We obviously need to set it around since we are taking it with us everywhere but we should refrain from throwing it or setting it on the floor. If a Muslim is coming to your home, you could keep your Bible on a Bible stand, or set it up on a bookcase or dresser. Muslims handle their Holy Book in a reverent way. They set it up high and often take it in their hands and kiss it. This is also a common Jewish practice. I accompanied my daughter to one of her friend's Bat Mitzvah ceremonies, and the honored child walked down all the aisles of the synagogue while members of the congregation kissed their prayer books and touched her with them. We can learn from the Muslims and the Jews respect of their holy books. When we moved to California, there was an Iranian Christian Church and I decided to visit it. I was overjoyed when I saw Iranians can come and worship in their own cultural context. Men can cry openly, some women cover their heads, if Islam is mentioned it is only with the utmost respect, and they have beautiful Iranian music! Now here is a place I can invite my Iranian friends and not worry about them being offended. Culture is very much a part of our worship.

Muslims make wonderful friends and we can feel very comfortable talking about our faith with them as long as our conversation is non-confrontational. Think of it as a part of your life. When you have a good friend, you share all things with them. Can you imagine having a good friend and never sharing with them about your family? Everyone loves to talk about the children in their family! In the same way, it is only natural for conversation about our God to enter into our friendship. Muslims have idioms about God sprinkled throughout their everyday conversation such as *God-willing, all praise be to God*, or *God forbid*. In fact, the Persian word for good-bye is *khoda hafez*, which literally means *may God keep you*.

I have an Iranian friend at a local university. One day she came wearing a sweatshirt that said Genesis-Revelations on it. I said, "What a beautiful shirt that is, do you know what that means?" She said she didn't; so I told her it meant the beginning and the end of God's story in the Bible. She seemed very pleased by that. Middle Easterners are very comfortable with religious conversation. Religion brings back memories of their home.

This open sharing may very well lead to discussions about Christian theology and comparative doctrine. The important thing to remember is that you don't necessarily have to comment on every thing; you don't have to agree on everything; but you do need to respect each other's faith. It is helpful to use the word God more than Jesus. Muslims do not understand our use of Jesus and God interchangeably. There is a new trend among Evangelical Christians to say "I believe Jesus is God." This as a modern day message that says one's theology is acceptable. Looking back to our discussions on the theology of the trinity, we see this as an oversimplification and it will be misunderstood by Muslims. This may be a good time to contemplate on the different roles of the trinity in our spirituality. Malcomb Smith, a radio teacher puts it very nicely, "Jesus came to bring us close to God, through the Holy Spirit." He based his statement on John 14:6...."no man come unto the Father, but by me."

For a Muslim to come to church in the first place is a sign he has an emotional or spiritual need, either for himself or for his children. We have discussed cultural problems involved with Middle Eastern families living in America. Muslims have been taught worship, fear of God, obedience and justice through Islam (submission to God) and most of them want their children to have that same training. In some cases the children have attended youth groups and have been told that their families are going to hell because they don't have Jesus. This is the one fear that Muslims have in sending their children to church: that their children will be turned against them. If the parents don't receive agape love through their children's relationship with the church, they will fall back into their old comfortable pattern of faith. But with no place to gather with others, their children will receive no religious training. Through a need, the Muslim is reaching out for spiritual help but the historical enmity is still there. Spiritual teaching is welcomed by them, but judgmental condemnation will drive them away. Hebrew 4:12 says the word of God is sharper than any two-edged sword but Hebrew 6:17 makes it clear it is the sword of the Spirit. It is not to hurt other people with. Ephesians 6:12 tells us our struggle is not against flesh and blood.

In conclusion, we must approach the Muslim with a new perspective; sharing God's love with them and giving the responsibility of their hearts to the Holy Spirit of God. We are to love and trust, and the spirit will do the rest.

Muslims have been coming to our churches, but our congregations are not prepared to receive them. They do not feel welcome because no one in the church makes an effort to truly become their friend. They never really become *one of us* and are often mistrusted for who they are rather than what they do. During the Gulf War, one of my own family members heard a Sunday school teacher read an Old Testament prophesy, about the destruction of Babylon. He then added Saddam Hossein should be killed. This person appeared to have no sympathy for a population of people in the Middle East that were being bombed and killed. We must try to put ourselves in their place. If the Middle East was a large powerful country, and they had bombed one of our states and just made remarks like, "It's their own fault." How would we feel? We must try to understand how offended they are.

To the people of the world, Jesus' message is of love and hope, and when the people that claim to represent Christ do not at least show compassion and concern, Muslims face a hopeless future. Jesus called his disciples *the salt of the earth,* Mark 9:50 (AET) says, "O how good is salt; but if the salt should lose its savor, with what could it be salted? Let there be salt in you, and be at peace with one another." James 3:9,10 (NIV) says, "With the tongue we praise our Lord and Father, and with it we curse men, who have been made in God's likeness. Out of the same mouth come praise and cursing. My brothers, this should not be."

There are many wonderful Christians making an effort to be friends with Muslims and with every offended Muslim their job becomes more difficult. One special speaker at the 1990 Urbana conference said, "If America goes to war with this Muslim country (Iraq) it will put Muslim-Christian relationships back 1000 years." II Corinthians 4:8(KJV) tells us, "We are troubled on every side, yet not distressed; we are perplexed, but not in despair." We must not give up hope that the mission of one Christian has more power than the work of many nations.

If you don't feel your church is ready for Middle Easterners, you could offer to have a Bible study with them. Our Iranian Christian church started out as a Bible study with seven people. Now the church is bursting at the seams and they need to enlarge the sanctuary. If you would like to do something to help in the peace process, find a Middle Eastern church and take them on as a mission project. Do they need funds for building, or for other programs reaching out to their own people? Making peace is much cheaper than making war, and take it from someone who lived through air raids of the Iran-Iraq war; it's a lot more fun.

If Christians don't welcome Muslims into their churches, Muslims will build Mosques and invite Christians to come. They have spiritual needs and they will be met. Downtown Chicago's Islamic center has used an annual traditional Islamic celebration as a time to reach out to those around them. Over two hundred invitations are sent to businesses and acquaintances for readings from the Quran and a question and answer time.[3]

We must learn from the great wise man of Israel, Solomon. As he dedicates the first temple built to worship God he says this beautiful prayer. It is recorded in the Chronicles of the Kings:

O Lord, God of Israel, there is no God like you in heaven or on earth—you who keep your covenant of love with your servants who continue wholeheartedly in your way....As for the foreigner who does not belong to your people Israel but has come from a distant land because of your great name and your mighty hand and outstretched arm—when he comes and prays toward this temple, then hear from heaven, your dwelling place, and do whatever the foreigner asks of you, so that all peoples of the earth may know your name and fear you, as do your own people Israel, and may know that this house I have built bears your name. [4]

May God richly bless you in your glorious adventure of traveling to the Middle East right here at home.

Notes:

1. Muhammad M. Pickthall, *The Meaning of the Glorious Quran* (New York, NY: Muslim World League-Rabita, 1977), Surah V:5.

2. Dr. Anis A. Shorrosh, *Islam Revealed* (Nashville: Thomas Nelson Publishers, 1988) p. 184f.

3. Terry Muck, *The Mosque Next Door,* Christianity Today magazine, February 19, 1988; p. 18.

4. *Disciple's Study Bible,* NIV (Nashville: Holman Bible Publishers, 1988), II Chronicles 6:14,32,33.

RECOMMENDED READING LIST

Bible Commentary on Middle Eastern Culture

George M. Lamsa, *Old Testament Light*, Harper & Row, 1964.

George M. Lamsa, *New Testament Light*, Harper & Row, 1968.

George M. Lamsa, *Idioms in the Bible Explained and a Key to Originals*, Harper & Row, 1985.

Iran

James A. Bill, *The Eagle and the Lion, The Tragedy of American-Iranian Relations*, Yale University Press, 1988.

Edwin M. Yamauchi, *Persia and the Bible*, Baker Book House, 1990.

The Arabs

Louis Bahjat Hamada, *Understanding the Arab World*, Thomas Nelson Publishers, 1990.

Judith Miller and Laurie Mylroie, *Saddam Hussein and the Crisis in the Gulf*, Random House, 1990.

Israeli-Palestinian Conflict

Elias Chacour with David Hazard, *Blood Brothers*, Chosen Books, 1984.

Audeh Rantisi & Ralph D. Beebe, *Blessed Are the Peacemakers*, Zondervan Publishers, 1990.

The Washington Report on the Middle East Affairs, American Educational Trust, P.O. Box 63062, Washington D.C. 20009. This magazine is published by retired U.S. Foreign Service officers to provide the American public with balanced and accurate information. The AET has an excellent Middle Eastern book list.

CIA Involvement in the Middle East

Bob Woodward, *VEIL: The Secret Wars of the CIA 1981-1987*, Simon and Schuster, 1987.

Being a Christian Example

Richard J. Foster, *Celebration of Discipline*, Harper & Row, 1978.